IDOLS-DEAD
OR ALIVE?

IDOLS—DEAD OR ALIVE?

Reuel J. Schulz

PUBLISHING HOUSE
Northwestern
MILWAUKEE, WISCONSIN

Scripture quotations from
the HOLY BIBLE
New International Version
Copyright ©, New York International Bible Society, 1978

Library of Congress Catalog Card Number 81-85921
Northwestern Publishing House
3624 W. North Ave., Milwaukee, WI 53208
© 1982 by Northwestern Publishing House. All rights reserved.
Published 1982
Printed in the United States of America
ISBN 0 8100 0151 9

CONTENTS

To my parents
GODFREY and VERA (nee KANSIER) SCHULZ
for their Christian training
patient support and love

❀

And to my wife
CHARLETTE (nee JOHNSON)
the beautiful Norwegian lass
who has given this gruff German
the goodness and favor
God promises in Proverbs 18:22

Foreword

There are books that ought not to be written and published, and then again there are books that ought to be written and published. This book by Pastor Reuel J. Schulz is one of the latter. What's more, it ought also to be read and digested, for it comes to grips with one of the basics of the saving faith.

Though the book's title places all the emphasis on idols — from the golden calf to Baal, from Diana of Ephesus to Hindu carvings, from CARC (common American religious creed) to atheism — the book really brings the reader face to face with the God of Scripture and what he expects of his creatures. It thus deals with a fact of life which everyone must face sooner or later even in an age that prides itself on being completely secular.

Reuel J. Schulz, pastor of a thriving WELS congregation in West Allis, Wisconsin, writes from a deep pastoral concern for young and old as he points out what ultimately is at stake: salvation, eternal life, heaven. He is a man who in his personal life and in his ministry has placed his confidence and his reliance in the Lord who said, "I am the way and the truth and the life. No one comes to the Father except through me" (John 14:6). He is fully aware that this same Lord and Savior spelled out the essence of God's first commandment in his commission to baptize "in the name of the Father and of the Son and of the Holy Spirit" (Matthew 28:19).

5

In looking at the world in which he and his parishioners live, Pastor Schulz has recognized that God's first commandment, "You shall have no other gods before me," is as pertinent today as yesterday, perhaps even more so. Though it is a sophisticated age in which we live, it is an age in which idolatry has by no means died out. It may at times be an idolatry that is more subtle than in past ages, but then again it can be just as blatant as ever before. In whichever form it appears, Pastor Schulz does a commendable job in exposing it for what it is — a soul-destroying error. If the world in which we live is ever to find a solution to the crime, immorality and materialism that are so rampant, it must find its way back to the one and only true God, the Triune God of Holy Writ.

Idols — Dead or Alive? is thoroughly documented. The reader will have no difficulty in grasping the points made by the author. He confesses his faith in Christ as clearly as Peter did in Jerusalem when he said, "Salvation is found in no one else, for there is no other name under heaven given to men by which we must be saved" (Acts 4:12).

Yes, this is a book that had to be written. Read it, and share it.

Harold E. Wicke

INTRODUCTION

This book has been stewing and simmering on the back-burner of my mind for more than two decades. It goes back to my Wisconsin Lutheran Seminary days when I began a filing system to accommodate clippings from magazines and newspapers on sundry subjects for use in writing sermons, class lectures, essays and articles. One of the categories in my highly individualistic filing system that attracted hundreds of news items over the years is entitled *GOD — Who are they talking about?*

Surely every Christian should be keenly interested in the basic doctrine of GOD. However, I believe that a Wisconsin Evangelical Lutheran Synod clergyman is likely to develop and cultivate an especially keen, above average interest in the subject of GOD because of several controversial, often unpopular, doctrinal positions taken by my church body over the years.

Lodges, Scouting, the military chaplaincy, prayer fellowship — these are issues which often have put WELS pastors and lay people on the spot. To question the value of the Scouting program, which seems to bring such positive benefits to American youth; to be in any way negative about perfunctory public prayers or a service organization like the Masonic Shriners which builds all those hospitals for terribly burned and crippled children, is, in the minds of many of our fellow Americans about the same as spitting on Old Glory or condemning motherhood, apple pie, Disneyland and the Golden Arches. As a result, many people are inclined to put Wisconsin Synod Lutherans in the same category with far-out, weirdo cultists such as the Jehovah's Witnesses who refuse to salute the flag and denounce blood transfusions as a device of the devil.

I believe the key to understanding and properly appreciating the stand of my church body on these issues lies in knowing and humbly accepting what God tells us about himself in the Bible, and being properly sensitive to any sins against his First Commandment. "Thou shalt have no other gods" — God unquestionably had good reason to put that commandment first. On page after page of the Bible we read of people who broke that commandment, fashioning and bowing down before idols, worshiping fake, counterfeit gods. In this book I will offer conclusive evidence that the sin of idolatry, so common in biblical times, is still widely practiced in our modern world in manifold forms.

It is my hope and prayer that this work may alert readers to the alarming prevalence of idolatry in the 20th century lest they slip into sins against the First Commandment unawares, and help them to warn and admonish, in a spirit of Christian humility and love, modern-day idolaters whom they are certain to encounter on their walk through this idol-littered world.

In summary let it be clearly said once more that the God of whom we speak insists, "I am the Lord, that is my name! I will not give my glory to another or my praise to idols" (Isaiah 42:8). The God of the Bible is the *only* true God and Savior. There is salvation in none other. He says simply but earnestly, "I, the Lord, am your Savior, your Redeemer" (Isaiah 49:26). Man rejects this Savior-God only at the peril of his immortal soul.

SOLI DEO GLORIA is a Latin phrase often used by

Christian writers to describe their motives and intentions. That phrase — to God alone be the glory — is most appropriate in connection with the contents of this book. The filing of items over the years, the research, organizing of materials, writing and rewriting have been undertaken to glorify the name of the one and only true Triune God, the God of Abraham, Isaac and Jacob, the God of Adam and Eve, the God of St. Paul and Dr. Martin Luther, the God of you the reader and of me the writer.

Reuel J. Schulz

Analysis

1. The Only True God — 17

A. Trinitarian Worship, Invocation and Benedictions
B. The Common American Religious Creed (CARC)
C. The Elks Lodge God
D. The "God Is Dead" theologians, Madalyn Murray O'Hair, James Watson, Carl R. Rogers, Arthur Schlesinger Jr., James A. Pike
E. The Athanasian Creed
F. Pope Paul VI's Universalism

2. Idols in Bible Times — 25

A. Egypt
B. Assyria-Babylonia
C. Persia
D. The Gods of Greece-Rome
E. Mystery Religions

    1. Eleusis
    2. Serapis-Isis
    3. Atargatis
    4. Mithras

F. Emperor Worship
G. Idols of the Bible

    1. Old Testament

        a. Adam and Eve
        b. Noah's contemporaries
        c. Babel
        d. Terah and Teraphim
        e. The Golden Calf
        f. Baal and Canaanite Deities
        g. Solomon and His Successors

CHAPTER ONE

THE ONLY TRUE GOD

This is life eternal, that they might know thee the only true God, and Jesus Christ, whom thou hast sent. (John 17:3)

Nearly every hour of worship in our churches begins with the significant words: "In the name of the Father and of the Son and of the Holy Ghost" (Matthew 28:19). That initial weekly reference to the one true Triune God is repeated throughout our liturgy: in the Confession and Absolution of Sins, in the Gloria Patri, the Kyrie, the Gloria in Excelsis, the Triple Hallelujah, the prayers and creeds (Apostles' and Nicene), the Sanctus, the Agnus Dei, the Nunc Dimittis — cf. *The Lutheran Hymnal*, pps. 5-31. This deliberately heavy stress on the fact that the God whom we worship is Triune, three distinct Persons in the one undivided and indivisible divine Essence (Mark 12:29,32; Isaiah 44:6), is also brought out in the closing benedictions in our services, the final words addressed to the assembled congregation by their minister. Both of our commonly used benedictions, the so-called Aaronic blessing taken from Numbers 6:24-26 with its three-fold "The Lord,"[1] and the Apostolic benediction, "The grace of the Lord Jesus Christ, and the love of God, and the communion of the Holy Ghost, be with you all" (II Corinthians 13:14), are intended to drive home to the worshiper the true identity of our Triune God.

How important is God's identity? Is the emphasis on the biblical doctrine of the Trinity referred to above really all that necessary? Shouldn't we be satisfied in the increasingly secular, agnostic, and downright atheistic society in which we live if people believe in a god, a supreme being, without bothering about difficult, hard-to-comprehend doctrines like the Trinity? Surely many Americans fail to see the need for an exact scriptural identification of God.

For several years I have served as a part-time chaplain at West Allis (Wisconsin) Memorial Hospital. Over the years I have heard hundreds of people in the hospital express what I like to call the Common American Religious Creed (CARC): "It really doesn't matter what or whom you believe in. After all, we all believe in the same god. As long as you're sincere in your belief and try to do your best, everything will turn out O.K. in the end." Although the preceding confession of faith is completely contrary to biblical teachings and is a blatant, blasphemous insult to the one true Triune God, people, especially the millions of unchurched people in our nation, desperately want to believe that it's true.

Most Americans think of themselves as being very broad-minded and open to new and different ideas, but over the course of time the Common American Religious Creed has become so firmly, if unofficially, established in our land that increasingly people impatiently dismiss any efforts to challenge or debunk it. The formulators of public opinion in the media seem to be committed to the CARC almost without exception. For example, under the heading "Should Girl Change Religion to That of Future Husband?" Ione Quinby Griggs, the personal advice columnist of the *Milwaukee Journal*, summed up her response to a troubled girl's letter with the following piece of CARC dogma: "Pray for guidance. Whatever church you join, you will be worshiping and praying to the same God."[2] The same vague religious philosophy was expressed in a Sunday supplement article some years ago about the folksingers Woody Guthrie and his son Arlo: "When he (Arlo) was born (on July 10, 1947) Woody told the nurse to put down 'All' on his birth certificate where it said religion. The hospital wouldn't do that, so Woody told them it was 'All' or 'None.' Woody was very religious — about life. He knew the Bible — he was raised a Protestant in Oklahoma — chapter and verse. And after he got married — I'm Jewish — he read the Talmud. But he never talked religion to the children. He used to say to them all religions were the same. . . ."[3]

I maintain that the "god" of Woody Guthrie and Ione Quinby Griggs has nothing whatsoever in common with the one Triune God as he identifies himself in his Word, the Holy Bible. Their god is a nonentity, a nothing, an idol, a figment of their imagination. However, it is apparent that Griggs and Guthrie have many co-religionists in our country who share their tragically misguided beliefs about God. Fraternal lodges in our land, for example, hold to a very similar misconcept of God. The following letter to the editor, which was written by the author about the Elks Lodge and their former whites only membership policy, exposes the shallowness of most lodges and their vague allegiance to their god:

> Recently you reported that the Benevolent and Protective Order of Elks voted at its San Francisco convention to continue its whites only membership policy. The same news item pointed out that the Elks' constitution states that prospective members must not only be white but also believers in God.
>
> It seems that the Elks' constitution contains a glaring contradiction. The true God of the Bible does not exclude anyone from membership in His organization on the basis of skin color. As far as the true God is concerned "there is neither Jew nor Greek, there is neither bond nor free, there is neither male nor female, for ye are all one in Christ Jesus" (Galatians 3:28).
>
> The Elks' constitutional requirement that members be believers in God would seem to indicate that they want to be very

religious men. Thus the Elks should be reminded that the true God "will have all men to be saved, and to come unto the knowledge of the truth" (I Timothy 2:4), and that He "so loved the world (not just people with white pigmentation), that He gave His only begotten Son, that whosoever believeth in Him should not perish, but have everlasting life" (John 3:16).

How strange that God offers His blessings to all men without exception but the godly Elks scrupulously restrict the benefits of their lodge to people whose skin color happens to be white!

My question: Just who is this "god" prospective Elks must believe in? Surely the "god" of the Elks is in no way connected with Jesus Christ. The Elks' "god" cannot be even remotely related to the true God of the Holy Bible.[4]

"Is God Dead?" — Those words in big, bold red letters against a black background on the cover of *Time* magazine in its April 8, 1966, issue introduced an article about the radical death-of-God theologians of that period, Thomas J. J. Altizer, William Hamilton and Paul Van Buron. These men maintained that God is indeed absolutely dead, but they nobly proposed to carry on and come up with a theology without *theos*, without God. Although the God-is-dead theologians (a contradiction in terms if there ever was one) have just about faded out of the public eye in the past decade and have been replaced by other theological fads, the denial of God's existence is still heard in many quarters. And Madalyn Murray O'Hair, the raucous and abrasive self-styled queen of the atheists, is not the only one making public attacks on God and those who believe in him. James Watson, a Harvard professor who won the Nobel prize for his discovery of DNA, the molecule of heredity, announced his disdain toward belief in God at a scientific symposium some years ago: "God is a copout . . . It would be nice to believe that there is something distantly wonderful that keeps everything in line, but there is no reason for it. I would like to think that there is something guiding our destiny. But there is nothing that is doing this but man himself. I don't believe in God at all."[5] For Watson God has been replaced by man; his supreme being is not the God of the Holy Bible, but the human being. In a similar vein the renowned psychologist Carl R. Rogers once described twentieth century man in the following way: "The emerging modern individual places his confidence not in society's norms, nor religion's rules, nor parents' dictates, but in his own changing experience as it occurs within himself. He is, in a very deep sense, his own highest authority. He chooses his own way."[6] Yet another example of modern man arrogantly declaring his independence of God took place at a bicentennial symposium sponsored by the Southeastern Pennsylvania Synod of the Lutheran Church in America where the famous historian Arthur Schlesinger Jr. told some 900 people: ". . . for better or for worse, religious faith hardly seems a living option for us today . . . God is dead; at least the serious God — the God of Augustine, Thomas Aquinas, Luther and Calvin — is dead. In how many lives nowadays is God, hour by hour, the decisive force?"[7]

There's no denying that allegiance to and respect for the one true Triune God whom Christians worship are on the wane in our modern world. Not only atheistic Communist comrades behind their Iron and Bamboo curtains, not only self-sufficient secular scholars like historian Schlesinger, psychologist Rogers, and geneticist Watson openly deny the reality of the God of Scripture. Regrettably even some clergymen who call themselves Christian do not hesitate to tear the heart out of the Bible's straightforward teaching about God. Typical of this type of liberal, Bible-denying theologian was the late Episcopalian Bishop James A. Pike who had the incredible audacity to suggest "that the church should abandon the Trinity, on the ground that it really seems to be preaching three Gods instead of one. Christianity, in his view, should stop attributing specific actions to persons of the Holy Trinity —just say that they were all the work of God."[8]

In sharp contrast to such vague, watered-down concepts of God stands that majestic masterpiece of our Christian faith, the Athanasian Creed, which drives home the scriptural teaching of the Trinity along with the deity of Christ and clearly reveals the damning consequences of rejecting these basic biblical doctrines: "Whosoever will be saved, before all things it is necessary that he hold the catholic [i.e., universal, Christian] faith. Which faith except everyone do keep whole and undefiled, without doubt he shall perish everlastingly. And the catholic faith is this, that we worship one God in Trinity and Trinity in Unity." After the Athanasian Creed goes into considerable detail (cf. *The Lutheran Hymnal*, p.53) concerning the Trinity, it sums up how vital this teaching is with the following uncompromising declaration: "He, therefore, that will be saved must thus think of the Trinity ... This is the catholic faith; which except a man believe faithfully and firmly, he cannot be saved."

Modern man may be inclined to dismiss the Athanasian Creed as much too rigid, dogmatic, and narrow-minded; indeed, many people of the 20th century recoil from statements like "must thus think," classifying that type of speech as brain-washing and smacking of simplistic thought control. Even the late Pope, Paul VI, parted company with the Athanasian Creed when he expressed his conviction that non-Christians and non-Trinitarians could be saved even without knowledge of the one true Triune God and without faith in the God-man, Jesus Christ. In an editorial published just after Pope Paul's death on August 6, 1978, at the age of 80, *Christian News*

Editor Herman Otten brought out the following facts about the Pope's beliefs:

> The Pope agreed with the liberals who teach that Christ is not the only way to heaven.
>
> Pope Paul's updated creed of 1968, which has even been praised by conservative Roman Catholics, leaves room for an anti-scriptural universalism. It does not uphold the scriptural position of the Athanasian Creed. The Pope's new creed says: "We give thanks, however, to the divine goodness that very many believers can testify with us before men to the unity of God, even though they know not the mystery of the Most Holy Trinity." Contrary to the Athanasian Creed and the words of Jesus Christ (John 14:6) and St. Peter (Acts 4:12), the Pope declared: "But the divine design of salvation embraces all men, and those who without fault on their part do not know the Gospel of Christ and His Church, but seek God sincerely and under the influence of grace endeavor to do His will as recognized through the promptings of their conscience, they, in a number known only to God, can obtain salvation."[9]

In Chapter Six we will point out the devastating effect that that sort of papistic dogma has to have on Christian evangelism and mission efforts. Although the Pope did not flatly deny the doctrine of the Trinity, the result is much the same as he arbitrarily opened the way to salvation to the sincere followers of other gods, such as Moslems, Hindus, and Buddhists. How tragic that the man who is looked up to by millions of people as the Vicar of Christ (correctly identified by our Lutheran Confessions as the Antichrist), as the visible leader of Christendom, should promulgate a creed so filled with deadly error and false comfort for non-Christians, and particularly so insulting to the one true Triune God who insists "I, even I, am the Lord; and beside me there is no Savior" (Isaiah 43:11), and "I am the Lord, that is my name! I will not give my glory to another, or my praise to idols" (Isaiah 42:8).

When we explore the subject of the Trinity and search

the Scriptures to learn the identity of the only true God, we dare not forget what is at stake, namely salvation, eternal life, heaven. Dead idols, graven images, whether they're fashioned by the skillful hands or fabricated by the ingenious, clever minds of mere men, do not and cannot save sinners from eternal death and hell. Fake and counterfeit gods, even if their promoters and false prophets manage to mislead and persuade millions of people to dedicate their lives to them, will not provide what only the true Triune God can give: eternal life in heaven, won for all mankind on Calvary's cross by the suffering and death of the true God's Son, Jesus Christ.

NOTES FOR CHAPTER ONE

[1] For a brief and clear explanation of the Trinitarian nature of this Aaronic blessing cf. Theodore Dierks, *The Order of Service* (Milwaukee: Northwestern Publishing House, 1952), pps. 39-42.

[2] *The Milwaukee Journal*, 16 Nov. 1963.

[3] Ibid., 23 Nov. 1969.

[4] Ibid., 25 July 1970.

[5] Ibid., 25 Nov. 1974.

[6] Ibid., 25 Nov. 1973.

[7] *Christian News*, 15 Nov. 1976.

[8] *Time*, 8 Apr. 1966, p. 86.

[9] Herman Otten, *Christian News*, 14 Aug. 1978, p. 12.

CHAPTER TWO

IDOLS IN BIBLE TIMES

Their land is full of idols; they bow down to the work of their hands, to what their fingers have made. (Isaiah 2:8 NIV)

It is not the primary purpose of this book to provide a comprehensive, exhaustive or complete catalog of idols. That would be all but impossible because of the bewildering variety of forms idolatry has assumed in the course of human history. However, it is in line with this book's purpose to give at least a brief glimpse of some of the prominent idols men have fashioned in the past with their minds and hands and have fervently worshiped in place of the true god.

A glance at any encyclopedia can give one a good idea of how important a role idolatry played in the lives of people who lived in Bible times. Under the heading of "Mythology" in the *World Book Encyclopedia*, for example, there is a lengthy article describing the various idols which were worshiped by misguided, myth-led people in ancient Egypt, Greece and the Roman Empire, as well as the mythic deities which developed and gained disciples under the influence of Celtic, Teutonic, Hindu, Pacific Islands, African and American Indian mythology.[1]

What was religion like in ancient times? What kind of gods and goddesses were worshiped by the people who surrounded the Children of Israel in Old Testament times and the Christians of the early New Testament era? A brief look at the religious beliefs in countries close to Palestine and adjacent to the Mediterranean Sea should answer these questions.

EGYPT

In his *World Book Encyclopedia* article on Ancient Egypt, Ricardo A. Caminos supplies the following facts about the idolatry that permeated life in ancient Egypt:

> Religion appeared in every part of life in ancient Egypt. The Egyptians believed that gods and goddesses took part in every human activity from birth to death. For the Egyptian, the good life depended on obeying the commands of the gods. After a person died, the gods would judge how well the person had obeyed their directions. The Egyptians believed that their king was a god who could keep the country prosperous by his divine powers.
>
> In the earliest period, the Egyptians worshiped the forces of nature, such as wind and water. As towns grew up, each adopted its own special god. In one part of the delta, the people worshiped Horus, the god of heaven.... In another district, the people worshiped Osiris, the god of vegetation, who later became the god of the dead.... Heliopolis, near Cairo, was the center for worship of the sun god Re, or Ra.... Heliopolis means city of the sun in Greek. About 2500 B.C., priests at Heliopolis developed the worship of Re as the nation's first state religion. Other members of Re's divine family included Osiris and his wife, Isis; Set, the evil brother of Osiris, and his wife Nephthys; Shu, god of air; Tefnut, goddess of moisture; Geb, god of earth; and Nut, goddess of the sky....
>
> The people of Thebes worshiped Amon, the god of the air and fertility. After Thebes became the political center of the empire, Amon became the empire's chief god. The people identified Amon with the sun god, Re, and Amon became known as Amon-Re....
>
> The Egyptians believed that certain animals might serve individual gods in a special way. For example, they regarded the ram as acceptable to Amon, and chose one ram to be the temple animal of that god. Other sacred animals included the

baboon, bull, cat, crocodile, and jackal.

The people of ancient Egypt took great care in preparing for life after death. They denied that death ended the existence of a person who had led a good life. They believed that the next world would be like Egypt in its richest and most enjoyable form. They built stone tombs and filled them with clothing, food, furnishings, and jewelry for use in the next world. They embalmed their dead and wrapped the bodies in layers of cloth. Preserved bodies were called mummies. . . .

The Egyptians carved inscriptions on the walls of their tombs. They also wrote on the insides of the coffins. They placed papyrus copies of the Book of the Dead in the tombs to protect the spirits of the dead. The Book of the Dead contained spells and prayers. . . .

The priests conducted the rituals and guarded the temples. They acquired much political power. For example, the king did not make them pay the Corvee, a tax in labor that furnished the government with workers. The priests used thousands of people to work in the temples and divine lands.[2]

Some students of mythology and scholars who specialize in the study of ancient Egyptian religion claim, falsely to be sure, that both the belief in one supreme being (monotheism) and the doctrine of the resurrection from the dead originally developed in ancient Egypt. They contend that during the 1300's B.C. the pharaoh Amenhotep IV chose Aton as the only god of Egypt and in his devotion to that deity changed his own name to Akhenaton. Although the Egyptians stopped worshiping Aton after Akhenaton's death, some scholars insist that the worship of Aton lingered among the Hebrews after their captivity in Egypt and that the Jewish and Christian belief in one God grew out of the cult of Aton. Such a theory, of course, ignores what the Bible teaches about the one God of Abraham, Isaac and Jacob, who was worshiped by those patriarchs and even earlier by Noah and Adam long before Amenhotep IV appeared on the world scene.

The so-called Osiris myth's connection with belief in a

resurrection also is not deserving of serious consideration. According to Egyptian mythology (idolatry) Osiris, Isis and Set were the divine children of Geb and Nut. When Geb retired to heaven, Osiris became pharaoh and took his sister Isis as his queen. Set grew jealous of Osiris' prominent position as pharaoh and killed him, cutting his body into pieces, stuffing the pieces into a box and setting the box afloat on the Nile. Isis would not accept the death of her husband-brother and searched for Osiris' remains with the aid of her sister Nepthys and several other gods and goddesses. Isis finally found the remains of Osiris, put his body back together and restored him to life. Thus Osiris cheated death and the Egyptians came to believe that if Osiris could triumph over death, so could man. Indeed, according to the scholars, every good Egyptian believed that, when he died, he himself became Osiris.[3]

To be sure, there may seem to be some superficial similarities between the Osiris myth with his alleged restoration to life and the scriptural account of the triumphant resurrection of our Savior from the tomb on the first Easter, but it would be blatant blasphemy to believe and insist that the Bible writers borrowed from the Osiris myth (with all its obvious idolatrous crudities) to come up with the majestic records of Christ's resurrection.

ASSYRIA-BABYLONIA

The Assyrian empire, so influential in ancient Bible times, was named for Ashur, god of military prowess and empire. The kings of Assyria served both as the supreme head of the empire and as the chief priest of the god Ashur. The chief Babylonian idol was Marduk who was called the "great lord, the lord of heaven and earth." His power was said to lie in his wisdom, which he used to govern the people of the earth, to support good people, and to punish the wicked. Marduk's temple and its buildings in the city of Babylon covered more than 60 acres. Babylonian kings usually were not religious leaders, but in the early Sumerian period the king sometimes ruled as a god himself. Babylonian religions combined scientific observation of the sky and the weather, prayer to the various gods who were believed to be in, control of these things, and magic, which soon led to the study of astrology. The number of gods worshiped by the Babylonians grew into the thousands. There were patron gods and goddesses of each city-state as well as gods representing such things as the sun, moon, and stars, the weather, crops, rivers and the land.

In addition to their supreme deity Ashur the Assyrians worshiped idols such as Nabu, the god of learning and patron of writers; Ninurta, the god of war; and Ishtar, the goddess of love. The goddess Ishtar was so famous in Nineveh (cf. O.T. Book of Jonah) that her statue was once sent from there to Egypt to help cure the Egyptian king of an illness. Assyrians offered food and precious objects to their gods. Priests tried to foretell the future by examining the innards of sacrificed animals and by observing and interpreting things in nature such as the weather and flights of birds.[4]

In Joshua 24:2 the great leader of Israel who was Moses' successor reminded his people how "Long ago your forefathers, including Terah, the father of Abraham and Nahor, lived beyond the River (the Euphrates) and worshiped other gods." The *Davis Dictionary of the Bible* describes the form of idolatry practiced by Abraham's father in ancient Babylonia as follows:

> Their worship was at least corrupted by the prevalent animism of Babylonia, which assigned a spirit to every object in nature, and which led to the conception of eleven great gods

besides innumerable minor deities. The great gods were the deities of the majestic and impressive objects in nature: of the sky, of earth's surface, of the ocean and all subterranean waters, of the moon, the sun, and the storm; and of the five planets visible to the naked eye. The gods were powerful, were active in nature, bestowed special care on favorite individuals and communities, heard and answered prayer.[5]

PERSIA

The early Persians believed in gods of nature, such as the sun, sky and fire. They believed these gods had social powers. Mithras, the sun god, for example, was supposed to control contracts. They had no temples, but prayed and offered sacrifices on mountains. Zoroaster (or Zarathustra), a prophet who lived about 600 B.C., reformed the ancient religion, preaching a faith based on good thoughts, words and deeds, emphasizing a supreme god called Ahura Mazda, "the wise spirit." Zoroaster's followers, called Zoroastrians, gradually spread his religion all over Persia. Zoroaster was a very early advocate of the doctrine of universalism, for he taught that even the wicked are finally saved. Righteous ones go directly to paradise, the wicked are first purified in a kind of hellish purgatory. After the conquest of Persia by Alexander the Great, Zoroastrianism began to die out. However, the religion revived during the early days of Christianity and even today the Parsis of India follow Zoroaster's form of idolatry.[6]

GREECE-ROME

Since this is just a brief survey or overview of ancient forms of idolatry, it seems to make good sense to combine the religions of Greece and Rome, because there are such close similarities and parallels in their forms of worship and the families of deities to which they are devoted.

Indeed, in *The World Book Encyclopedia* the following list of gods and goddesses appears, emphasizing how the Romans were indebted to the Greeks for their ideas about divinities:

Greek Name	Roman Name	Position
Aphrodite	Venus	Goddess of love
Apollo	Apollo	God of music, poetry, and purity
Ares	Mars	God of war
Artemis	Diana	Goddess of hunting and childbirth
Asclepius	Aesculapius	God of healing
Athena	Minerva	Goddess of crafts, war, and wisdom
Cronus	Saturn	In Greek mythology, ruler of the Titans and father of Zeus; In Roman mythology, also the god of agriculture
Demeter	Ceres	Goddess of growing things
Dionysus	Bacchus	God of wine, fertility, and wild behavior
Eros	Cupid	God of love
Gaea	Terra	Symbol of the earth and mother and wife of Uranus
Hephaestus	Vulcan	Blacksmith for the gods and the god of fire and metal-working

Hera	Juno	Protector of marriage and women. In Greek mythology, sister and wife of Zeus; In Roman mythology, wife of Jupiter
Hermes	Mercury	Messenger for the gods; god of commerce and science; and protector of travelers, thieves, and vagabonds
Hestia	Vesta	Goddess of the hearth
Hypnos	Somnus	God of sleep
Pluto, or Hades	Pluto	God of the underworld
Poseidon	Neptune	God of the sea. In Greek mythology, also god of earthquakes and horses
Rhea	Rhea	Wife and sister of Cronus
Uranus	Uranus	Son and husband of Gaea and father of the Titans
Zeus	Jupiter	Ruler of the gods[7]

The Greeks worshiped many gods, as the list above indicates. Most Greeks believed their gods were superhuman beings who were friendly to mankind. They felt that men could anger the gods only by impiety or insolence. They seemingly did not live in terror of their gods, as other ancient peoples did. Each city-state had its own minor gods and worshiped them in its own way. Many festivals were held in honor of their gods with programs featuring dramas, prayers, animal sacrifices and athletic contests such as the original Olympic Games.

A feature of Greek religion, as well as Roman, were the

oracles. The word oracles has several meanings. It can refer to the answers given by a god to some question, to the priest or other means by which the answer was given, or the place where the answer was given. Both the ancient Greeks and the Romans believed that their deities took a personal interest in human affairs. When the people sought advice and answers to perplexing problems, the gods were supposed to answer them through oracles. The meanings of the answers were often difficult to understand, so special priests or priestesses interpreted the god's meaning. The people rewarded the priests and priestesses with gifts, a custom that often led charlatans to pretend to be oracles and to reap tidy profits from their religious racket, a despicable practice that is still carried on by many false prophets and fortune tellers in our own time. Two very well-known Greek oracles were the oracles of Apollo at Delphi and of Zeus at Dodona.

At Dodona the people wrote their questions on lead tablets. They believed the rustling of the leaves of a sacred red oak tree answered them. Temple priests called *Selli* interpreted the rustlings and provided the answers. At the Delphic oracle a woman, called Pythia, would utter weird sounds while in a frenzy. The petitioners believed these were the words of Apollo. Here also temple priests provided interpretations for the public. Entire cities, as well as private individuals, sought the oracle's advice and as a result Pythia, or more accurately the temple priests, greatly influenced Greek religion, economics and politics.

Did people actually believe the answers supplied by the oracles? Did they really think that there were superhuman beings like Zeus, Mars or Poseidon who watched over and even intervened in their affairs? Those are questions we are quick to raise at the close of our sophisticated, science-conscious 20th century. We wonder how people could be so simple, so gullible, so steeped in superstitions, so susceptible to the schemes of religious racketeers. In the chapters to come, however, we will show that such spiritual ignorance is still very common in our own supposedly more enlightened modern times. There can be no doubt that millions of people in ancient Greece and Rome did fervently believe in their mythic deities with all their hearts and souls. Indeed they provided eloquent evidence of their misbelief and dedicated idolatry by building impressive temples to their gods that still can be seen today. Tourists visiting Athens can still see the temple of Zeus, which was built over a period of more than six hundred years, and the majestic Parthenon, the peak of Doric architecture, which was erected as a temple to the glory of the goddess Athena Parthenos (the virgin).

It is true that shortly before the coming of Christ there was a considerable decrease in religious fervor among the Greeks and Romans. The older state religion declined and as the population shifted from the country to the city there was a diminishing in the worship of local and village deities. Merrill C. Tenney aptly describes the cooling off of the religious climate in Greece and Rome at the time of Christ and also gives a devastating description of paganism as follows:

> Paganism is a parody and a perversion of God's original revelation to man. It retains many basic elements of truth but twists them into practical falsehood. Divine sovereignty becomes fatalism; grace becomes indulgence; righteousness becomes conformity to arbitrary rules; worship becomes empty ritual; prayer becomes selfish begging; the supernatural degenerates into superstition. The light of God is clouded by fanciful legend and by downright falsehood. The consequent confusion of beliefs and of values left man wandering in a maze of uncertainties. To some, expediency became the dominating philosophy of life; for if there can be no ultimate certainty, there can be no permanent principles by which to guide conduct; and if there

are no permanent principles, one must live as well as he can by the advantage of the moment. Skepticism prevailed, for the old gods had lost their power and no new gods had appeared. Numerous novel cults invaded the empire from every quarter and became the fads of the dilettante rich or the refuge of the desperate poor. Men had largely lost the sense of joy and of destiny that made human life worthwhile. . . . Among the educated classes a growing skepticism decreased religious leadership, though many maintained an outward allegiance to the ancestral gods for the sake of public relations.[8]

When the Emperor Octavian became the sole ruler of Rome in 27 B.C., he tried to rehabilitate the old Roman religion in order to promote the solidarity and integrity of the state. He rebuilt eighty-two temples of the gods, subsidized them with costly gifts, recruited new candidates for the priesthood and the Vestal Virgins, and restored some of the ancient rites and festivals, such as the Lupercalia and the Compitalia, annual games which celebrated respectively fertility rites and the honor of the spirits that guarded the homes of the people.[9] At the dawn of the New Testament era it appears that in Rome religious practice was intertwined with patriotism and loyalty toward the government. The Vestal Virgins are an example of this mixing of religious sentiment with patriotic feelings. In the center of Rome stood a circular temple to Vesta, the goddess of fire on the hearths of home and state. She was the symbol of the home, each house had a shrine to her, and every meal began and ended with an offering to her. In her Roman temple a sacred fire, guarded by six young Vestal Virgins, burned constantly and the Romans believed the fire was a safeguard against national disaster.

Just as it would be difficult, if not impossible to describe the religious beliefs of the average American in the 1980's, so it is hard to be certain about the convictions of the average Greek or Roman in the days of Jesus and Paul. Undeniably allegiance to the ancient idols had declined, but many undoubtedly were still under their influence. Tenney states that

> It would be inaccurate to say that the old religion of Rome was dead when the temples of the gods still maintained their ascendancy in civic life and commanded the allegiance of a considerable part of the population. . . .
>
> Whatever may have been the individual attitudes of the populace toward the ancestral pantheon (all the gods of a people), ranging from cool skepticism to hysterical devotion, the massive temples and gilded shrines that adorned the heights and highways of every city and town exercised a powerful though silent influence. They may have been the monuments of a moribund faith, but they still marked the highest aesthetic and religious achievement of the past. In Athens, the cultural center of the Hellenic world (replete with an estimated 30,000 gods and goddesses, plus the UNKNOWN GOD of Acts 17:23), Paul, gazing at the magnificent buildings dedicated to the Olympian deities, exclaimed, "I perceive that in every way you are very religious" (Acts 17:22, NIV). The entire religious culture of the past was represented by the buildings and rites of pagan worship; its legends and ethics were ingrained into the people; and as Christianity slowly penetrated the fabric of society, it met the resistance of these antecedents.[10]

MYSTERY RELIGIONS

As the ancestral gods seemed to become more distant and unreal the Greeks and Romans began to look elsewhere for religious fulfillment and satisfaction. Many of them turned to the mystery religions which were so called because of the esoteric character of their worship. These religions promised more personal and immediate involvement with deity. Indeed they retain their aura of mystery to this day because their initiates were sworn to secrecy concerning the precise nature of their rites and ceremonies and most of their adherents kept their vows not to divulge the secrets. The oldest of the popular mysteries was the cult of Eleusis, a town twelve miles from Athens.

Candidates for initiation gathered at Athens, washed themselves in the sea, made various sacrifices, and on their way to Eleusis sang hymns to Iacchus, the infant Dionysus, god of wine. After more bathing, sacrifices, a sacred banquet and a consecrated drink, they witnessed a sacred drama, enacted by the priests of the shrine. The initiates were conducted on a pilgrimage through a dark passageway to represent the cheerless wanderings of the dead in the underworld, and then were brought back to the upper air and light, where they were shown the sacred objects of the cult. The vision of these objects was the culmination of the initiation, for they represented the personal revelation of deity to the individual.[11]

The mystery religions of Greece and Rome also borrowed heavily from idol worship that originated in other lands such as Egypt, Syria and Persia. The cult of Serapis, for example, was derived from Egypt. The name was a Hellenization of the Egyptian Asor-hapi, the appearance of the god Osiris in the guise of a bull. The worship of Serapis could be classified as monotheistic pantheism. The precise nature of the god was not clearly defined, but it was opposed to polytheism and asserted the pervasive power of his deity through all nature. His devotees called Serapis "Lord of Totality" and identified him with the sun-god. They saw him as a protector, healer and savior of men, who could be approached through sacred ritual. The worship of Isis, the consort of Osiris, often went hand in hand with the Serapis cult. The cult of Isis had a strong attraction for women. The Roman emperors were inconsistent in their treatment of the Serapis and Isis cults. Augustus once expelled the priests of the Serapis cult for complicity in a case of flagrant immorality and in 30 B.C. destroyed the temples of Isis and Serapis. Similarly in A.D. 19 Tiberius destroyed the Isis shrine and crucified the priests. Nero and Caligula, on the other hand, looked with favor on these Egyptian cults. In fact Caligula introduced the worship of Isis into his palace and participated in celebrating the mysteries.

The cult of Atargatis came to Rome from Syria. Together with her consort, Baal-hadad, she was worshiped throughout the Middle East as the fish goddess. The first part of her name is related to the names of the goddess Ishtar, Astarte, or Ashtoreth, who was likewise the deity of fertility, love and life. Her worship was accompanied by ritual prostitution and human sacrifice until it was outlawed by Hadrian (A.D. 76-138). Her priests were eunuchs who on fast days danced in her honor and scourged each other in orgiastic frenzy. Much attention was paid to astrology and its concomitant teachings of good fortune guided by the stars and planets.[12] Lest we dismiss the Atargatis cult as an example of ancient primitive paganism which modern man has outgrown, we should not overlook the Playboy Clubs in major American cities or the obsession with astrology that persists in our society. If the cult of Atargatis were still around, it would surely attract hordes of disciples in 20th century America.

Persia's contribution to the mystery religions was Mithraism, named after the Persian deity, Mithras, "the Heavenly Light," which came into the Roman world about 76 B.C. and became the strongest rival of Christianity for two centuries. The followers of Mithras, the sun-god, the apotheosis of light, purity and righteousness, underwent an elaborate initiation, proceeding step by step from the first rudimentary rites to the final test which presumably prepared them for immortality. This cult of Mithras was less tainted by sexual indulgences than the other mystery religions and appealed strongly to the more heroic qualities of human nature. Its emphasis on the virtues of fidelity and courage made it very popular in the army and it became predominantly a soldier's faith. Women were excluded from Mithraic worship and it seems to have been free from the sensuality and orgiastic excesses of the other cults.[13] Again it would seem that this mystery religion dedicated to Mithras is far removed from our modern life. However, I believe that the followers of Mithras would feel very much at home today in a secret organization like the Masonic Lodge with its emphasis on work-righteousness, human virtues and the worship of a Christless deity that is just as much a dead idol as Mithras of old.

Some scholars make much of the superficial similarities between some aspects of the mystery religions and our Christian faith and even insist that Christianity borrowed some basic doctrines such as the resurrection from the pagan cults. While it is true that the mystery religions dedicated to Attis, Osiris and Odonis teach that those deities allegedly returned to life two to four days after death, any real relationship with Jesus' death and resurrection on the third day is clearly absurd. J. N. D. Anderson hits the nail on the head when he insists that:

> If borrowing there was by one religion from another, it seems clear which way it went. . . . The difference between the mythological experiences of these nebulous figures (the idols of the mystery religions) and the crucifixion under Pontius Pilate of one of whom eyewitnesses bore testimony to both his death and resurrection is . . . obvious.[14]

Similarly E. O. James asserts that:

> There is no valid comparison between the Synoptic story of Jesus of Nazareth and the mythological accounts of the mystery divinities of Eleusis, Thrace, Phrygia, or Egypt. . . . Similarly, the belief in the Resurrection of Christ is poles removed from the resuscitation of Osiris, Dionysus, or Attis in an annual ritual based on primitive conceptions of mummification, and

the renewal of the new life in the spring. The resemblance between the Christian Easter and the Hilaria in the Attis mystery on March 25th is purely superficial, there being no real points of contact. . . .[15]

There was, indeed, a fundamental flaw in the mystery religions. Although they speak of savior-gods and resurrections, they were clearly based on far-fetched religious fantasies and extravagant mythology rather than the simple, majestic historic facts which the Holy Scriptures communicate.

EMPEROR WORSHIP

When the state religion declined, emperor worship arose to fill the religious vacuum in the Roman regime. In the Oriental and Hellenistic world the divinity of royalty was long established and gradually that idea also gained ground among the Romans. The first Roman emperor, Augustus (63 B.C. — A.D. 14), did not seem to take himself seriously as a divine ruler, but he gave support to the custom of deifying the ruler at death by building a temple to his great-uncle Divus Julius Caesar in the Forum. The eastern Greek-speaking provinces of the empire, where kings had long been regarded as gods, insisted on deifying Augustus even before his death and altars were erected in his honor also in Gaul and Lyons. In Palestine Herod the Great named his new city of Samaria *Sebaste*, the Greek equivalent of Augustus, and dedicated the temple, its most imposing structure, to Roma and Augustus. After his death, the people of the Roman Empire worshiped him as Divine Augustus.

Augustus' successor, Tiberius (42 B.C. — A.D. 37), who was proclaimed emperor when Augustus died in A.D. 14 and ruled during the life of Jesus, tried to discourage emperor worship. He restrained the popular impulse to worship the imperial statues and scarcely allowed his birthday to be noticed. He permitted his image to be erected in public only if it were not to be classed with likenesses of the gods, and he would not allow anyone to address him as "Lord."

The next emperor, Caius Caligula (A.D. 12-41), was a madman who still managed to rule for four years, from A.D. 37-41. He was murdered when he insulted the army and threatened to kill the members of the Roman Senate. Although he was obviously insane, he apparently was most responsible for injecting the idea of emperor worship into the minds of the Roman people. In A.D. 40 he began to seek worship for himself; he claimed to be all gods at once, ordering that a statue of Zeus with his features be placed in the Temple in Jerusalem and demanding that he be worshiped at Rome as well.

Although Claudius (10 B.C. — A.D. 54), who followed crazy Caligula, was considered an excellent emperor during his thirteen-year reign, A.D. 41-54, and rejected the proposal that a high priest and temple be dedicated to him, still even during his lifetime writers described him as "our god Caesar," and after his death (possibly murdered by his niece-wife Agrippina) he was exalted to the company of the gods by vote of the Senate.

The notorious Nero (A.D. 37-68), who became emperor in A.D. 54 after the death of Claudius, is best remembered for his alleged fiddling while Rome burned and the fierce persecution of Christians whom he blamed for the fire. At first Nero refused to allow the dedication of a temple in his honor built at public expense, but later he placed in front of his new palace a colossus of the sun-god with his own features and represented himself with a radiant crown, the emblem of the sun-god, in the coins of the realm.

Vespasian, (A.D. 9-79), builder of the famous Roman

Colosseum, apparently had no illusions of grandeur about his divine status. On his death bed, he is reported to have said: "Alas! I think that I am about to become a god." After the brief rule of Titus, Vespasian's son, from A.D. 79-81, Domitian, Vespasian's second son, became emperor and unabashedly demanded divine status. He was a confirmed egotist and during his years in power (A.D. 81-96) he executed Christians and Jews and insisted that he be hailed as Dominus and Deus, "Lord and God." He seemingly was deadly serious in his claims and with arrogant conceit assumed the prerogatives of a god. He wanted to be hailed as Jupiter's son and heir, the earthly vice-regent and representative of the king of the universe.[16]

It is easy to exaggerate the influence of emperor worship in the Roman Empire and its effect on the early Christians. Many Roman citizens, especially among the intellectuals, and even most of the emperors themselves, must have considered the deification of the rulers almost a joke. However, it is equally true that many people were dead serious about emperor worship. Indeed, up to the end of World War II the Japanese were giving divine status to their Emperor Hirohito. The inclination of people to worship the creature rather than the Creator must never be underestimated.

Tenney provides the following perceptive summary of emperor worship and the problems that it caused Christianity, especially in the first century:

> With the exception of madmen like Caligula, or egotists like Domitian, none of the emperors seems to have taken his putative divinity very seriously. Politically, however, emperor worship was a very effective bond of unity. Whatever gods the several peoples of the empire may have worshiped, they could unite on the adoration of the ruler who was the visible guardian of their peace and prosperity. There were some who refused to

participate in such worship. Political opponents of the empire, particularly those who had mourned the demise of the Republic, would not endorse any such claims. The Jews would not elevate any man to the place of God, nor would the Christians. As Paul said, "For us there is one God, the Father . . . and one Lord, Jesus Christ" (I Corinthians 8:6).

Emperor worship was a political rather than a religious cult, though it eventuated in the worship of the state: Evidently it was not uniformly enforced; it seems to have been much more prevalent in the provinces than in Rome, particularly in the Middle East. Christians were placed in the irreducible dilemma of being compelled to apostatize by token worship of Caesar if they would save their lives, or of appearing unpatriotic because they would not conform to state requirements. Irregular and perfunctory as emperor worship was, it symbolized the desire for protection by some visible power that was more real than the older gods who had proved ineffectual. The Romans felt that their security was personified in the head of the state, who was responsible for their food, their pleasures, their safety and their future. The result was a state cult which set the emperor in the place of God and created an atmosphere of man-worship. Such an attitude was hostile to Christianity, which was as rigidly uncompromising toward idolatry as Judaism had ever been. The constant pressure of the state was an unremitting threat to Christianity even under those emperors who did not take it seriously and who consequently did not promote an active persecution of dissidents. On the other hand, the very name "Christian" became synonymous with subversion and in the eyes of the general public Christians came to be classed with criminals (I Peter 4:15,16).[17]

Tenney also sums up the spirit of the times very accurately and describes the devastating effect of idolatry on pagan people in the Graeco-Roman world as follows:

Into such a superstitious and materialistic world Christianity was born. Fate, demons, and gods of every description haunted the atmosphere; spells, incantations, and magic were the means by which the individual could fend off the dangers that encircled him. Security was obtained by bribing the deities, or by ascertaining from horoscopes what course of action to pursue, or by discovering some potent charm to keep the threatening powers of darkness at bay. The uncertainty of the future held the masses of mankind in mental and spiritual bondage. Not until the light of the gospel of Christ penetrated to the Gentiles did men begin to lose their dread of the unseen powers and to achieve a true freedom. . . .

The prevailing laxity in sexual behavior, the gluttonous and idolatrous feasts, the incessant holiday-making in honor of the emperor or of the gods, and the interchange of entertainment in pagan homes must have affected many Christians.[18]

In the preceding pages of this chapter we've just barely scratched the surface of the ever-prevalent idolatry that was practiced in Bible times in the countries that surrounded the Promised Land of the Children of Israel. Aton, Attis, Athena, Ahura Mazda, Apollo, Aphrodite, Artemis, Ares, Asclepius — just a preliminary listing of the idols that begin with the letter "A" is a reminder of the mind-boggling numbers of deities that attracted devotees and kept people of Bible times locked fast in damning misbelief. How pleased Satan must have been to lead most of the people in ancient times to believe in literally thousands of idols and to remain far removed from the true God, the almighty Maker of heaven and earth. How tragic that so few people knew that "all the gods of the nations are idols, but the Lord made the heavens" (Psalm 96:5).

IDOLS OF THE BIBLE

Most of the idols mentioned above are not referred to directly in the Bible. Surely their worshipers came in contact on many occasions with God's chosen people, notably through trade, and the widespread practice of idolatry outside of Palestine (Canaan) helped to pave the way for the introduction of idolatrous activities among the Israelites. At this point it would be in place to get at least an overview of the idolatrous beliefs and some of the idols that are mentioned in the Holy Scriptures.

Old Testament

It could be said that Adam and Eve were guilty of idolatry when they took the word of a creature of God (Satan) and disobeyed the clear command of their Creator. Of course, every transgression of God's Law involves the breaking of the First Commandment, "Thou shalt have no other gods." The thief, the adulterer, the false witness, the despiser of God's Word, the individual who disobeys parents and superiors, the covetous person, the person who takes God's name in vain, the hate-poisoned murderer — all fracture the First Commandment as well as whatever commandment more directly forbids their sin. Thus it is correct to classify Cain, Lamech (Genesis 4:23,24) and the people who perished in the flood in Noah's day as idolaters. In fact, what Jesus said about the contemporaries of Noah, namely that those "people were eating and drinking, marrying and giving in marriage, up to the day Noah entered the ark" (Matthew 24:38 NIV), strongly suggests that the form of idolatry which contributed to their destruction was the same kind that has captured the devotion of millions in our modern age, namely blatant materialism, the worship of worldly pursuits, pleasures, property and possessions, and giving such things of the world higher priority than love and service to God.

BABEL

Idolatry also appeared to be in the picture when God confounded the language of mankind at the Tower of Babel at a time when the whole world had one language and a common speech. When the people declared, "Come, let us build ourselves a city, with a tower that reaches to the heavens, so that we may make a name for ourselves and not be scattered over the face of the whole earth" (Genesis 11:4), they were defiantly pitting their self-will against God's will which had decreed that men should "fill the earth and subdue it" (Genesis 1:28). Egotism in defiance of God seems to be the idol which caused the confusion of tongues at Babel and this too is a form of idolatry that's still very powerful and popular today. In fact, Pastor Immanuel Frey has stated in the *Northwestern Lutheran* that " 'Me' seems to have emerged as the idol of our generation."[19] Also in connection with the Babel incident Kenneth Hamilton maintains that idolatry has not changed much over the centuries, except that it has discarded its more blatant forms for something a little more subtle. He has observed that in idolatry today, at least in the Western world, the external image (statues of metal, wood and stone) has given place to the internal one (idolatrous ideas like evolution, atheism, etc.). Hamilton perceptively makes the point that whereas modern man imagines (see the word *image* in that word) that there is no heaven "up there," at Babel the people imagined that they could build a tower that would reach "up there." In both cases, however, idolatry is the root sin.[20]

TERAH AND TERAPHIM

According to Joshua 24:2 Terah, the father of Abraham, "lived beyond the River (Euphrates) and worshiped other gods." We have no exact details about the form of idolatry that held sway over Abraham's father, although it may have involved the worship of the moon-god because there was a celebrated temple dedicated to this heathen deity at Ur of the Chaldees, which was Terah's home city. By God's grace Abraham did not indulge in idolatry as his father had. He was led to worship the true God who promised that through him and his Seed (the

Savior) all the people on earth would be blessed. But idolatry was never far away from Abraham and his descendants. At all times the Israelites lived in an idol-worshiping world where a plurality of gods was commonplace and taken for granted.

The prevalence of idolatry can be seen in the presence of teraphim or household gods that wormed their way into the lives of Rachel, one of the patriarch Jacob's wives, and of Michal, the wife of King David. Though the word teraphim in English is superficially similar to Terah, the father of Abraham, there is no real connection. The teraphim were images, statues or figurines probably regarded as good luck charms and they were consulted with respect to the advisability of proposed actions (Ezekiel 21:21; Zechariah 10:2). The precise motivation of Rachel in stealing her father Laban's teraphim (Genesis 31:19ff.) is not revealed in the Bible. Most Bible commentators believe that it was idolatrous superstition that prompted Rachel to sneak away those household gods, to hide them inside her camel's saddle, and when Laban came to her tent looking for the missing teraphim, to divert his attention from her and the saddle on which she was sitting by telling him that she couldn't stand up because she was having her menstrual period.

James Kelso believes that Rachel's motive may have been covetous rather than idolatrous, for he theorizes that

> . . . these teraphim were doubly significant to Laban, since legally the person who possessed the family gods thereby had title deed to the family's property. Naturally Laban accused the crafty Jacob of this double crime. Laban did not find the teraphim and therefore he made a covenant that each party would leave the other alone and the marking of a boundary is this memorial pillar (Genesis 31:51, 52.)[21]

There is a question about the size of the teraphim. Most of them seemed to be little figurines, small enough for

Rachel to hide in her camel's saddle. Such tiny idols are still being found by archeologists in the Holy Land today. However, when David's wife Michal protected him from the fierce hatred of her father, King Saul, when he sent some of his soldiers to kill David, we're told that "Michal let David down through a window, and he fled and escaped. Then Michal took an idol (Hebrew — *teraphim*) and laid it on the bed, covering it with a garment and putting some goats' hair at the head. When Saul sent the men to capture David, Michal said, 'He is ill.' But Saul sent the men back to see David and told them, 'Bring him up to me in his bed so that I may kill him.' But when the men entered, there was the idol in the bed, and at the head was some goats' hair" (I Samuel 19:12-16, NIV). Thus it seems that most teraphim were tiny statuettes, with some exceptions, like the life-size idol which Michal utilized to cover up David's escape from Saul's murderous plan.

THE GOLDEN CALF

When one thinks of idolatry practiced in the Old Testament period, the worship of the golden calf by the Israelites at Sinai comes immediately to mind. From beginning to end this incident, described in considerable detail by the prophet Moses in Exodus 32, reeks of blasphemy, blatant unbelief, rebellion against the true God and unspeakable tragedy. How tragic, indeed, that Moses' brother Aaron did not have the backbone to go against the demands of the people: "Come, make us gods who will go before us" (Exodus 32:1). How tragic that God's chosen people gave credit to that golden calf for bringing them out of bondage in Egypt (Exodus 32:8) and gave themselves over to drunken revelry, running wild in their idolatrous orgies (Exodus 32:6,25)!

Why did Aaron fashion a calf of gold in response to the people's clamor for an idol? Some Bible scholars believe that Aaron's image of the calf, or young bull, was an imitation of the Apis Bull of Memphis worshiped by the Egyptians, since that form of idolatry would still be very fresh in the minds of Aaron and the Israelites after their exodus from Egypt. James Kelso, however, insists that

> The golden calf was not a heresy picked up in Egypt, for in that land bull worship demanded a living bull, not an idol. No, the golden calf was an old Mesopotamian heresy going back to the pre-Abraham generation which came out of Ur. But these fertility cults of Mesopotamia and Canaan with their bull symbolism will be in almost constant competition with Yahveh until Israel returns from her exile.[22]

Martin Noth maintains that

> . . . the "golden calf" recorded in the Old Testament was certainly not thought of originally as an image of deity, but only as a pedestal of a deity, in this case not depicted, but rather conceived as invisibly standing on it.[23]

Noth's understanding of the golden calf is unusual and intriguing, but it cannot be harmonized with the plain words of Scripture, such as Exodus 32:32 where we're told that "Moses went back to the Lord and said, 'Oh, what a great sin these people have committed! They have made themselves gods of gold.' "

Some scholars insist that Aaron's action in fashioning the golden calf should not be condemned too severely, that he was guilty, not of gross idolatry, but merely of a misguided syncretism, the blending of a mild form of pagan idolatry with the worship of the true God, because he announced, after an altar was erected in front of the calf, that "Tomorrow there will be a festival to the LORD" (Exodus 32:5). However, we dare not minimize the heinousness of the idolatry perpetrated by Aaron and the children of Israel who pressured him into fashioning that golden calf. St. Paul sums up the sad shoddy affair in I Corinthians 10:7 — "Do not be idolaters, as some of them were; as it is written: 'The people sat down to eat and drink and got up to indulge in pagan revelry.' "

Several centuries after Aaron fashioned the original golden calf during the wilderness wanderings of the Israelites, a very similar form of idolatry was introduced by Jeroboam, the first king of the ten northern tribes which came to be called Israel. In order to keep the people away from the temple in Jerusalem and to prevent them from giving their allegiance and obedience to his rival, Rehoboam, king of Judah, "the king (Jeroboam) made two golden calves. He said to the people, 'It is too much for you to go up to Jerusalem. Here are your gods, O Israel, who brought you up out of Egypt.' One he set up in Bethel, and the other in Dan. And this thing became a sin; the people went even as far as Dan to worship the one there. Jeroboam built shrines on high places and appointed priests from all sorts of people, even though they were not Levites. He instituted a festival on the fifteenth day of the eighth month, like the festival held in Judah, and offered sacrifices on the altar. This he did in Bethel, sacrificing to the calves he had made. . . ." (I Kings 12:28-32).

BAAL AND CANAANITE DEITIES

The aforementioned golden calves at Dan and Bethel set up by Jeroboam reflected the influence of the worship of Baal, the chief deity of the Canaanite pantheon, who was also associated with the bull. There are scores of references in the Scriptures to Baal. No idol is mentioned more frequently in the Bible. Even before the children of Israel entered the Promised Land, Baal worship reared its ugly, lascivious head and brought condemnation and death upon several thousand of the Israelites (cf. Numbers 25). St. Paul later described that disgraceful behavior of the Israelites in I Corinthians 10:8 — "We should not commit sexual immorality, as some of them did — and in one day twenty-three thousand of them died." Again and again, for hundreds of years, the Baal form of idolatry with countless variations cropped up as a device of Satan to seduce and deceive God's people. Probably the best known and most dramatic encounter took place in the time of Elijah when that great prophet challenged wicked King Ahab, the fickle, double-minded children of Israel and 450 pagan prophets of Baal to a test to demonstrate the superiority and supremacy of the Lord over impotent idols (I Kings 18). A short time before the seventy year Babylonian exile of God's people the Prophet Jeremiah revealed why that judgment was to descend upon them. As God's mouthpiece Jeremiah declared: ". . . they have forsaken me and made this a place of foreign gods; they have burned sacrifices in it to gods that neither they nor their fathers nor the kings of Judah ever knew, and they have filled this place with the blood of the innocent. They have built the high places of Baal to burn their sons in the fire as offerings to Baal" (Jeremiah 19:4,5). ". . . They set up their abominable idols in the house that bears my Name and defiled it. They built high places for Baal in the Valley of Ben Hinnom to sacrifice their sons and daughters to Molech, though I never commanded, nor did it enter my mind that they should do such a detestable thing and so make Judah sin" (Jeremiah 32:34,35).

The reference above to sacrificing children to Molech (an aspect of Baal known also as Moloch, Milcom, Malcam or Melcarth) proves how correct is James Kelso's description of Canaanite idolatry:

> One feature of Canaanite religion stands out above all others — its depravity. It was the most degenerate of all the religions of antiquity. Its deities were murderers, adulterers and degenerates.[24]

Kelso gives a good description of the principle Canaanite deities, including a quotation from W. F. Albright's *Archaeology and the Religion of Israel*, in which Albright tells of the goddess Anath's lust for blood:

The Canaanites had a polytheistic faith with emphasis on a fertility cult which was much more primitive than that of other nations. El, the progenitor of both gods and men, was the oldest of their gods and the chief of their pantheon. But he was little concerned with men and earth. "He dethroned his own father, Heaven (Uranus), and castrated him; he slew his own favorite son, probably Iadid (Beloved), with the latter's iron weapon; he cut off his daughter's head; he offered up his 'only begotten son' as a sacrifice to Heaven (Uranus)." Now contrast Yahweh with El.

The god closest to the Canaanite people themselves was Baal whose throne name was Hadad. He was the storm god. As the giver of rain he was a fertility deity, although he had to share a part of that honor with Mot (the god of death and harvest). Baal is often pictured holding the lightning bolts in one hand and a war club in the other. The latter symbolized him as the warrior king. He is often portrayed standing on a bull. Compare the use of the bull pedestal in Jeroboam's temple to Yahweh at Bethel.

The Canaanites considered Baal to be a son of El; but the Amorites, whose theology was later blended into that of the Canaanites, considered him to be the son of Dagon. In ancient Ugarit Dagon's temple was larger than Baal's. Dagon was also a Philistine grain god. After the ark of the covenant was captured by the Philistines in their attack on Shiloh, it was taken as a votive offering and placed in Dagon's temple in Ashdod (I Samuel 5:1ff).

There were three major goddesses: Astarte, Anath and Asherah; but it is difficult to separate them and their functions. They were primarily sex goddesses serving both as mother goddesses and sacred prostitutes, but the emphasis was on the latter. A secondary function was that of goddess of war. So it was only natural that later the armour of the dead Saul was placed in the temple of Astarte (Ashtaroth) in Beth-shan.

"There is a harrowing description of Anath's thirst for blood. For a reason which still escapes us she decided to carry out a general massacre: 'With might she hewed down the people of the cities, she smote the folk of the sea-coast, she slew the men of the sunrise (east).' After filling her temple (it seems) with men, she barred the gates so that none might escape, after which 'she hurled chairs at the youths, tables at the warriors, footstools at the men of might.' The blood was so deep that she waded in it up to her knees — nay, up to her neck. Under her feet were human heads, above her human hands flew like locusts. In her sensuous delight she decorated herself with suspended heads, while she attached hands to her girdle. Her joy at the butchery is described in even more sadistic language: 'Her liver swelled with laughter, her heart was full of joy, the liver of Anath (was full of) exultation(?).' Afterwards Anath 'was satisfied' and washed her hands in human gore before proceeding to other occupations." (W. F. Albright, *Archaeology and the Religion of Israel*, p. 77.)

One of the great truths of Revelation is retributive justice and since this is the bloody ideal of the Canaanite gods the extermination of the Canaanites referred to in Joshua is just what they asked for.

One of these prostitute goddesses was called "the holy one," which is the last word in blasphemy to the Hebrews as the term "Holy" was used only of Yahweh. Asherah was also the goddess of the sea and as such appeared with Baal in the Mt. Carmel episode of Ahab and Elijah. Asherah seems to appear as Baal's wife more often in later myths, but Anath held that position earlier.

The following minor deities had sanctuaries in Palestine and gave their names to the cities where these sanctuaries were located. Hauron was the god of the underworld. Shemesh was the sun god. Lahum was the god of war and his sanctuary was at Bethlehem. The Canaanite spelling of that city was Beth-la-hum.

In striking contrast to these Canaanite deities, remember that Yahweh was neither "god or goddess." Yahweh was infinitely beyond gender, i.e. beyond anything human. The Canaanites on the other hand made their gods in their own image and likeness. The only true blending of humanity and deity was to come later in the person of Jesus the Christ.[25]

We in the 20th century who are accustomed to think of

ourselves as highly advanced, sophisticated and civilized are tempted to dismiss Canaanite idol perversions as the abnormal behavior of a backward, primitive pagan people who simply didn't know any better. Surely people living in this modern day of intercontinental communication systems and spectacular space explorations would not behave like those idolatrous Canaanites. Yet when we turn to modern mass media devices like television and movies, we see that they are often obsessed and saturated with mindless violence and sexual perversions, which would make the Canaanites feel right at home.

What James Kelso writes about Sodom and Gomorrah and Canaanite religion as practiced later by Ahaz and Manasseh could fit the kind of behavior permitted and even promoted in modern cities like Las Vegas and San Francisco:

> The immorality displayed in the Sodom and Gomorrah episode (Genesis 19) is typical of Canaanite religion. Since the highest gods of the Canaanites went in for immorality, their worshipers naturally did so also. Sex orgies were common and the temples had their male and female prostitutes. And along with these were self-made eunuch priests and a guild of homosexuals. Anath and Astarte (Ashtaroth), their two chief goddesses, were both mother goddesses and divine courtesans; but the emphasis was seldom on the maternal. Most startling of all is the portrayal of a naked prostitute goddess referred to as "the holy one." Child sacrifice to their deities was the final Canaanite blasphemy. No wonder Yahweh ordered the Israelites to wipe out the Canaanite religion for "Yahweh our God is Holy."
> . . . Human sacrifice was their most heinous religious act. Little children were sacrificed in Jerusalem under such kings as Ahaz and Manasseh who practiced all the worst of heathen religions. The sacrifice of children continued on in Carthage, a Canaanite colony in North Africa, until that city was destroyed by Rome. The emphasis upon fertility in their cult ritual went the whole way with sacred prostitution. There were male and female prostitutes, eunuch priests and homosexual guilds.[26]

Is there any modern-day parallel to the sickening, stomach-turning Canaanite religious practice of human sacrifice, and of children at that? Well, what about the million or so infants, just in the United States in recent years, who annually are slaughtered in the name of women's rights? What about those precious unborn babies being sacrificed on the altar of the goddess, Abortion on Demand, in compliance with the sacred slogan of radical women's libbers who insist that every woman has the right to do what she wants with her own body? Although St. Paul wrote: "Do you not know that your body is a temple of the Holy Spirit, who is in you, whom you have received from God? You are not your own; you were bought at a price. Therefore honor God with your body" (I Corinthians 6:19,20), a million American girls and women and the physicians who are their advisors and accomplices in the abortion of their babies, each year behave more like the ancient Canaanites rather than as Christians. The Canaanites believed it was O.K., even god-pleasing, to sacrifice their children. Christians surely will recognize that snuffing out a baby's (even when it could be called a fetus) life to cover up the shame of premarital sex or to get rid of an unwanted child is no way to honor God with your body. Idolatry, indeed, is not dead in our day. The widespread perversion of sex and the performance of millions of abortions in recent years prove beyond any doubt that idolatrous beliefs and attitudes are still very much alive.

SOLOMON AND HIS SUCCESSORS

King Solomon, the son of David, was one of Israel's greatest kings, the builder of the temple, a holy man chosen and moved by God to write part of the Old Testament, a man justly renowned for his God-given wisdom. However, in his old age Solomon proved the truth of the adage: "There's no fool like an old fool." In spite of the clear commands and prohibitions which God had announced to the Israelites before they entered Canaan and with which Solomon must have been familiar (cf. Exodus 34:11-17 and Deuteronomy 17:17), Solomon permitted himself to be led astray from the Lord by a spiritually poisonous potion of polygamy and idolatrous polytheism. This sad chapter in Solomon's otherwise distinguished royal career is described as follows in I Kings 11:1-10:

> King Solomon, however, loved many foreign women besides Pharaoh's daughter — Moabites, Ammonites, Edomites, Sidonians, and Hittites. They were from nations about which the Lord had told the Israelites, "You must not intermarry with them, because they will surely turn your hearts after their gods." Nevertheless, Solomon held fast to them in love. He had seven hundred wives of royal birth and three hundred concubines, and his wives led him astray. As Solomon grew old, his wives turned his heart after other gods, and his heart was not fully devoted to the Lord his God, as the heart of David his father had been. He followed Ashtoreth the goddess of the Sidonians, and Molech the detestable god of the Ammonites. So Solomon did evil in the eyes of the Lord; he did not follow the Lord completely, as David his father had done.
>
> On a hill east of Jerusalem, Solomon built a high place for Chemosh the detestable god of Moab, and for Molech the detestable god of the Ammonites. He did the same for all his foreign wives, who burned incense and offered sacrifices to their gods.
>
> The Lord became angry with Solomon because his heart had turned away from the Lord, the God of Israel, who had appeared to him twice. Although he had forbidden Solomon to follow other gods, Solomon did not keep the Lord's command.

After Solomon's kingdom was divided about 1000 B.C. into the northern kingdom of Israel with ten tribes and the southern kingdom of Judah made up of the two tribes of Judah and Benjamin, the plunge into idolatry by God's chosen people picked up momentum. None of the 19 kings of Israel who were in power from about 975-722 B.C. could be classified as God-fearing. Of the seventh king of Israel, it was said that "Ahab son of Omri did more evil in the eyes of the Lord than any of those before him. He not only considered it trivial to commit the sins of Jeroboam son of Nebat (recall that Jeroboam had begun worship to golden calves in Dan and Bethel), but he also married Jezebel daughter of Ethbaal king of the Sidonians, and began to serve Baal and worship him. He set up an altar for Baal in the temple of Baal that he built in Samaria. Ahab also made an Asherah pole and did more to provoke the Lord, the God of Israel, to anger than did all the kings of Israel before him" (I Kings 16:30-33). To be sure, Ahab with his 450 priests of Baal and his wife Jezebel who employed 400 priests in lewd devotion to the moon goddess Ashtoreth of her native country, were champions of idolatry. About the only bright spot in the whole sordid history of Israel is the reign of Jehu who was commissioned to destroy the house and family of Ahab. He obediently killed Ahab's son, King Jehoram, and ordered the death of Jezebel, who was flung from a window and killed. Jehu also destroyed Baal worship in Israel by summoning and then slaughtering all the prophets, priests and ministers of Baal. After that methodical massacre, described so vividly in II Kings 10:18ff., it was said: "They demolished the sacred stone of Baal and tore down the temple of Baal, and people have used it for a latrine to this day" (I Kings 10:27). However, even though Jehu eradicated Baal worship in Israel as God had commanded him, "he did not turn away from the sins of Jeroboam . . . the worship of the golden calves at Bethel and Dan" (II Kings 10:29).

In the kingdom of Judah eight of the 20 kings who ruled from 975-588 B.C. more or less upheld the worship of the true God. Hezekiah and Josiah especially stand out as God-fearing reformers who made significant efforts to root out idolatry when they were in power. But the efforts of Hezekiah and Josiah also remind us of kings of Judah like Ahaz and Manasseh who matched and even perhaps surpassed Israel's King Ahab in the depravity of their idolatrous practices. The corrupt religious principles and practices of Ahaz and Manasseh, Hezekiah's father and his wicked son, are summed up by James Kelso as follows:

> . . . Ahaz introduced the gods of Assyria for political reasons. Refusing to accept the grace of God to save his throne for him, he voluntarily surrendered to Tiglath-pileser III, king of Assyria. This action demanded that he worship Assyrian gods and he therefore introduced a pagan altar into the Yahweh temple in Jerusalem. For religious worship, however, Ahaz preferred Baal and burned incense to him on the high places. He also introduced Moloch worship in which he burned his own children in the fire of that demonic ritual (II Chronicles 28:3,4). This rite had been imported from Syria (II Kings 17:31). This tragic cult is known best through the work of the Carthaginian archaeologists who have found thousands of these cremated infants.
>
> Hezekiah's reformation only temporarily cleared away the blasphemies of his father Ahaz, for as soon as Hezekiah was gone Manasseh (Hezekiah's son) reintroduced everything of Baalism. He also expanded Assyrian worship putting special emphasis upon the celestial deities, "The host of heaven," putting their altars in Yahweh's temple (II Kings 21:5). Most significant were the horses and chariots of the sun, which remind us at once of the Greek god Apollo. He even named his son Amon after one of the most influential Egyptian deities (as in King Tutankh*amon*). It is startling to find the name of this Egyptian god given to one in the Messianic line! After the brief respite of Josiah's reformation, Judah's sins came full cycle, and Jerusalem and Judah were destroyed; and the covenant people transplanted to Babylon.[27]

New Testament

As one might expect, since the Gospels and Epistles describe in considerable detail the life and teachings of our Savior, there are not nearly as many references to idolatry in the New Testament as in the Old Testament. During the three years of his public ministry the Lord Jesus did not have any direct confrontations with any gross forms of idolatry in the land of Palestine. It could be said that his most persistent adversaries, the self-righteous scribes, Pharisees and chief priests, were idolaters in the sense that they trusted in themselves and their works for salvation, but Jesus did not have to deal in any obvious way with idols like Baal, Moloch, Dagon or Asherah, which are referred to so frequently in the Old Testament. Judas, the betrayer of his Master, might be classified as an idolater, and a very modern one at that. His love of money, in the form of thirty pieces of silver, prompted him to turn Jesus over to his enemies and put him in the same category with so many people in our 20th century who are devoted worshipers of the Almighty Dollar, the idol which makes it impossible for them to fear, love and trust in the true God above all things.

The clearest examples of idol worship in the New Testament, however, come to view in connection with the missionary journeys of the Apostle Paul and his experiences in the cities of Lystra, Athens and Ephesus.

LYSTRA

On his first missionary journey St. Paul, accompanied by his missionary colleague Barnabas, came to the Roman colony town of Lystra in Asia Minor. When Paul in the course of his ministry was instrumental in healing a crippled man who had been lame from birth, the crowd which witnessed the miracle reacted in harmony with their heathen background by shouting: " 'The gods have come down to us in human form!' Barnabas they called Zeus (Jupiter), and Paul they called Hermes (Mercury) because he was the chief speaker. The priest of Zeus, whose temple was just outside the city, brought bulls and wreaths to the city gates because he and the crowd wanted to offer sacrifices to them. But when the apostles Barnabas and Paul heard of this, they tore their clothes and rushed into the crowd, shouting: 'Men, why are you doing this? We too are only men, human like you. We are bringing you good news, telling you to turn from these worthless things to the living God, who made heaven and earth and sea and everything in them. In the past, he let all nations go their own way. Yet he has not left himself without testimony: He has shown kindness by giving you rain from heaven and crops in their season: he provides you with plenty of food and fills your hearts with joy.' Even with these words, they had difficulty keeping the crowd from sacrificing to them" (Acts 14:11-18).

ATHENS

On his second missionary journey Paul visited the renowned city of Athens, which could be called the idol capital of the ancient world. The city was named after the goddess Athena, whose 75 foot statue, perched on the Acropolis, a hill 150 feet high, served as a landmark for sailors. The city had literally thousands of idol statues, so many that Paul "was greatly distressed to see that the city was full of idols" (Acts 17:16). Pagan writers make it clear that Paul had plenty of reason to be disturbed about the large number of idols in Athens and that Luke was not exaggerating when he described the city as "full of idols." Petronius sarcastically said that it was easier to find a god than a man in Athens; Xenophon described Athens as "one great altar, one great offering to the gods;" Pausanias claimed that Athens had more idol images than all the rest of Greece put together; Livy wrote that "in Athens are to be seen images of gods and men of all descriptions and made of all materials."

In this stronghold of idolatry Paul encountered some

Stoic and Epicurean philosophers who were slaves to a different kind of idol, their own proud reason and intellect. These learned men invited Paul to share with them his strange ideas, for they prided themselves on their open-mindedness toward and interest in new philosophies. Paul made the most of his opportunity by saying: "Men of Athens, I see that in every way you are very religious. For as I walked around and observed your objects of worship, I even found an altar with this inscription: TO AN UNKNOWN GOD. Now what you worship as something unknown I am going to proclaim to you" (Act 17:22,23).

Paul then proceeded to tell the Athenians about the true Triune God who gives all men life and breath and everything else. In that city filled with all sorts of idolatrous statues Paul courageously declared that "we should not think that the divine being is like gold or silver or stone — an image made by man's design and skill" (Acts 17:29). Paul then concluded his address with a call to repentance, a reference to God's raising his Son Jesus from the dead and the prediction that a day of just judgment will be coming.

Some Bible scholars believe that Paul failed in Athens, that he blew a golden opportunity to win over to Christianity the Athenian intelligentsia. It's true that "when they heard about the resurrection of the dead, some of them sneered, but others said, 'We want to hear you again on this subject' " (Acts 17:32), which may have been their polite way of saying: "Don't call us; we'll call you." But it would be as much a mistake to dismiss Paul's mission work in Athens as a failure as it would to claim that Christ failed because he attracted only a few followers and finally was nailed to a cross. "Many are called, but few are chosen" (Matthew 22:14), Jesus had predicted, and confronted by the formidable idolatry in Athens, Paul preached a powerful and effective message with the gratifying result that "a few men became followers of Paul and believed. Among them was Dionysius, a member of the Aeropagus (one of the twelve judges of the Athenian court who very likely became the first Christian bishop of Athens), also a woman named Damaris and a number of others" (Acts 17:34).

EPHESUS

On his third missionary journey Paul spent three years in the metropolis of Asia Minor, the prosperous trade center of Ephesus. Here stood one of the seven wonders of the ancient world, the great pagan temple of the goddess Diana (Gk. Artemis). This impressive structure, four times as large as the Parthenon in Athens, had 127 sixty-foot columns of white marble and glittered in brilliant splendor at the head of Ephesus' bustling harbor. In this stronghold of heathen idolatry Paul's mission efforts were blessed with significant success as "the word of the Lord spread widely and grew in power" (Acts 19:20). Prior to Paul's coming Satan had reigned supreme in Ephesus. When he saw the success of the gospel, he pulled out all the stops to destroy the Christian church. He stirred up a silversmith named Demetrius, who made silver shrines of Artemis, to call together other heathen craftsmen and warn them that the powerful gospel preaching of the apostle Paul would wipe out their idol-fashioning trade if they didn't do something to protect their interests. F. Rupprecht offers this description of the goddess and the thriving business generated by her idol worship:

> The Ephesian Diana was presented as a standing idol. The upper part of the body, in front, was covered with rows of breasts, symbolizing her as the mother of all life, while the lower part was merely an upright block representing robes, covered with symbols and figures of animals. The shrines were small

models of the goddess standing on a pedestal, over which a canopy was erected; some were so small that they could be carried about on a person. The silver shrines (also bronze) were for the rich; the models for the poorer classes were made of terra-cotta marble, many of which are still to be found in the neighborhood of Ephesus.[28]

Demetrius, as the devil's mouthpiece, pleaded with his fellow craftsmen: "Men, you know we receive a good income from this business. And you see and hear how this fellow Paul has convinced and led astray large numbers of people here in Ephesus and in practically the whole province of Asia. He says that man-made gods are no gods at all. There is danger not only that our trade will lose its good name, but also that the temple of the great goddess Artemis will be discredited, and the goddess herself, who is worshiped throughout the province of Asia and the world, will be robbed of her divine majesty" (Acts 19:25b-27).

Demetrius proved to be a diabolically-skilled rabble-rouser as he triggered a riot in the Ephesian amphitheater, the largest in the world at the time, holding 24,500 people. St. Luke gives the following classic description of mob psychology which was set in motion by Demetrius: "The assembly was in confusion: Some were shouting one thing, some another. Most of the people did not even know why they were there . . . they all shouted in unison for about two hours: 'Great is Artemis of the Ephesians!' " (Acts 19:32,34).

Finally the cool-headed city clerk calmed the crowd by challenging Demetrius and his fellow craftsmen to take the matter to court and to press charges against Paul and the Christians if they felt they had a legitimate grievance. The influence of Roman law and order in Ephesus is shown by the city clerk's insistence that rioting would do no good and that the issue must be settled in a legal assembly.

Also in Ephesus Paul faced two forms of idolatry just as

he did in Athens. Not only was there the gross worship of a heathen goddess, Artemis (Diana), to contend with, but even more formidable was the love of money which motivated Demetrius and his fellow craftsmen to stir up mob action against Paul because they feared that their lucrative business would be ruined by Paul's preaching of the gospel and his exposing the folly of idolatry. In Athens Paul faced gross idolatry and the idol of human reason and philosophy; in Ephesus he encountered gross idolatry again in the worship of Artemis, but the almighty dollar or Greek drachma was the more powerful idol that stirred up Demetrius and his cohorts.

Paul's experiences in Athens and Ephesus bring to mind the observation of James Kelso, who noted a turning point in history at the time of Cyrus, the Persian monarch who conquered Babylon in 539 B.C. Instead of keeping for himself and the Persian people all the idols which Nebuchadnezzar had captured and which he found in Babylon, Cyrus sent all those idols back to their original sanctuaries in various countries. Kelso says:

> ... something new happened in world history. . . . This was one of the greatest political moves in all of ancient history! And Persia profited by it for two centuries. But Yahweh had already proved these idols worthless. Nevertheless idolatry will still go on but from now on it will be the more subtle idolatry of MONEY and the INTELLECT. Pagan idolatry must now share her throne with the almighty dollar and the omniscient (all-knowing) philosopher.[29]

During his missionary career Paul came into contact with various kinds of idolatry. At Lystra it was idolatry in its more primitive pagan form when Paul and Barnabas were seen as Hermes and Zeus after the miraculous healing of the lame man. At Athens Paul had to address himself not only to that idol-cluttered city of thousands of statues, but he faced an even more formidable idol, the INTEL-

LECT of the Stoic and Epicurean philosophers. At Ephesus MONEY was the real idol that stirred up all the trouble along with the common people's devotion to their heathen goddess, the Asiatic Artemis, Diana of Ephesus, who was a union of the Greek Artemis with the lusty Semitic moon-goddess, Ashtoreth.

GALATIANS 5:12

In his letter to the Galatians Paul had to contend with the Judaizers, false teachers who insisted that faith in Christ was not sufficient for salvation, that works of the Old Testament ceremonial law like circumcision were also required. Paul pulled no punches in denouncing those Judaizers who were trying to promote among the Galatians a different gospel — which was really no gospel at all (Galatians 1:6,7). In Galatians 5:12 Paul revealed the depth of his displeasure and disgust with the following shocking denunciation of those errorists: "As for those agitators, I wish they would go the whole way and emasculate themselves." Most Bible commentators believe that Paul's harsh condemnation of the Judaizers is closely connected with the worship of Cybele and Attis, one of the mystery religions that had become popular in Asia Minor and with which Paul and his Galatian readers would have been very familiar (cf. Mystery Religions above).

R. C. H. Lenski says this in connection with Galatians 5:12:

> Paul's hot indignation against these Judaizers who stoop to anything they think may further their cause is expressed in the ironic wish that they might have themselves even castrated. . . . The point of castration was highly effective in the case of the Galatians, who had among them the castrated priests of Cybele, a Phrygian goddess, who was by the Greeks identified more or less with Rhea, the mother of their gods. Castration appears in various other pagan cults. So these Judaizers, who had advanced to castration, would be out and out pagans![30]

Harold Willoughby gives a vivid description of the heathen rites of Attis-Cybele worship that Paul most likely was referring to in his condemnation of the Judaizers in Galatians 5:12:

According to the myth, the goddess-mother loved the youthful, virgin-born shepherd Attis with a pure love. But Attis died, either slain by another or by his own hand. In the latter instance, he was unfaithful to the Great Mother (Cybele) and in a frenzy of regret he emasculated himself and died. The goddess-mother mourned her dead lover and finally effected his restoration. Thus, in the end the mortal Attis became deified and immortal. These were the main elements in the developed myth which bulked largest in the mind of the devotee as he participated in the rites of the cult. . . .

These rites came on the twenty-fourth of March, a day that was called significantly enough, the "Day of Blood." At this time the Great Mother of the gods inspired her devotees with a frenzy surpassing that which the followers of Dionysus knew. It was a madness induced not by wine, but by the din of crashing music, the dizzy whirling of the dance, and the sight of blood. The music which accompanied these rites was wild and barbaric, made by clashing cymbals and blatant horns, shrilling flutes and rolling drums. It was maddening music, noisy and savage. . . . Music of this kind — the Anatolian prototype of modern jazz (or punk rock in the '70s? — R. J. S.) — was popularly known as Phrygian music. . . .

(The) cruel custom of lacerating one's own flesh during the frenzied ritual was a distinctive characteristic of the Great Mother's cult. Slashing their arms with knives, or gashing their bodies, the worshipers sprinkled with their own blood the sacred tree that was Attis. . . . It is probable . . . that the devotees, wrought up to a very high pitch of excitement by the din of the noisy music and the frenzy of the wild dance, were largely insensible to the pain. . . . But the devotees of the Great Mother did not stop with the shedding of blood merely. Keyed up to the highest pitch of religious excitement, they followed the example of Attis and emasculated themselves. With this final act of self-sacrifice and consecration, the Dies Sanguinis (Day of

Blood) was crowned and the devotee became one of the *Galli*, a eunuch-priest of the Asian goddess. . . .

In his account Willoughby includes the following description by the pagan writer Lucian:

"As the *Galli* sing and celebrate their orgies, frenzy falls on many of them, and many who had come as mere spectators afterwards are found to have committed the great act. Any young man who has resolved on this action, strips off his clothes, and with a loud shout bursts into the midst of the crowd and picks up a sword. He takes it and emasculates himself and then runs wild through the city."

Undoubtedly for the devotee of Cybele the rite of self-mutilation had distinct religious values. By the very act the devotee himself became another Attis. He had done in the service of the goddess what Attis had already done. . . . Just as Attis was believed to have attained the state of deity by the passion of emasculation so by the way of self-mutilation, the *Gallus* became a god instead of a mortal. . . .

The act that made an Attis of the votary placed him in peculiarly intimate relationship to the Mother Goddess herself. The broken instruments of his manhood were treated as an oblation (offering) to the goddess. Perhaps they were thrown into the lap of her statue. . . . As a new Attis the votary assumed the role of a bridegroom to the goddess. . . . By the fact of emasculation he had assimilated himself to the nature of the goddess. As an indication of this transformation he henceforth wore feminine dress and allowed his hair to grow long. . . . The orgiastic rite reached its climax in the irrevocable sacrifice of manhood, an act whereby the devotee physically assimilated himself to divinity. He himself became Attis, a god, mystically united as a divine lover to the great Goddess. In the resurrection of his god he felt himself personally participant and he found therein the assurance of a happy future life. The experience was a crudely physical one and realistic in the extreme. Yet it had a strange fascination because of its very realism, and it held out to the devotees who were willing to make the supreme sacrifice the promise of a divinization of human nature and an immediate communion with deity.[31]

Although the Cybele-Attis cult with its glorification of

castration may not be typical of ancient idolatry, it does give us some insight into the poisoned and perverted moral climate in which the apostle Paul lived and proclaimed the gospel and which prevailed also, in even greater measure, in Old Testament times.

Biblical Descriptions and Denunciations of Idolatry

The Bible, especially the Old Testament, abounds with vivid descriptions and uncompromising denunciations of the idolatry which so often seduced God's chosen people. In Psalm 115:3-8 the sharp contrast between the unlimited might of the true God and the complete impotence of heathen idols is set forth, as well as the utter folly and stupidity of idolaters:

> Ps. 115:3-8 — Our God is in heaven; he does whatever pleases him. But their idols are silver and gold, made by the hands of men. They have mouths, but cannot speak, eyes, but they cannot see; they have ears, but cannot hear, noses, but they cannot smell; they have hands, but cannot feel, feet, but they cannot walk; nor can they utter a sound with their throats. Those who make them will be like them, and so will all who trust in them. (cf. Ps. 135:15-18 for a nearly identical description of idols.)

The Prophet Isaiah exposed the vanity of idolatry, and the fanatic, misguided zeal of idol makers and worshipers in Isaiah 44:9-20 as follows:

> Is. 44:9-20 — All who make idols are nothing, and the things they treasure are worthless. Those who would speak up for them are blind; they are ignorant, to their own shame. Who shapes a god and casts an idol, which can profit him nothing? He and his kind will be put to shame; craftsmen are nothing but men. Let them all come together and take their stand; they will be brought down to terror and infamy. The blacksmith takes a tool and works with it in the coals, he shapes an idol with hammers, he forges it with the might of his arm. He gets hungry and loses his strength; he drinks no water and grows faint. The carpenter measures with a line and makes an outline with

a marker; he roughs it out with chisels and marks it with compasses. He shapes it in the form of man, of man in all his glory, that it may dwell in a shrine. He cut down cedars, or perhaps took a cypress or oak. He let it grow among the trees of the forest, or planted a pine, and the rain made it grow. It is man's fuel for burning; some of it he takes and warms himself, he kindles a fire and bakes bread. But he also fashions a god and worships it; he makes an idol and bows down to it. Half of the wood he burns in the fire; over it he prepares his meal, he roasts his meat and eats his fill. He also warms himself and says, "Ah! I am warm; I see the fire." From the rest he makes a god, his idol; he bows down to it and worships. He prays to it and says, "Save me; you are my god." They know nothing, they understand nothing; their eyes are plastered over so they cannot see, and their minds closed so they cannot understand. No one stops to think, no one has the knowledge or understanding to say, "Half of it I used for fuel; I even baked bread over its coals, I roasted meat and I ate. Shall I make a detestable thing from what is left? Shall I bow down to a block of wood? He feeds on ashes, a deluded heart misleads him; he cannot save himself, or say, "Is not this thing in my right hand a lie?"

A similar devastating description of idolatry, its foolishness and powerlessness in contrast to the omnipotence and majesty of the true God, is recorded by the Prophet Jeremiah, chapter 10, verses 3-16:

> For the customs of the peoples are worthless; they cut a tree out of the forest, and a craftsman shapes it with his chisel. They adorn it with silver and gold; they fasten it with hammer and nails so it will not totter. Like a scarecrow in a melon patch, their idols cannot speak; they must be carried because they cannot walk. Do not fear them; they can do no harm nor can they do any good. No one is like you, O Lord; you are great, and your name is mighty in power. Who should not revere you, O King of the nations? This is your due. Among all the wise men of the nations and in all their kingdoms, there is no one like you. They are all senseless and foolish; they are taught by worthless wooden idols. Hammered silver is brought from Tarshish and gold from Uphaz. What the craftsman and goldsmith have made is then dressed in blue and purple all made by skilled

workers. But the Lord is the true God; he is the living God, the eternal King. When he is angry, the earth trembles; the nations cannot endure his wrath. "Tell them this: 'These gods, who did not make the heavens and the earth, will perish from the earth and from under the heavens.' " But God made the earth by his power; he founded the world by his wisdom and stretched out the heavens by his understanding. When he thunders, the waters in the heavens roar; he makes clouds rise from the ends of the earth. He sends lightning with the rain and brings out the wind from his storehouses. Everyone is senseless and without knowledge; every goldsmith is shamed by his idols. His images are a fraud; they have no breath in them. They are worthless, the objects of mockery; when their judgment comes, they will perish. He who is the Portion of Jacob is not like these, for he is the Maker of all things, including Israel, the tribe of his inheritance — the Lord Almighty is his name.

Several forms of idolatrous activity are described and condemned by Ezekiel in the eighth chapter of his book as follows:

In the sixth year, in the sixth month on the fifth day, while I was sitting in my house and the elders of Judah were sitting before me, the hand of the Sovereign Lord came upon me there. I looked, and I saw a figure like that of a man. From what appeared to be his waist down he was like fire, and from there up his appearance was as bright as glowing metal. He stretched out what looked like a hand and took me by the hair of my head. The Spirit lifted me up between earth and heaven and in visions of God he took me to Jerusalem, to the entrance to the north gate of the inner court, where the idol that provokes to jealousy stood. And there before me was the glory of the God of Israel, as in the vision I had seen in the plain.

Then he said to me, "Son of man, look toward the north." So I looked, and in the entrance north of the gate of the altar I saw this idol of jealousy.

And he said to me, "Son of man, do you see what they are doing — the utterly detestable things the house of Israel is doing here, things that will drive me far from my sanctuary? But you will see things that are even more detestable." Then he brought me to the entrance to the court. I looked, and I saw a hole in the wall. He said to me, "Son of man, now dig into the wall." So I dug into the wall and saw a doorway there. And he said to me, "Go in and see the wicked and detestable things they are doing here." So I went in and looked, and I saw portrayed all over the walls all kinds of crawling things and detestable animals and all the idols of the house of Israel. In front of them stood seventy elders of the house of Israel, and Jaazaniah son of Shaphan was standing among them. Each had a censer in his hand and a fragrant cloud of incense was rising.

He said to me, "Son of man, have you seen what the elders of the house of Israel are doing in the darkness, each at the shrine of his own idol? They say, 'The Lord does not see us; the Lord has forsaken the land." Again, he said, "You will see them doing things that are even more detestable." Then he brought me to the entrance to the north gate of the house of the Lord, and I saw women sitting there, mourning for Tammuz. He said to me, "Do you see this, son of man? You will see things that are even more detestable than this."

He then brought me into the inner court of the house of the Lord, and there at the entrance to the temple, between the portico and the altar, were about twenty-five men. With their backs toward the temple of the Lord and their faces toward the east, they were bowing down to the sun in the east. He said to me, "Have you seen this, son of man? Is it a trivial matter for the house of Judah to do the detestable things they are doing here? Must they also fill the land with violence and continually provoke me to anger? Look at them putting the branch to their nose! Therefore I will deal with them in anger; I will not look on them with pity or spare them. Although they shout in my ears, I will not listen to them."

In the preceding eighth chapter Ezekiel emphasized how idolatry arouses God's righteous wrath and calls for divine retribution and judgment such as the Babylonian Captivity which the Jews brought upon themselves. Again and again the word "detestable" is used by Ezekiel in connection with the idolatrous activities of God's people. James Kelso supplies some enlightening insight into the visions of idolatry which Ezekiel wrote about in chapter eight:

Ezekiel devotes the eighth chapter of his book to four brazen heathen worship practices in God's holy Temple. The first is the "image of jealousy." This was some heathen idol whose very presence aroused the jealousy of Yahweh. Scholars differ as to what deity is referred to. It may have been Marduk, the chief god of Babylon, who is called Bel in Isaiah and Jeremiah. Since Israel was a tributary state of Babylon her god must be set up in Judah's temple. Babylon was the agent which Yahweh was to use in punishing wicked Judah, and therefore Marduk would be doubly blasphemous. Or it might have been an image of Baal or Ashera or the still more sadistic Moloch. Such heathen Moloch worship has its climax in Ezekiel 23:39. "For when they had slaughtered their children in sacrifice to their idols, on the same day they came into my sanctuary to profane it. And lo, this is what they did in my house."

The second false worship practice appears to have been Egyptian, as this nation was the most primitive of all the ancients in the importance they placed on all kinds of animals, birds and insects in their pantheism. This sin strikes directly at the Ten Commandments for in Exodus 20:4-5, "You shall not make yourself a graven image, or any likeness of anything that is in heaven above, or that is in the earth beneath, or that is in the water under the earth; you shall not bow down to them or serve them; for I the Lord your God am a jealous God...." Before the exile there had always been a strong pro-Egyptian party in Judah and this worship was doubtless a part of their influence. Isaiah tells us that wicked Israel sacrificed swine and mice. And a serpent was at the heart of Canaanite worship.

The third false worship was that of the women wailing for Tammuz. He was the old Sumerian god of the spring vegetation who was betrayed by Ishtar, the goddess of love. He came over into Greek mythology where we know him under the name of Adonis. His most sacred red river was in Phoenicia. His death symbolized the death of vegetation in the hot summer months and the whole Near East observed a period of mourning in his honor. Tammuz actually gave his name to the fourth month of the Palestinian calendar when this service was held. In Ezekiel the rite took place in the sixth month. This Tammuz worship was just another phase of Baalism.

The last heresy was sun worship with some of Yahweh's

temple priests themselves turning their backs on Yahweh's temple to face the rising sun in adoration! This was doubtless a phase of Mesopotamian sun worship introduced into Jerusalem by the Assyrian conquerors and continued by the Babylonians. The Greeks gave Apollo the honor of driving the chariot of the sun. But the sun was also one of the older but lesser gods of the Canaanites. Beth-shemesh was his major sanctuary in Palestine.

But Judah's days of heresy were short. For Nebuchadnezzar's second seige of the city ended its history and the history of the land of Judah for seventy years. Every city the archaeologists have dug up in Judah was annihilated by Nebuchadnezzar![32]

The Prophet Hosea stresses that idolatry and adultery frequently go hand in hand. By worshiping idols God's people were spiritually unfaithful to him and, as has been noted above, that spiritual adultery was often accompanied by actual physical adultery because temple prostitution and all sorts of other lewd and lascivious practices were commonly featured in pagan religions. The following is a sample of idolatry according to God's Prophet Hosea:

Hosea 4:10-14 — "They will eat but not have enough; they will engage in prostitution but not increase, because they have deserted the Lord to give themselves to prostitution, to old wine and new, which takes away the understanding of my people. They consult a wooden idol and are answered by a stick of wood. A spirit of prostitution leads them astray; they are unfaithful to their God. They sacrifice on the mountaintops and burn offerings on the hills, under oak, poplar and terebinth, where the shade is pleasant. Therefore your daughters turn to prostitution and your daughters-in-law to adultery. I will not punish your daughters when they turn to prostitution, nor your daughters-in-law when they commit adultery, because the men themselves consort with harlots and sacrifice with temple prostitutes — a people without understanding will come to ruin!"

The New Testament has much less to say about idolatry than the Old Testament. However, in his first letter to the Corinthians St. Paul points out that although all idols are in reality "nothing", yet they are deadly devices of the devil when people believe they are real and put their faith in them instead of in the Triune God "from whom all things came and for whom we live" (1 Corinthians 8:6). In 1 Corinthians 8:4-6 and 10:19,20 Paul wrote: "So then, about eating food sacrificed to idols: We know that an idol is nothing at all in the world and that there is no God but one. For even if there are so-called gods, whether in heaven or on earth (as indeed there are many 'gods' and many 'lords'), yet for us there is but one God the Father, from whom all things came and for whom we live; and there is but one Lord, Jesus Christ, through whom all things came and through whom we live. . . . Do I mean that a sacrifice offered to an idol is anything, or that an idol is anything? No, but the sacrifices of pagans are offered to demons, not to God, and I do not want you to be participants with demons."

There are, of course, scores of other Scripture sections that could be brought forward to describe and denounce idolatry and to demonstrate how this basic sin permeated the whole atmosphere of life in Bible times, both outside and within the borders of Israel's Promised Land. The passages of God's Word which are quoted above from the Psalms, the Old Testament Prophets and the Apostle Paul supply just a small sample of how widespread was the diabolical influence of idolatry, and explain why it is condemned and warned against by the writers of God's Word again and again. And those warnings and condemnations of idolatry are still timely today. Although it would be difficult today to find someone worshiping Baal or sacrificing their children to Moloch, that does not mean that idol worship has died out. We contend that idolatry is still very much alive in the twentieth century and in the next chapter we will look at some modern-day manifestations of those idols or "nothings" which Satan employs so cleverly to lead people away from the one true Triune God.

NOTES FOR CHAPTER TWO

[1] *The World Book Encyclopedia*, 1976, s.v. "Mythology."

[2] Ibid., s.v. "Ancient Egypt."

[3] Ibid., s.v. "Osiris."

[4] Ibid., s.v. "Assyria," "Babylonia," "Marduk."

[5] John D. David, *A Dictionary of the Bible*, (Grand Rapids: Baker Book House, 1958), pp. 9, 10.

[6] *The World Book Encyclopedia*, 1976, s.v. "Persia," "Zoroaster," "Zoroastrianism."

[7] Ibid., s.v. "Mythology."

[8] Merrill C. Tenney, *New Testament Times*, (Grand Rapids: Wm. B. Eerdmans Publishing Company, 1965), p. 108.

[9] Ibid., pp. 108, 109.

[10] Ibid., pp. 109-111.

[11] Ibid., pp. 117, 118.

[12] Ibid., pp. 118-120.

[13] Ibid., pp. 120, 121.

[14] J. N. D. Anderson, *Christianity and Comparative Religion*, (Downers Grove, Illinois: Inter Varsity Press, 1970), p. 39.

[15] E. O. James, *In the Fullness of Time* (SPCK, 1935), pp. 87f. quoted in op. cit. by Anderson, p. 41.

[16] The material for emperor worship was taken from *The World Book Encyclopedia* and Merrill C. Tenney's *New Testament Times*, op. cit., pp. 112-116 and 324.

[17] Merrill C. Tenney, *New Testament Times*, pp. 116, 117.

[18] Ibid., pp. 124, 125.

[19] Immanuel Frey, *Northwestern Lutheran* editorial, 1 May 1977, p. 131.

[20] Kenneth Hamilton *To Turn from Idols*, (Grand Rapids: Wm. B. Eerdmans Publishing Company, 1973), p. 55.

[21] James L. Kelso, *Archaeology and the Ancient Testament*, (Grand Rapids: Zondervan Publishing House, 1968), p. 65.

[22] Ibid., p. 102.

[23] Martin Noth, *The Old Testament World*, (London: Adam and Charles Black, 1964 — translation by Victor I. Gruhn for Fortress Press, 1966), p. 285.

[24] Kelso, *Archaeology and the Ancient Testament*, p. 19.

[25]Ibid., pp. 73-75.

[26]Ibid., pp. 55, 56, 98.

[27]Ibid., pp. 160, 161.

[28]F. Rupprecht, *Bible History References*, (St. Louis: Concordia Publishing House, 1957), Vol. II, New Testament Stories, p. 578.

[29]Kelso, *Archaeology and the Ancient Testament*, p. 182.

[30]R. C. H. Lenski, *The Interpretation of St. Paul's Epistles to the Galatians, to the Ephesians and to the Philippians,* (Columbus, Ohio: The Wartburg Press, 1946), pp. 271, 272.

[31]Harold R. Willoughby, *Pagan Regeneration*, (The University of Chicago Press, 1929 Midway Reprint 1974), pp. 117, 118, 123-127, 129.

[32]Kelso, *Archaeology and the Ancient Testament*, pp. 194, 196.

CHAPTER THREE

TWENTIETH CENTURY IDOLS

This is the testimony: God has given us eternal life, and this life is in his Son. He who has the Son has life; he who does not have the Son of God does not have life. I write these things to you who believe in the name of the Son of God so that you may know that you have eternal life. . . . We know also that the Son of God has come and has given us understanding, so that we may know him who is true. And we are in him who is true — even in his Son Jesus Christ. He is the true God and eternal life. Dear children, keep yourselves from idols. (I John 5:11-13,20,21 NIV)

In the previous chapter we acknowledged that we were offering only a very few examples of the numerous idols which were worshiped in Bible times. The same admission must be made as we now turn our attention to modern-day idols. We make no claims to completeness; by no means will the reader find in this chapter a comprehensive or exhaustive catalog of 20th century idols. We present those idols only which have caught this writer's attention over the years and aroused his interest, in the hope that they will be of interest to others also and that learning about them will help us heed St. John's admonition above: "Dear children, keep yourselves from idols" (1 John 5:21).

We agree with Kenneth Hamilton that "contemporary man probably has a greater variety of beliefs than his forefathers. . . . The modern idolatrous imagination still refuses to believe that the promises of the living God are sure and that his grace is sufficient for all our needs. It still looks to other powers and authorities for support and guidance, transferring to them what belongs to the Creator alone. . . . Because idolatry is a product of the 'imagination of men's hearts,' it is always with us. The forms taken by the idolatrous imagination are constantly changing: the thing itself remains and finds ever new expressions. . . . The failure of the imagination to form images according to the revealed truth of the living God is the root of idolatry."[1]

GROSS IDOLATRY IN OUR DAY

The distinction has been made between gross idolatry and fine idolatry, the former referring to visible idolatry like the ones described in the previous chapter which are coarse, vulgar, obvious and glaring while the latter type would not be as readily recognized because of their subtle, even secret or invisible character. In modern times most idolatry would be classified as fine, especially in Western countries. Worshipers of the Almighty Dollar, for example, usually do not publicly proclaim their devotion to that idol and may not even be fully aware of their love of money.

Gross idolatry, however, is far from dead in our day. Millions of Hindu pilgrims still come from all corners of India to throw cash, gold, precious stones and even the hair they've shaved from their heads before the 7-foot statue of Lord Thirupathi, the consort of the Hindu goddess for wealth. In a land where the average monthly income is $13 that idol, Lord Thirupathi, raked in a cool $12.5 million in offerings in 1978.[2] Blind devotion to a gross idol also motivated an African religious zealot to accomplish one of the most amazing climbs in mountaineering history. In August, 1979, two British climbers came upon a fanatic idolater who had scaled 17,000-foot Nelion Peak on Mt. Kenya — barefoot and without any climbing equipment, protected from the cold on the snow capped peak only by a light jacket. That man made one of the most difficult climbs in the world because he was determined to pray to the Kikuyu tribal god, En-gai, who is supposed to reside in the mountain's peaks.[3] In my files I have a picture of a man from Bangkok, Thailand, walking briskly over a bed of burning coals to show faith in Kuah Yin, goddess of mercy. In that diabolical display of an idolatrous mind over matter, the man apparently suffered no burns from the hot coals.[4]

Just as the ancient Romans deified their emperors, the belief that some special human beings should be recognized as divine is still to be found in the Himalayan kingdom of Nepal. Consider the following Associated Press story of how idolaters in that far-off land set apart three-year-old girls and recognize them as goddesses:

Lonely Child Adored as Nepalese Goddess

Katmandu, Nepal — (AP) — She is a living goddess but she must be one of the loneliest little girls in the world.

This is the 6 year old Kumari of Katmandu, a slender, solemn faced little girl worshiped by thousands of Nepalese who keep her a virtual prisoner.

She leads a life of seculsion and in accordance with ancient religious law is kept in a dusty old temple off Durbar square away from her family and away from the world.

... The Kumari never is permitted to play or even walk in the courtyard. Her world is the dim inner recesses of the temple, where she is guarded from the world by attendants and the ever present guruma, a woman who teaches and has charge of the little girl.

A few times each year, during important religious festivals, the Kumari is dressed in fine robes and a rich headdress, hoisted to a palanquin on men's shoulders and paraded through the street. But even then, released from her temple prison, she cannot act like a little girl.

The Kumari must sit correctly, without smiling, receiving the shouted adoration of those who worship her.

. . . Each Kumari is selected at about age 3 and reigns until the onset of puberty or until (heaven forbid, Nepalese say) an accident scratches her or otherwise causes her to bleed.

When a vacancy occurs, word goes out to Nepal's priest-goldsmith community: A new Kumari is among you. The Nepalese, eager for the honor of providing a living goddess, trek to Katmandu with their young daughters. Priests from the temple off Durbar square take over from there.

All the tiny girls, some separate from their mothers for the first time, are put in a dark room filled with the bloody heads of sacrificial buffalo, goats and chicken. Huge drums are beaten, horns are blown as priests put up a frightening din. With one exception, the priests say, the little girls dissolve into tears and wails of fright. That exception, the priests add, obviously is the new Kumari — composed, stately and unafraid, even at the age of three.

The present Kumari has been in the temple three years — three years of no running, no laughing and even no weeping. If a Kumari were to weep, a great calamity of some sort would strike Nepal. Disaster, or so it is believed, would sweep down from the Himalayas.

The 20th century has made many inroads in Nepal, a closed kingdom for hundreds of years. But Nepalese faith in the Kumari and their guarded watch over her have not been shaken.[5]

The inclination of human beings to idolize and worship other humans instead of the true God was demonstrated also by the Tibetan Dalai Lama's seven week tour of twenty-two U.S. cities in the fall of 1979. Although the present Dalai Lama does not see himself as divine, many of his Tibetan Buddhist followers still recognize him as a "god-king," the incarnate Lord of Compassion and the reincarnation of his predecessor. The forty-four-year-old Dalai Lama, who has lived in exile in India since the Chinese Communist takeover of his country in 1959, was chosen at the age of two. He was found in a peasant's hut in Taktser after a long search during which monks used divinations and sought miraculous signs to reveal his whereabouts. They allegedly confirmed their discovery of reincarnation by having the child identify objects associated with his predecessor. Sad to say, the idolatrous background of the Dalai Lama did not discourage hundreds of so-called Christians from gathering in New York's St. Patrick's Cathedral for an ecumenical, interreligious prayer service, where they greeted him with a standing ovation and heard him declare that "all the world's major religions are the same." Farther along on his tour, as another misguided expression of ecumenism, Carroll College of Waukesha, Wisconsin, an institution of the United Presbyterian Church in the U.S.A., granted the Dalai Lama an honorary doctor of divinity degree. At a luncheon in his honor the Dalai Lama's desire to usher in a syncretistic one-world religion, which would make a mockery of the Christian faith, was favorably recognized. A Milwaukee Presbyterian minister opened the meal with a "Christian" prayer and at meal's close an hour later the Dalai Lama chanted a Buddhist benediction. Indeed, gross idolatry is not dead in our day. It is warmly welcomed right in our own American backyard in Roman Catholic Cathedrals and on college campuses all across the country where more and more of our young people are being drawn to Oriental religions that explore inner spiritual resources through meditative techniques and reject the unique revelation of the Triune God recorded in the Holy Bible.[6]

For an excellent description of the gross idolatry which still exerts considerable influence in Africa in the form of animism, demi-gods, ancestor worship and high gods, we recommend that you read *Of Other Gods and Other Spirits,* Northwestern Publishing House, 1977, by Professor Ernst H. Wendland, longtime missionary-teacher in Africa.

IDOLATRY IN NON-CHRISTIAN CULTS

Some of the fastest growing and most highly publicized religious movements in our country must be classified as idolatrous and non-Christian. Again, it is not our purpose to offer a complete list of such cults or to make a thorough study of all their teachings. A brief glimpse at a few of the better known organizations will have to suffice.

Armstrongism

In recent years the Worldwide Church of God, founded in 1934 by Herbert W. Armstrong, has been rocked by internal division, controversy and scandal. Herbert W. and his eloquent son, Garner Ted who seemed to be his successor and heir apparent, are now estranged. Garner Ted has had to go his own way and to found his own church. Herbert W., now in his eighties, was one of the first false prophets in America to recognize and utilize the potential of radio and the printing press to fund a false faith. By filling the airwaves with his message and by sending out many millions of "free" copies of his slick publication, the misnamed *Plain Truth*, Armstrong managed to build a multi-million dollar religious empire, featuring a plush campus for his Ambassador College in Pasadena, California, palatial mansions as residences for him and his associates, and jet travels in style and luxury around the world to interview gullible world leaders who were persuaded by Armstrong's expensive gifts to give him the appearance of importance and legitimacy.

It's bad enough that hundreds of thousands of people over the years have been taken in by the unscrupulous false prophet and heeded his pleas for their double and triple tithes to finance his flashy projects and to send him flying around the world, but, worst of all, the god of Herbert W. Armstrong is nothing but an idol as Paul N. Benware points out:

> The Worldwide Church of God teaches many things in common with orthodox Christianity on the Godhead. Its view is that God the Father is both personal and powerful, possessing most of the attributes generally ascribed to Him by biblical Christianity. The majesty and authority of the mighty Creator God continually finds emphasis in Armstrongism. However, in several vital areas there is a departure from the orthodox position. First, the view that God is a family is at total variance with the biblical position. The denial of the Trinity puts the Worldwide Church of God outside the circle of biblical Christianity. Second, it holds that God is a Spirit, but nevertheless has Him possessing physical form and shape. This view resembles that of Swedenborgism, but doesn't go as far as Mormonism. Spirit is not a refined form of matter, but rather an immaterial substance. Third, its view that God has imposed a restriction on his own knowledge damages the attribute of omniscience.
>
> . . . The denial of the personality of the Holy Spirit naturally affects this entire doctrine. The Spirit's ministries in the believer, in the unbeliever, and in the life of Christ are all greatly changed when he is viewed as a force or power from God. As a result, there is no agreement at all in this doctrinal area between biblical Christianity and Armstrongism.
>
> . . . The Christology of the Worldwide Church of God is difficult to comprehend entirely because of the confusion and contradiction within the system. In viewing the Person of Christ it seems that Armstrongism believes that Christ is both God and man — the biblical teaching. However, a number of statements show that its position is not of Orthodox Christianity. First, Armstrongism actually has three Christs who have no relationship to one another, except on paper. The pre-existent Christ is said to be Jehovah the Eternal One of the Old Testament. (It should be noted that Armstrongism is not careful when dealing with the Persons of the Godhead.) At the incarnation, an entirely different person is presented. He is definitely not the God-man of the Scriptures who is truly human, and yet, who is also undiminished deity. He is not the one who veiled his preincarnate glory,

took on the likeness of sinful flesh and voluntarily gave up the use of certain attributes. In Armstrongism, Christ is totally a man (having "emptied himself of being God") and only by the force of God retained the ability to reveal the will and character of God. However, it is an elementary fact of theology that giving up the attributes of deity means that he ceased to be God. The "second" Christ theoretically could have been eternally lost, a concept impossible to understand. The idea of one of the Persons of the Godhead being eternally separated from the other is incomprehensible, yet that is the position of the Worldwide Church of God.

At his resurrection, He was then converted into a spirit Son of God. He did not retain the human body or nature, so this is a "third" Christ. Thus, when putting the pieces together, the Worldwide Church of God has a pre-incarnate Christ who is the Great God Jehovah, who then changed into a human being with sinful flesh, but having no deity. He was then changed into a spirit Son of God, something He was not before becoming a man. There is simply no logical or biblical way that these "Christs" can be the same person.

There are other major problems in the Christology of the Worldwide Church of God. Christ, as a human being, can only be rightly understood in the light of its position on the nature of man — that he is mortal, material and having no distinct entity as soul or spirit. As it will be seen later, this position colors the thinking in a great many areas. In this system, then, Christ could never become a God-man in the biblical sense.

The position of Armstrongism on the person of Christ raises some questions on such things as the equality of the Father and Son, the place of God the Father in the Old Testament, and the problem of imputed sin in relationship to Christ.

On the work of Christ the position of Armstrongism is more understandable, but not more biblical. Christ's death paid for the repentant, baptized sinner's past sins. Then, by Christ living through him, the sinner is eventually brought to sonship.

Christ died and ceased to exist for three days according to the theology of Armstrongism. It holds that the Second Person of the Godhead actually ceased to exist. How can God be God, with such attributes as immutability, eternality, and unity, and still cease to exist? Among other things, the "God Family" ("Elohim") would have gone out of existence for three days since there was no plurality left in the Godhead.

The resurrection of Christ was spiritual. Nothing is said about the old human body of Christ, as to what happened to it. Christ, according to Armstrongism, received immortality at this time. This raises many more questions, such as, if Christ, as a person did not previously have immortality, which is an attribute of God, then how could he be God? If He did have it, then how could He cease to exist? Before the incarnation and resurrection, what was the relationship of the two Persons in the Godhead, if it were not Father-Son? How can the Father be qualitatively greater than the Son? . . . The whole Christology of the Worldwide Church of God is replete with contradictory positions as well as outright error. This most critical of doctrinal areas shows Armstrongism found wanting.[7]

Bahai

On the shores of Lake Michigan at Wilmette, Illinois, stands a famous nine-sided structure, the Bahai temple, the U.S. headquarters and worship center of the inclusive Bahai faith. For years Bahai leaders have been claiming that their faith will become the foremost world religion of the future and that a majority of people will come to accept it. With the increasing mania for ecumenism which is so popular at the end of the 20th century, they just might be correct. Already many people who are not officially Bahai nevertheless believe what the Bahai religion teaches: that all religions are true and that all their scriptures, the Christian Bible, the Moslem Koran, the Jewish Torah, the Hindu Bhagavad-Gita are all equally inspired. This faith which emphasizes the unity of God, of mankind and of all religions, was founded more than a hundred years ago by Baha'u'llah, a Persian seer who proclaimed himself "him whom God manifests," offering what he and his followers have described as revelations for the modern age. He is regarded by the Bahai faithful as the latest in a line of divine messengers, including Abraham, Moses, Buddha, Zoroaster, Christ and Mohammed. The "god" of the Bahai religion obviously is an idol, but their insistence that there is but one God and therefore only one religion is shared by millions of people all around the globe. Their inclusive, syncretistic belief could catch on in our country at any time and could spread like wildfire among the multitudes who choose to ignore doctrinal differences and want to see all religions worshiping together.[8]

Jehovah's Witnesses

"Transfusion Refused, Patient Dies" — Over the years I've read many tragic news items with that kind of headline. This one told of thirty-one-year-old Eleanor L. Maurer of Teaticket, Massachusetts, who died of uncontrolled bleeding after childbirth because she and her husband refused to permit doctors to give her a blood transfusion which would have saved her life.[9] Mrs. Maurer, of course, was another victim of the death-dealing false doctrine of the Jehovah's Witnesses' sect which teaches that blood transfusions are prohibited by several Old Testament ceremonial law passages which forbid the eating of blood. Jehovah's Witnesses also are known as a doomsday cult which has been preoccupied for many decades with the subject of Judgment Day. In my file I have a 1974 article describing a Jehovah's Witnesses' assembly at Milwaukee County Stadium at which it was predicted that at most only 10 years remain before Armageddon or doomsday.[10] A year later, however, F. F. Garrett, a circuit overseer for Milwaukee area Witnesses, was saying that they "were convinced that it (the end of the world) would happen at least within the next two or three decades — in other words, before the year 2000. 'It could happen this year, next year, or, very possibly, sometime within the 1970's,' Garrett said."[11]

This dabbling in possible dates for doomsday has a long history among Jehovah's Witnesses, going back to 1914 when the founder of their false faith, Charles Taze Russell, predicted that Christ would appear visibly on earth in that year to begin his reign.

We wonder how so many people can be taken in by this sect which strays so far from the Scriptures, saying that it's sinful to salute the American flag, to serve as a soldier or to celebrate Christmas. Actually, the secret of their success in bringing souls under their spell is self-evident. They are zealous, tireless propagators of their false doctrines, going from door to door in their communities again and again so that by now its almost impossible to find anyone in our country who has never had Jehovah's Witnesses at his door trying to sell some Watchtower literature. Their zeal, fueled though it may be by fanaticism and the perverse pleasure of suffering rejection as Jehovah's martyrs, ought to be more than matched by us Christians who are privileged to be genuine witnesses unto Christ and the pure truth of the gospel (Acts 1:8).

Who is their Jehovah, anyway? Since the Jehovah's Witnesses reject the biblical teaching of the Holy Trinity, claiming that it's a pagan myth, no different from the polytheism of the ancient heathen religions; since they mock and ridicule the Bible's doctrine of God and Christ as trinitarian nonsense, unscriptural and unreasonable; since they deny the deity of Christ and claim that he's merely a creature and not the Creator, they should be told with tact and love, the next time they come to your door, that their Jehovah is a man-made idol, a false god, dreamed up by men like Russell.

Moonies

"Brainwashing" and "deprogramming" — those words became synonymous with what was probably the most controversial religion to catch the public eye in America in the 1970's, the Unification Church of the Rev. Sun Myung Moon (popularly known as the Moonies). This cult quickly gained notoriety for its heavy-handed methods of effecting conversions: isolating prospects from all past and outside contacts; surrounding them with new instant comrades and a new authority figure; wearing them down physically, mentally and emotionally by the use of a special diet and strenuous recreational activity; inculating new beliefs and applying psychological pressure to achieve total commitment. With perhaps no more than 10,000 hard-core, fulltime devotees in this country the Moonies are said to have a $10 — $50 million or more national budget. Most of the income comes from dedicated Moonies who sell flowers on streetcorners or pester people to make donations to their "educational foundation." Moonies are brainwashed to believe that the cash in other people's pockets is "crying" because it wants to be blessed by Father Moon, who claims he is the new Messiah and that he must become the richest and most powerful man in the world to achieve God's will.

Moon's tactics are similar to the methods of Herbert W. Armstrong of the Worldwide Church of God. Like Armstrong Moon is not hesitant to spend large amounts of money to hobnob with influential people and to provide a seemingly respectable platform for his peculiar type of idolatrous teachings. In late 1977, for example, Moon spent about half a million dollars for a three-day conference on "science and absolute values" in San Francisco, which drew 450 social scientists, theologians and learned academics, four Nobel prizewinners among them.[12] Such extravaganzas undoubtedly help Moon to maintain his hypnotic hold over his devoted followers and help to blunt the criticism directed against him for his dictatorial rule over his church. The extent of his disciples' loyalty and single-minded obedience can be seen in the announcement that Moon was the matchmaker, who arranged engagements and marriage plans for 1410 of his church members, many of whom had never met or seriously contemplated marriage to one another. Three years after their Moon-made matches, the 705 couples, representing every race and every continent, will be married by Moon in a mass ceremony that surely will attract more publicity.[13]

Although Moon has described himself as a Christian evangelist, it has become increasingly apparent over the years that he is in actuality the megalomaniacal messiah of a new religion, that he sees himself not only as a successor to Christ, but even superior to our Savior, who supposedly failed in his mission because he was not married. *Time* magazine offered the following excerpts from speeches Moon allegedly gave to disciples in the inner sanctum of his cult: "He (God) is living in me and I am the incarnation of Himself. The whole world is in my hand, and I will conquer and subjugate the world. God is now throwing Christianity away and is now establishing a new religion, and this religion is Unification Church. All the Christians in the world are destined to be absorbed by our movement. There have been saints, prophets, many religious leaders . . . in past human history. . . . Master (Moon) here is more than any of those people and greater than Jesus himself."[14] That Moonism is blasphemous and idolatrous soon becomes evident when Moonies claim that their leader is a second Messiah who will exceed Jesus Christ in glory and when they honor and even pray to Moon and his wife as their "true parents."

Mormonism

The Church of Jesus Christ of Latter-day Saints has come a long way since its official beginning with a membership of thirty souls on 6 April 1830 at Fayette, New York. Its founder, Joseph Smith, claimed that the Lord had commissioned him to "restore" the true gospel of Christ to Christendom. The early history of this "made in America" religion was marked by persecution, including the brutal murder of Joseph Smith and his brother by a mob in Carthage, Illinois, in June, 1844. The practice of polygamy by Smith, by his dynamic successor, Brigham Young, and by many other members of Mormonism also aroused opposition and controversy until a Mormon manifesto (directly contrary to the express words of Prophet Smith) belatedly prohibited it, thanks to considerable pressure by the U.S. government. This checkered early history of Mormonism seems to have been forgotten by most Americans today. The public image of Mormons at the present time is very positive as a result of their excellent Mormon Tabernacle Choir, their shunning of alcohol, tobacco, and caffeinated beverages, their commitment to hard work and wholesome family life and the 1978 revelation received by their President Spencer Kimball, which dramatically opened the Mormon priesthood to blacks after 148 years of second-class church membership. Prominent Mormons like Ezra Taft Benson and George Romney, as well as the popular entertainers, Donny and Marie Osmond, have prompted many people to react to Mormonism with admiration and profound respect.

In the words of *Time*: "Just as the Saints once made the desert bloom through honeybee-like enterprise, so have they made their church into the biggest, richest, strongest faith ever born on U.S. soil. It has grown fourfold since World War II to 4 million members, including 1 million outside the U.S. Church income is rumored to exceed $1 billion a year, though Kimball insists it is 'much less than that.' "[15]

That tremendous surge in Mormon church membership undoubtedly is due primarily to the Mormon practice of sending out thousands (26,500 in 1978) of their clean-cut young men who are supposed to serve as missionaries for two years between their education and their careers.

Who is the god of these ambitious and enterprising Latter-day Saints? Although Mormon leaders have sometimes described their deity with terms like Holy Trinity, even a superficial look at some of their theological statements makes it clear that the god of Mormonism has nothing in common with the true Triune God of the Holy Bible. Consider the following Mormon description of their god: "He (Adam) is our Father and our God, and the only God with whom we have to do." (Brigham Young) "God Himself was once, as we are now, and is an exalted man — and you have to learn how to be gods yourselves, the same as all gods have done before you." (Joseph Smith) "Are there more gods than one? Yes, many." (Mormon Catechism) "The Father has a body of flesh and bones as tangible as man's." (Doctrine and Covenants) "The Father has begotten Him (Jesus Christ) in His own likeness. He was not begotten of the Holy Ghost. And who is the Father? He is the first of the human family." (Brigham Young) "We say it was Jesus Christ who was married (at Cana to the Marys and Martha), whereby He could see His seed before He was crucified." (Apostle O. Hyde) "We believe that through the atonement of Jesus Christ all mankind may be saved by obedience to the laws and ordinances of the Gospel." (Summary of Mormon Belief, 1884).[16]

The doctrine of God that seems to emerge from the

confusing hodge-podge of Mormon declarations goes something like this: There are many gods who once were human; devout Mormons can aspire to godhood by obeying the laws of their gospel; by their own works they can become members of a kind of god-family. Again, the judgment must be made: Joseph Smith, Brigham Young and their so-called apostolic successors must be classified as false prophets who have led their disciples into blasphemous and patently unscriptural idolatry.

Eastern Religions

Many Americans are fascinated by Eastern religions which promise that happiness and peace with God can be found by looking within oneself rather than through teachings such as are found in the Bible where God reveals the truth about us and himself. "Happiness is yourself" is the slogan I heard recently on the radio in a commercial concerning the coming of a Hindu swami to our local university. For a while Zen Buddhism was the "in" religion, the latest fad faith for young intellectuals who were convinced that Christianity had been hopelessly corrupted because it was the religion of the establishment. More recently young Americans in search of truth and meaning for their lives have been passionately chanting, "Hare Krishna, Hare Krishna, Krishna Krishna, Hare Hare, Hare Rama, Hare Rama, Rama Rama" in fervent praise of a Hindu idol, Krishna, who is supposed to be the eighth incarnation or avatar of the Hindu god, Vishnu. Most American air travelers have been approached by aggressive Hare Krishna devotees, who either ask them for a handout or try to sell them some Hindu literature. Why the chanting? The Hare Krishnas believe they can realize God by chanting his names in order and that they can liberate their souls from the influence of their bodies by this yoga-related discipline. Through the constant chants of the various names of their god, the Krishna convert eventually goes into a state of trance-like ecstasy. He feels that he is liberated from his body and is suspended in a state of pure spirit. It is the repetition of his god's name and total abandonment of self to him that accomplishes it. In his book, *Those Curious New Cults*, William J. Peterson offers the following reasons for the success of the Hare Krishna movement in attracting disciples and transforming them into fanatic, stubbornly persistent beggars who brazenly and often belligerently accost travelers in airports all across America:

> Why has Krishna Consciousness gained such a following among youth today?
> 1. Because it is anti-materialistic. Reacting against the hard-driving, success-oriented culture today, youth realizes that money and material possessions haven't brought satisfaction to their parents. Science has brought us the H-bomb; materialism has brought us an endless chase after unhappiness; competition has brought us ruthlessness and failure. Krishna says, "Why worry about material things: they are all unreal anyway!"
> 2. Because it is the ultimate drop-out. Not having answers to the complex problems of the world, youth decides that the easiest thing is to negate the physical by Hare Krishna chants, which are certainly less dangerous than LSD trips. Drugs, as more and more young people are discovering, are not the answer. But they still want to drop out some other way.
> 3. Because it is the ultimate protest. It seems ridiculous to think of Hare Krishna as a protest movement, but perhaps that is what it is in America. Young people have protested violently against the system, and they have participated in active politics against the system. But their protests have seemed to be to no avail. Perhaps Hare Krishna is just a simple way of thumbing their noses at the system that refuses to change.
> 4. Because it is as close as Hinduism ever comes to Christianity. Lord Krishna has evolved into a pale imitation of Jesus Christ, although Krishna's liberation is not Christian salvation, and Krishna's reincarnation is not Christian regeneration.[17]

Peterson also believes that the famous Beatle, George Harrison, helped to spread Krishna Consciousness when his Hare Krishna record, "My Sweet Lord," a song praising Lord Krishna, became a best seller both in the U.S. and in Europe.

Celebrities like the Beatles, the Rolling Stones rock group, actresses like Mia Farrow and Shirley McLaine and T.V. talk show host Merv Griffin undoubtedly have also contributed to the popularity and spread of another idolatrous offshoot of Hinduism, namely Transcendental Meditation. TM, as proclaimed by a diminutive, giggling (all the way to the bank?) Indian guru named Maharishi Mahesh Yogi, says that you can eliminate suffering and unhappiness merely by meditating, by repeating your special mantra (Hindu words like Rama or Om) for 30 or 40 minutes twice a day. For a while the TM apostles managed to spread their teachings into factories, offices and even public schools and stoutly insisted that they were merely promoting a way to achieve relaxation and respite from the rat race, rather than a religion. Before long, however, the inseparable relationship between TM and Hindu idolatry became clear, as reported by Professor Joel Gerlach in *The Northwestern Lutheran*:

Federal Judge H. Curtis Meanor has banned the teaching of transcendental meditation in New Jersey public schools. Judge Meanor ruled that the practice violated the doctrine of separation of church and state. While the decision affects only public schools in New Jersey, the decision will doubtless influence the practice in other states which have budgeted tax dollars for teaching TM.

Judge Meanor said in part that "the underlying teachings fall well within the concepts which courts previously have found to be religious."

We are grateful for the judge's long-awaited decision. But we suspect that TM's future was nipped in the lotus bud prior to the judge's ruling when the Maharishi Mahesh Yogi publicly claimed to be able to teach TM practitioners to levitate. At any rate we can hope that this Hinduism in sheep's clothing will soon fade from the scene so that millions more are not deceived by it.[18]

Barnum was supposed to have said, "There's a sucker born every minute!" How true that is also in religion we can see as millions of Americans, often highly educated and of superior intelligence, turn to various Eastern religions for answers that have been revealed for all time to all mankind by the Triune God in his book, the Holy Bible. The following excerpt from a news article by Donald Pfarrer about the Divine Light Mission's Maharaj Ji demonstrates how false prophets claiming to be God can fool gullible souls:

Does God hire billboards?

Does He suffer His face to be displayed on lapel buttons? Does He wear jewels, ride in a Mercedes and have a public relations man?

Does He sum up His message with "That's the whole deal"?

And with apologies to our corpulent brethren, is God fat?

The disciples of Guru Maharaj Ji answer: Why Not?

They acknowledge the contrast between their 15-year-old Guru and God the Father as painted by Michelangelo on the ceiling of the Sistine chapel in Rome.

Michelangelo's God is masculine to the limit — muscular and potent and full of the power of judgment.

The guru waddles when he walks, he is approximately spheroidal in shape, his voice squeaks and he claims he doesn't judge anyone.

But the followers of the guru — guru is Hindu for one who brings light out of darkness — believe he is God. He is the "perfect master" of our time, the one who in this age brings the message that Jesus, Mohammed, Krishna, Buddha and other perfect masters brought in theirs.

The guru's Divine Light Mission claims more than 5 million adherents in the world and 40,000 in the United States, including about 120 from Milwaukee, who have "received knowledge" through the mahatmas, or chosen disciples, empowered by the guru to transmit his techniques of meditation.

The followers are forbidden to discuss the techniques with outsiders but they assert that through them and only through them can a human being find the divine light within.

If it seems unlikely to you that the Indian boy who was hit in the face with a pie last summer in Detroit should be the perfect master of our time, the disciples say, try him.

Seek his knowledge. Search the planet, search humanity, search nature, politics, drugs, religion and sex. You'll find momentary satisfaction perhaps but not lasting peace, not that "pure and perfect peace" that the Bible calls the peace that passes all understanding.

For that, the guru says, you must search "within inside yourself" and to find it you need the boy from India or one of his 2,000 mahatmas. There are presently two mahatmas in the United States, and their physical touch is necessary for the transmission of "the knowledge."

You will know the perfect master by his fruits, the followers say, so laugh at the "fat boy" guru if you wish; he even laughs at himself.

But when you want more than a laugh, when you want to be blissed out, as they say, you need him. The world is full of false gurus but there is only one Satguru, or true guru — and even the true gurus of past ages, such as Christ, can't give you "the knowledge" because they are dead, the followers says.

It isn't learning or the amassing of facts. Neither is it the mastery of concepts or skill in reasoning. It's "practical experience," including the secret techniques of meditation leading to the union of the self with the essence of God within the self.[19]

An article with a Berkeley, California, dateline and a *New York Times Service* copyright comments on the appeal of so-called Eastern religions, like the ones mentioned above, and expresses the opinion that such religions will steadily gain greater acceptance, legitimacy and respectability in American society and will be with us for many years to come. Under the heading, "New Religious Sects Taking Hold" the article states:

There are growing signs here and elsewhere across the country that the youth oriented religious sects that sprung into existence a few years ago are gaining a foothold for an enduring future.

The emergence of a wide assortment of spiritual movements — from Eastern religions to Jesus people — has been the principal feature of a recent resurgence of interest in religion among America's young people. Many movements, demanding intensive commitment, have evoked strong criticism from parents of members and public officials.

The groups represent a highly diverse variety of cults, meditation centers, rural communes, loosely organized associations and highly structured churches.

However, if religion is defined as any cluster of values around which people shape their lives, a growing number of Americans appear to be taking part.

According to a Gallup survey last fall, 12% of those polled indicated that they had participated in one of several groups. The largest number, 4% or a projected 6 million Americans, had been involved with transcendental meditation. Next was yoga with 3%, or 5 million, followed by charismatic renewal, 2% or 3 million; mysticism with the same number, and Oriental religions, 1% or 2 million.

After nearly a decade of this ferment, the question is whether these groups will last.

The answer appears to be that most of them, though faced with high attrition rates and continuing obstacles to survival, have retained a small core of devoted followers and are acquiring the resources needed to continue their work.

If historical patterns prevail, even the most controversial movements may find greater acceptance in America's religious pluralism. Much the same process of harsh criticism and later toleration has followed such groups as the Mormons, Christian Scientists and Jehovah's Witnesses.

In the interim, said Harvey Cox, a Harvard theologian, many of these groups will bear the brunt of certain historical "myths" believed by the religious and cultural majority — that they are subversive, that they encourage sexual perversion, that they refuse to tell the truth about themselves and that they employ means of duping followers.

But among the most significant indications that these new groups are preparing for the long haul is the increasing willingness of sect members to seek legitimacy through the courts.

At least six lawsuits have been instigated against "de-programmers," who removed followers from their sects and tried to dissuade them from returning. The plaintiffs include members of Hare Krishna, the Unification Church of Sun Myung Moon and The Way.

"Members of these groups are asking the system to support them," said Jeremiah Gutman, head of the privacy committee of the American Civil Liberties Union. "They have gone from defensive thinking toward taking the offense."

The new religious groups are raising fundamental cultural and legal questions that are attracting growing attention from scholars.

"The new religious movement, in its broadest sense, can no longer be taken as a transitory cultural aberration," Prof. Jacob Needleman of San Francisco State University said, "but rather as a central feature of the profound change through which the American civilization is now passing."

Until now, scholars say, little has been learned about most of the sects, partly because they have only recently been seen as important cultural factors.

Academicians disagree as to how great that impact has been. But most who have studied the question concur that the groups signify deep longings for meaning and a search for a more satisfactory sense of self. They also appear to represent serious challenges to Western thought that have caused many people to turn away from material gain, competition and the success ethic.

Theodore Roszak, historian and author, said the lesson taught by this religious renaissance is that "we can use its conception of human potentiality to challenge the adequacy of our science, our technics, our politics."

Outsiders have shown by far the greatest concern about the high intensity groups such as the Unification Church and Hare Krishna.

Preliminary studies of both groups indicate a small though steady growth rate.

The vigor and general acceptability of the new movements vary greatly. The dropout rate is high among these groups, and researchers have found that only 25% of those who had some contact with a new religious movement were still involved.

But whatever the reasons, scholars generally agree that the old and the new religions in this country have begun to influence each other and will continue to do so. To a degree out of portion to their relatively small numbers, the small groups are causing organized religion to do considerable thinking about their mission and purpose.[20]

If the above article's assessment is accurate, it is imperative that we work harder to help our young people be on guard against the manifold forms that idolatry assumes in our modern world. It is unlikely that Eastern religions are just a passing fad that will quickly fade away. They will continue to pose a significant threat to the faith of impressionable youth, especially when they are promoted and proclaimed on university campuses by personable and persuasive false prophets.[21]

IDOLATRY WITHIN CHRISTIANITY?

Immaculate Conception, Holy Assumption, Immaculate Heart of Mary, Mary, Queen of Heaven — those are the names of Roman Catholic churches in the community in which I live. They indicate that Mary holds a key position in Roman Catholic theology. But do Catholics see Mary as a goddess? Is it accurate to maintain that Mary has been deified by the Church of Rome and that Catholics are guilty of Mariolatry? The following news article discussed those questions some years ago:

Do some Christians worship a goddess as well as a God? Roman Catholics show great reverence for the Virgin Mary. And to many outside the church, the pious fervor seems to equal or exceed worship of Jesus. And so, it has been charged that Christianity has a female deity. Catholics deny that Mary is thought of as a goddess. They explain that she is venerated, not worshiped, and that she is very highly honored because of her role as Jesus' mother.... It is said that Jesus would not deny His mother any favor she asked of Him. Mary is petitioned in prayer

99

to intercede with her Son on behalf of mortals. An Episcopal priest here said that although Roman Catholic theology did not deify Mary, the distinction in the public mind between great veneration and worship could eaily become dim. The faith which some Catholics have in Mary is great and almost childlike. Last year, an Italian peasant, carrying a six foot wooden cross, walked 2,000 miles to the shrine of Our Lady of Fatima in Portugal. There, he claimed, he was cured of a gastric ulcer. . . . Mary has been interpreted — in psychological terms without any supernatural meaning — as a mother figure who, like the female representation of Buddha, is thought to have attributes of gentleness and compassion. In reports of apparitions, Mary has taken the role of a mother who asks for prayer and penance and the conversion of sinners, warning that her Son will punish His children unless they mend their ways. . . . Mary's place is highest, most defined in dogma, in the Roman Catholic church. The dogma of the Immaculate Conception was proclaimed in 1854, and the dogma of the Assumption was proclaimed by the pope in 1950. . . . The beliefs were held long before the dogmas were proclaimed. The dogma of the Immaculate Conception holds that from the first instant of her conception, Mary was preserved from the stain of original sin. Many people, including some Catholics, have thought erroneously that the doctrine deals with the belief in the virgin birth of Jesus. The dogma of the Assumption is that Mary was assumed into heaven in body as well as in soul.[22]

A *Time* magazine article in 1962 quoted a Jesuit seminary professor, Father Walter J. Burghardt, S.J., as follows on the problems that Protestants find with the Roman position on Mary:

"She (Mary) is for the Protestant the visible symbol of Catholic idolatry, the Roman abandonment of Scripture, of the history of Christ. Divine Maternity and perpetual Virginity and Immaculate Conception and a glorious Assumption — these are already stones of stumbling. But the end is not yet. It may soon be defined as part and parcel of God's public revelation that in union with her son the Virgin redeemed the world."[23]

Another *Time* magazine article in 1964 pinpointed the

problem caused by the excessive devotion to Mary on the part of many Roman Catholics:

> Next to papal infallibility, the biggest barrier to Catholic-Protestant unity is the humble Jewish girl who gave birth to Jesus of Nazareth. By popular piety and papal decrees, Roman Catholics elevated Mary to the queen of heaven, born free of sin and assumed bodily into heaven. Marian "maximalists" even yearn for the day when a Pope will promulgate new dogmas that in union with her son she is redemptress of the human race and mediatrix of God's grace to men. For centuries, Protestants have reacted by condemning Catholic "Mariolatry" as paganism and ignoring the Virgin as much as they decently could.[24]

In the 15 years since that *Time* article appeared, no pope had the audacity to produce a new dogma declaring Mary as co-redemptrix. On the contrary, the Second Vatican Council appeared to bring about a deemphasis on Marian devotion, a development that was deplored by disappointed Mary maximalists within Catholicism. A UPI article in 1972 described how the Vatican II leaders had headed off an attempt by extreme mariologists to depict the mother of Jesus as co-redemptrix — a title that many Catholics and virtually all Protestants regard as tantamount to the idolatrous elevation of a human person to divine status. As a result of that action many American Catholics felt their leaders were cutting back on the reverence due Mary. This led to a decline in public and private devotions to the Virgin Mary and to many Catholics it seemed as if the elaborate structure of Marian Piety suddenly collapsed.[25]

A year later, in 1973, Father Luke Zimmer of Los Angeles, founder of the Apostolate of Christian Renewal, described his efforts to bring back devotions to the Virgin Mary as "an uphill battle." Zimmer acknowledged that traditional Catholic devotion to Jesus' mother "was eclipsed through misinterpretation of the Vatican Council." But he added: "Actually, the Vatican Council didn't lessen her role, but that was the impression given by some theologians after the council. As the ecumenical spirit grew, some Catholics also thought it would be less offensive to other Christians if they didn't play up the role of Mary so strongly." Zimmer conceded that, in the past, Marian devotion might have been exaggerated, but he insisted that legitimate traditional devotions to her should be practiced. He expressed disappointment that among young people, devotion to Mary had "dropped to almost nothing" because it generally was not encouraged in schools or homes. "Teachers in Catholic schools don't deny the role of Mary," Zimmer said. "They just don't talk about it." Zimmer offered the following explanation of Mary's role: "Jesus is the only mediator between God and man, and she (Mary) is an intercessor. We ask her to pray for us. She is the mother of Christ, and when a mother asks her son for something, that is a very powerful intercession. But we are not giving her worship. We cannot make a goddess of her."[26]

Are charges of Mariolatry against Catholicism made by Protestants, this writer among them, unwarranted? Are such charges possibly motivated by bigoted anti-Catholic bias, especially in the face of such fervent denials by Catholic leaders like Father Zimmer, who maintain that they do not mean to worship Mary or make her into a goddess? Yet, in spite of such statements by responsible Roman Catholic spokesmen, the Mariolatry charge just won't go away nor can it be casually dismissed. We maintain that there is no real difference between veneration and worship and that prayers should be addressed to God alone. Jesus himself is our intercessor with the Father; he needs no assistance in that role from Mary. Our Savior is very approachable and promises every Christian: "Whatsoever ye shall ask the Father in my name, he will give it you" (John 16:23).

No, the charge of idolatry, especially in light of the actions and statements of Marian maximalists, is not excessive. Consider the following facts. All Roman Catholics are instructed that Mary made special, supernatural visits to various places on the earth to guide and warn her followers. In 1531, for example, we are supposed to believe that she spoke to a young Indian named Juan Diego and gave him a most unusual gift, her own portrait painted on his cloak. Catholics are told that they can see this same cloak, miraculously provided by Mary, hanging in the basilica in Guadalupe, Mexico. A similar appearance allegedly took place at Lourdes, France, to one Bernadette; and at Fatima, Portugal, Mary is said to have appeared to three children in 1917 and subsequently triggered the awesome spectacle, witnessed by 70,000 people, of the sun spinning and dancing on its axis and then seeming to plunge toward the earth. We are also told that Mary has prophesied that Russia will be converted and that she has provided a peace plan from heaven as follows: "Mary comes to us with a plan for peace — the peace the world cannot give — the peace she can obtain for our hearts, our country, our world through her intercessory power. Listen to what Mary is saying: 'I come from heaven. I am the Lady of the Rosary. I have come to warn the faithful to amend their lives and to ask pardon for their sins. They must not offend our Lord anymore, for He is already too grievously offended by the sins of men. People must say the Rosary. If people do as I ask many souls will be converted and there will be peace.' "[27] What idolatrous blasphemy! Attributing the conversion of many souls to their doing what Mary asks. "One day through the Rosary and Scapular I will save the world. . . . Who piously wears my (Mary's) Scapular shall not suffer the fires of hell." When one reads statements like these attributed to Mary, the fervent denials made by Catholic leaders that they do not intend to deify her sound rather hollow.

How many Catholics have been misled by Mariolatry away from the Savior and the Holy Scriptures which need no amendments from Mary? Several years ago I came across this item in the In Memoriam section of the newspaper, placed there by a devoted son two years after his father's death: "William C. Jones (not his real name) 2 years ago, Dec. 5, Founder and Director of Holy Mary of Perpetual Helps Boys' Home. While on earth, all his thoughts, his deeds and his sacrifices were always done within the Image of Her."[28] Superstitious idolatry also triggered this news item: "A statue of the Blessed Virgin, set facing west the night before, brings good weather on the wedding day, according to Polish tradition. The bride's mother, Mrs. Stanley V. Smith (not her real name) had this statue (a picture went with the news item) in the window for two weeks 'to be sure the message got through,' her husband said. The day was sunny."[29]

An Associated Press article by Dennis Redmont reports that devotion to Mary will undoubtedly be promoted by the pope who is reigning at the time of this writing, Pope John Paul II. If there was a decline of Marian piety in the wake of the Second Vatican Council, it seems certain that the first Polish pontiff will push Mary into prominence once again. Redmont asserts:

> Pope John Paul is making the Roman Catholic cult of the Virgin Mary into one of the cornerstones of his pontificate.
>
> During his four months as pope, he has sprinkled dozens of speeches with devotional words for the mother of Christ, made prayers to the Virgin one of the major themes of his trip to Latin America, and kept the "M" of Mary flying high on his blue papal coat of arms.
>
> "The cult of the Virgin is an element which brings down to earth and humanizes religion . . . just as family life involves the affection of children for the father and the mother," says Father Virgilio Levi, a Vatican prelate and writer.
>
> Veneration of the Virgin — a popular tradition in Latin

America, southern Europe and the pope's native Poland —frequently has been identified with old fashioned conservative theological positions. Protestant churches in the past have cited the cult as a potential obstacle to efforts for Christian unity.

During his Mexican trip, the pope bestowed crowns as a sign of church esteem on two of the leading Virgin images of Latin America — Our Lady of Guadalupe, patroness of Mexico and Latin America, and Our Lady of Altagracia, madonna of the Dominican Republic.

Pope John Paul devoted four major speeches to the Virgin Mary and her teachings of the religious virtues of fidelity and perseverance.

Opening the Latin American Bishops' conference at the sanctuary of the Virgin of Guadalupe, the pope lauded her lyrically as "the mother of God, the mother of Mexico, the queen of the apostles and the queen of peace," asking her "to save the nations and peoples of the whole continent from wars, hatred and subversion."

In the central address of his trip Sunday, he invoked "the spiritual presence of Our Lady of Guadalupe" to reaffirm that the church is not tied to any political system and seeks the liberation of man only within the framework of the church.

Interest in the 17 day conference revolved around the church's role in political and social affairs, but one of the key points in the preliminary document cited "the need to strengthen Marian piety, one of the pillars of popular religion and of faith." It called the Virgin Mary "a symbol, a pillar, a mode."

Vatican prelates accompanying the pope said the huge crowds brandishing portraits of the pope and the Virgin Mary showed that the cult of the Madonna responds to deep spiritual needs.

Close friends say that John Paul, who lost his mother when he was 9, always has been deeply moved by the Virgin Mary as a mother figure. The pope's church in Poland, dedicated to the Virgin Mary, was built with pebbles from a riverbank after communist officials refused to allow him to use the materials he wanted for construction.

After being elected, one of the first images the pope ordered brought to his private chapel from Poland was that of Virgin of Czestochowa. His papal coat of arms, dedicated to the Virgin, shows the cross with a capital "M" dominating the shield and the motto "totus tuus" (all yours).

Other popes also have pressed the development of the cult of the Virgin Mary, but none with such initial vigor as Pope John Paul.

Pope Paul VI, in a major 1974 document, called her "the new woman" who took an active role in the early church and championed the rights of the weak against the powerful. But he criticized soft hearted devotion, calling it "sterile and emphemeral sentimentality."

In a reference to purported appearances of the Virgin Mary, particularly frequent in Latin American and European countries, Paul VI deplored "vain credulity and . . . the exaggerated search for novelties or extraordinary phenomena."[30]

Under the dynamic, crowd-pleasing leadership of this diabolical false prophet, Pope John Paul II, more and more Roman Catholic people surely will be singing and praying words of idolatrous praise to Mary:

> Mother dearest, Mother fairest,
> Help of all who call on thee,
> Virgin purest, brightest, rarest,
> Help us, help, we cry to thee.
> O purest Mary, O sweetest Mary,
> let thy name henceforth be ever
> (sic) on my lips. Delay not, O
> blessed lady, to help me whenever
> I call on thee, for in all my needs,
> in all my temptations, I shall never
> cease to call on thee, ever repeating
> thy sacred name, Mary, Mary.[31]

What is the origin of Mariolatry and why is it so popular with millions of people? In *The Religions of the Roman Empire*, in his chapter on "The Great Mother" John Ferguson observes that "the worship of a feminine archetype is deeply embedded in human nature." Ferguson obviously looked upon Mary as being in the same category as pagan female deities, some of whom we mentioned in Chapter Two, including Atargatis, Inanna, Ishtar, Anat, Artemis-Diana of Ephesus, Baubo, Aphrodite, Rhea-Dictynna, Demeter, Orthia, Bendis, Isis, Cybele, Ma, or Bellona, to name just a few. At the conclusion of his chapter on the above female idols, Ferguson states that "the hunger for adoration of the power of woman was not quenched within orthodox(?) Christianity. In parts of Italy today the statue of Mary is ceremoniously washed (just as was done with the statues of heathen female idols), and the Mother of Christ has attracted the devotion which once was attached to the Great Mother of the Gods."[32]

This section on Mary is not meant to dishonor that blessed woman who was highly favored by God and who with God-given eloquence so beautifully confessed her faith in God's promises and her own need for a Savior from sin in her Magnificat (Luke 1:46-55). Yet in a book on idols, the blasphemous deification of the Virgin Mary by Roman Catholicism cannot be ignored. This Lutheran Christian has to point out that nowhere in the Holy Scriptures is there any hint or the slightest suggestion that Mary was immaculately conceived or assumed bodily into heaven. Nowhere does the Bible lead Christians to believe that Mary would appear at Guadalupe, Lourdes or Fatima to bring messages God supposedly forgot to include in his Holy Scriptures (cf. Revelation 22:18,19).

We must agree with the anonymous tract-writer that

> The Bible knows of only one Person who was immaculately conceived and born without sin, and that is Jesus Christ. "God made Him to be sin for us who knew no sin, that we might be made the righteousness of God in Him" (2 Cor. 5:21).
>
> Protestants are happy to remember Mary as the one woman whom God honored above all others — by selecting her to be the human mother of Jesus Christ, His only Son.
>
> But Protestants refuse to share in the idolatry of the Roman

Catholic Church, which down through the ages has added fiction to fiction until today the mother of Christ has been exalted to a position almost equal to that of her divine Son.

Protestants still believe that fiction is fiction, no matter who proclaims it as fact.[33]

IDOLATRY IN THE LODGES—SCOUTING ORGANIZATIONS

Lodges

In a small sixteen page undated (probably late in the 1950's) tract, put out by the Concordia Publishing House, there appears the following statement attributed to Prof. Winfred Schaller on April 25, 1951 and reaffirmed by the secretary of the Evangelical Lutheran Joint Synod of Wisconsin and Other States (now Wisconsin Evangelical Lutheran Synod), the Rev. Theodore Sauer, on November 27, 1956: "As lodges and similar organizations have in general a deistic religion, are anti-Christian in character, and teach synergism (man cooperating with God in his own conversion) in its crassest form, we consider it a contradiction in itself to try to be a member of the Lutheran Church and a member of such a society at the same time. Joining such organizations is an act which severs the true fellowship with the Lutheran Church. The simple command of the Lord: Flee from idolatry! covers the situation nicely."

Several years later a similar Concordia Publishing House tract, "The Lutheran Churches View Fraternal Organizations," offered this April 25, 1962, quotation from the sainted Wisconsin Synod president, the Reverend Oscar J. Naumann:

> Our Synod has steadfastly opposed membership in Fraternal Organizations with objectionable religious features, such as the lodges. We consider it wisest to oppose such membership and to deal with members involved in or contemplating such membership on the basis of the Word of God itself, rather than on the basis of synodical resolutions or congregational constitution.

We oppose such membership in lodges because it involves unionism and syncretism, the denial of the Holy Trinity, and the denial of the cardinal teaching of Holy Scripture, namely, justification of the sinner before God by grace, through faith, because of the all-sufficient merits and sacrifice of Jesus Christ.

Our suggested model constitution for congregations stipulates in Article III, Membership: "Only such can be and remain members and enjoy the rights and privileges of membership in this congregation, who . . . 7) do not hold membership in an organization conflicting with the Word of God, like groups with false religious confessions, services, or prayers (lodges, etc.)."

When congregations apply for membership in our Synod and their constitution is reviewed by the membership committee, they are asked to add a similar paragraph if the constitution does not already contain one.

We consider it a part of the faithful shepherding of his flock that a pastor should continue to guard his congregation against such involvements and to instruct and admonish them to this end in an evangelical manner.

Is the Wisconsin Synod making a mountain out of a molehill when it continues its opposition to the principles and teachings of Masonry and similar fraternal orders? Is it accurate or fair to employ the inflammatory word "idolatry" in connection with the worship practiced in lodges? Could respected American heroes and presidents, like Benjamin Franklin, George Washington, Andrew Jackson, Theodore Roosevelt, William Taft, Franklin Roosevelt, Harry Truman, Gerald Ford, (14 U.S. presidents in all were Masons), as well as thousands of other pillars of American society in the past 200-plus years really have been involved in idol worship through their membership in Masonry and other lodges? Would the Prophet Elijah and the Apostle Paul really put the Christless god of the lodges in the same category with the idols they had to denounce, such as Baal and Diana (Artemis) of Ephesus?

To answer the above questions, consider the following words written more than 50 years ago by Roy D. Linhart, a Lutheran minister in Detroit, in the pamphlet, "The Evil of Lodgery":

> Another reason why we as a Christian Church do not sanction the lodge is because most secret societies of the day stand charged with idolatry, since the God that is worshiped in the lodge is not the true God, the God of the Bible. Most lodges today require a mere belief in a supreme being, and this satisfies many people. But, what does it mean to believe in a supreme being, or in some deity called god? There is hardly a person on this earth but what believes in some kind of a god. Even the heathen believes in a god or a supreme being. The fact, therefore that the lodge requires a mere belief in a supreme being does not bar hardly anyone from becoming a member, as long as he can say that he believes in some kind of a god. But the god of Masonry is not the Christian God, nor is its worship the true Christian worship. Masonry itself says: "Masonry is not a Christian institution. If it were, the Jew and the Moslem, the Brahman and the Buddhist could not conscientiously partake of its illumination. But, its universality is its boast; in its language, citizens of every nation may converse; at its altars men of all religions may kneel; to its creed disciples of every faith may subscribe."
>
> But, pray tell me, how is it possible to bring all these believers, unbelievers, deists, rationalists and idolaters together and unite them in a common worship, before a common altar, and join in united prayers to a common god? Do you mean to say that the true God is worshiped there where there is the Jew with his Christless god, the Mohammedan with his strange god, the deist with his self-invented god, the Christian with his Triune God? But, with all these the Christian man in the lodge is united in oath-bound brotherhood, joins with them in common prayers, goes with them before a common altar, etc. Whether all of these various classes can ascend to the same height on the ladder of degrees or not, does not change matters in the least; for they all enter the same door, are brothers of the same lodge, are bound by the same oath, and worship the same god.
>
> How, therefore, can a Christian explain and justify such a union of believers and non-believers, true worshipers and idol worshipers, as we find them in the lodge? Let him try to justify it in whatever way he may; the Lord God condemns it in clear and

solemn words. Hear what He says in II Corinthians 6,14-18: "Be ye not unequally yoked together with unbelievers; for what fellowship hath righteousness with unrighteousness, and what communion hath light with darkness? And what concord hath Christ with Belial? Or what part hath he that believeth with an infidel? And what agreement hath the temple of God with idols? for ye are the temple of the living God; as God hath said, I will dwell in them and walk with them; and I will be their God and they shall be My people. Wherefore, come out from among them and be ye separate, saith the Lord, and teach not the unclean thing; and I will receive you, and will be a Father unto you, and ye shall be My sons and daughters, saith the Lord Almighty."

And the fact that Masonry does attempt to make use of the name of Christ in one or two of the higher degrees only makes the matter worse. In the 26th degree of the Scottish Rite, as well as in the Knight Templar degree of the American Rite, you will find mention made of the name of Christ. But, if you will examine it closely, you will find that not one mention is made of the saving work of Christ, but that He is mentioned as a great example or teacher. But, does such use and mention of the name of Christ characterize Masonry in those certain degrees as being Christian in character? Most certainly not; for there is not one in the world today who would not gladly refer to Christ as having been a great Teacher and example, be he Jew, Mohammedan, heathen or who he may. But, will they refer to His atoning work and speak of Him as the Savior of men? Certainly not. Therefore, we can see that this mention of the name of Christ as we find it in one or two of the higher degrees of Masonry is an empty symbol and is a veneer which deceived many a Christian. For, while the name is used, everything that is connected with that name is idolatrous and unchristian. For example, consider the fact that the Templars, who make use of Christ's name, unite with the 32nd degree Masons of the Scottish Rite to form the Mystic Shrine; and the Shrine uses a Mohammedan ritual. Its symbol is the scimitar and crescent of the Turk. Do you mean to say that there Masonry has a Christian aspect and character when Christ is surrounded with Mohammedanism? To all of this, Christ solemnly says: "What concord hath Christ with Belial?" (II Cor. 6:15) And, what a sight it is to stand on the street and watch the Shriners' parade,

111

and see the Christian adorned in the attire of the Turk (who is a worshiper of heathen gods), and to see these Christians and Mohammedans keeping step as the band plays: "Onward, Christian Soldiers." How beautiful, you say, to see those white plumes waving as they march in the form of a cross! But, what do you suppose is the verdict of the Savior who looks down upon it all and beholds that sacred symbol of His suffering and death, the cross, used in such a display, especially when it is formed by some who reject Him as the Savior of the world — yea, who would spit upon His name?

Dear brother, do you not see the sinfulness of all of this? And, do you not see what a deception it is when it is claimed that Christ is worshiped in certain degrees of the Masonic lodge because His name happens to appear in such a manner as mentioned above? Indeed, it would be a thousand times better if Masonry had never attempted to use the name of Christ, than to use it in such dishonor. And the fact that it appears in one or two places in such a manner does not off-set the idolatry of the lodge. And, remember, that there is no greater sin before God than that of idolatry; for it is the sin condemned in the first great commandment, when God says: "Thou shalt have no other gods before Me." Yea, he says: "I am the Lord thy God, and My glory will I not give to another." And, of the idolater He says: "He shall not enter the kingdom of Heaven." We take it for granted, dear Christian brother, that it is your intention in life to worship none other than the true God of the Bible. But, by being a member of the lodge, you become a partaker of that idolatrous worship and God says: "Be not a partaker of other men's sins." (I Tim. 5,22.)[34]

In a more recent publication, "Should I Join a Fraternal Society?" Walter A. Maier Jr. repeats the solemn, deadly serious accusation that lodgery and idolatry are inseparable:

Who is the god of the lodge? Which god is worshiped?

Masons pride themselves on the international character of their brotherhood and make it clear that men all over the world (except members of non-white races and persons who have been physically disabled) are eligible to membership in the order, providing they are willing to subscribe to the existence of a Supreme Divine Being. To this ultimate deity, who requires universal homage, Masonic nomenclature variously assigns the titles, "God," "Deity," "Divine Artist," "Great Architect of the Universe," "Grand Warden of Heaven," "Supreme Grand Master," and similar designations. The god of Masonry is not —and indeed could not be — the Christian God, the true and triune God: Father, Son, and Holy Ghost. Such a specification of the deity would be offensive to the Jewish, Mohammedan, and all other non-Christian members of the international Masonic brotherhood. Specifically unacceptable would be the Christian belief that Jesus Christ is the divine Son of God and the one Mediator between God and men.

Surely the God of the Bible is not glorified in the Masonic delineation of deity, ritual, and worship. Jesus declares: "All men should honor the Son, even as they honor the Father. He that honoreth not the Son honoreth not the Father which hath sent Him" (John 5:23; cf. 2 John 9); and again, "I am the Way, the Truth, and the Life; no man cometh unto the Father, but by Me" (John 14:6). It is absolutely hopeless to attempt to reach, worship, and serve the true God in any other way than by acknowledging Him as triune and approachable solely through the merits of Christ. The god of the Masonic lodge is a figment of Masonic imagination, not the exalted Lord of heaven and earth. To put the matter crassly but altogether correctly: The god of Masonry is an idol; the worship of their deity on the part of the Masonic fraternity is rank idolatry, and idolatry, nakedly exposed, is devil worship (cf. 1 Corinthians 10:19,20). Since this is so, the Christian's course ought to be clear: He should in no way become involved in an association which requires him to participate in idolatrous worship. He should not join the lodge. He should "flee from idolatry" (I Corinthains 10:14).[35]

The testimony of Joseph K. Peaslee, a Lutheran minister and former Masonic lodge chaplain, is very enlightening and has the ring of accuracy and authority based on his direct personal experience in the lodge. How he finally came to recognize the idolatry and spiritual adultery promoted by Masonry is forcefully described in a June 26, 1962, *Lutheran Witness* article entitled "Is Masonry Heresy?":

"The lodge question" is constantly raised among concerned Lutherans in all national Lutheran bodies. Frequently spokesmen on both sides of this continuing debate are handicapped for they lack sufficient knowledge of what the other side is talking about. After many years of relative silence I joined the debate for the first time.

Eighteen years ago I was ordained by a constituent synod of the United Lutheran Church of America. Shortly afterward I followed in the footsteps of several generations of my forebears and applied for membership in a "blue" lodge. After all, my grandfather had been a thirty-second degree Mason, and the synod president at that time held a thirty-third degree. Many fine men in my church were already members. The character of these men and their faithfulness to their Bible class impressed me.

In weeks, after rigorously memorizing the ritual, I became a Master Mason and was soon made chaplain of my lodge. The visible use of the Bible, the Scripture quotations, the altar, certain symbols, prayers, and ritual, did not then convince me that I was being made an accessory to a false religion.

Now I am convinced that many devout Lutheran men apply for lodge membership, little realizing that they are compromising their faith in Jesus Christ.

This is not their fault. First of all, they have no way of knowing the teachings of Masonry until after they are in the lodge. Secondly, not all pastors preach the Word of God with such vigor and clarity that men will recognize the conflict of thought between the church and the lodge.

Most of us have been conditioned to believe that whatever is good is good and is not contrary to Scripture and, therefore, is of God. Actually such is not the case. This is only the foolish wisdom of the world. In the robust language of Martin Luther, when we trust in anything except Jesus Christ and His holy work of redemption for us, we are guilty of "vomiting grace."

Precisely where do Masonry and Christianity run into open conflict? The answer is as old as the church: Salvation by grace through faith — faith in Jesus Christ and Him only. Masonry assumes the natural goodness of man, Christianity teaches man's utter depravity — that even the "good" that man does is done by him for selfish reasons.

114

Masonry at its very best is theistic — God is in heaven; if life gets rough enough, you can turn to Him. The way to Him is not specified; so any good Jew or Moslem can be a Mason on this basis. But Jesus Christ said, "No man comes to the Father but by Me."

At its worst Masonry is deistic. This really means that God made the world and then ran away from it — abandoning it to man. According to deism, man can pretty much make heaven out of earth if he keeps his nose clean, keeps a stiff upper lip, and sings "Smile, darnya, smile." Oh, yes — and if he does his good deed every day!

This sort of thinking is theological adultery. Many a lodge member, I have found, considers himself a Protestant simply because he hates Roman Catholicism. I have discovered more in common with my Roman brethren in Christ — despite our differences — than with any pseudo religious group.

The church of Jesus Christ is founded on the rock of Peter's confession "Thou art the Christ, the Son of the living God." It is not dependent upon the wisdom of man. Even though that wisdom may have existed before the birth of Christ and comes from the mouth of Solomon himself — if it does not point us to Jesus Christ, it is trash and garbage.

I have officiated at many a Masonic funeral. I shall never do so again. The "phony" philosophy, lifted, I suspect, from the ancient mystery religions of the East, has so many solid reassurances — except to a sinner convicted by his sin. Such "reassurance" dwells upon human character and attainment — all that humanistic "con" game of reputation — the flattened dimension of man horizontally worshiping the glory of man.

Despite all of this, I am convinced that there are many devout Christians who do not yet realize what they have done in taking vows in the Masonic order. They read into Masonry a Christian content it simply does not contain.

I do not condemn them. But if they hear the Word of God purely preached, they must come to conclude concerning their lodge ritual: "This does not quite say what I thought it meant to say." And one day they will awaken to the fact they have become a party to their own betrayal.

But — and this is a large but — we do not club brothers in Christ into accord or into mutual understanding. A ball bat is no substitute for truth. Truth is a leaven which works slowly but stubbornly, leavening the whole lump. And truth is needed to leaven even a pastor's life!

Today — after many years — I know and I speak the truth. I say: "As for the plumb, square, and level, MAKE MINE THE CROSS!"

In recent years there have been some signs that lodge membership and interest have been waning. In an August 8, 1976, *Milwaukee Journal* article, "Old Orders Facing a Time of Change," Donald H. Pfarrer described the decline of Milwaukee fraternalism "in some ways and for some orders." Pfarrer stated that "ritual (worship?) is declining and the orders that cling to it most tenaciously are paying the price. But even the flourishing orders, such as the Knights of Columbus and the Eagles, maintain an irreducible minimum of ritual and form, and consider it essential to their identity. The membership began moving out of the center of the city before the lodges realized it, and they are only now catching up. . . . Something else is gone, something less tangible. In countless homes, 'lodge night' used to be inviolable. Now it competes with a six-pack and a Packer game and often loses. The overt, active race discrimination of the past has lingering effects today. Scarcely any of the lodges have black members." Pfarrer then went on to give some statistics on the individual lodges in the Milwaukee area and throughout Wisconsin as follows: **Masons** — Membership down by 10% from 1966-1976; 282 lodges in Wisconsin with 45,698 Masons. "Aside from charity (support of hospitals for crippled children and burn centers) and fraternity, the Masons have a spiritual (sic) mission. They say that making bad men good is the role of a church, and making good men better is the role of the Masonic orders." They face a dilemma. "If they maintain their ritual and stan-

116

dards they risk attrition, and if they relax them they risk the loss of their reason for being."

Moose — Membership increased in Milwaukee area from 2500 in 1971 to 4600 in 1976 due primarily to their move to the periphery of the city. Statewide, in Wisconsin, the Moose reached a new high: 19,500 members in 43 lodges. **Elks** — 26,000 in 38 lodges in 1976 in Wisconsin; in Milwaukee the Elks membership had dropped from 5500 in 1954 to about 1,000 in 1976, but they are making a comeback in new quarters and are attracting younger men. **Eagles** — Thanks to an ambitious building program with top notch athletic facilities the Eagles grew from 3500 in 1966 to 8400 in 1976 in Milwaukee. The average age is 30 and the average Eagle seems to be more interested in working out for physical fitness than in ritual and fraternalism. In Milwaukee the Eagles attract most of the judges, aldermen and local state legislators, as well as more than a 1,000 policemen and firemen. **Knights of Pythias** — They have preserved their ritual virtually unchanged since 1864. The ritual has to do with how they can live better lives and how they can conduct themselves in the best interest of humanity. In Wisconsin their membership has declined from 5,109 members in 80 lodges in 1960 to 3,000 members in 35 lodges in 1976.[36]

On the basis of quotations like those above and as a result of many conversations with lodge members I see a broad streak of self-righteousness and work-righteousness running through lodge organizations, a Pharisaic, holier-than-thou spirit, as well as a thinly disguised attitude of bias and bigotry toward blacks and other minorities who are systematically blackballed from membership by these "good" men who imagine they can better themselves and think that they already are much better than others. However, the primary objection Christians must lodge against lodges remains the idolatry which such organizations promote. The Reverend L. James Rongstad nails down this glaring error in a recent booklet on lodges as follows:

The first and most glaring contradiction between the lodge and Christianity centers on God. Although the lodge demands belief in a "Supreme Being," although it uses the terms "god," "Lord," "The All-Seeing Eye," etc., and although they form a theology about their "god" as to what he does, the lodge very carefully refuses to confess the God of the Scriptures. A definition of the Person of God is avoided. There is no identification of the Father, Son, and Holy Spirit in the lodge, nor any phrase which would identify God as the Trinity. The lodge simply by omission denies the revealed God of the Bible. This offends the Christian — or it should! The Christian is taught from the Bible that there is no salvation, no god other than the Lord of Lords, the Holy Trinity, and that to be saved it is essential to believe and confess this God.

Jesus is the "Word made flesh." He is the great "Light" the Masonic order tries to discover in its search for Truth but never finds. "Whoever has seen Me has seen the Father," Jesus said.

So strongly do the Masons regard a belief in a "Supreme Being" that they ousted an entire atheistic congregation from their premises. An atheistic Rabbi and his 140 member congregation in Birmingham, Mich., were refused further use of the Masonic Temple in early 1965. The *St. Louis Post-Dispatch*, on March 21, 1965, said that "theological reasons" were given as the reason for the decision. The Masons insisted that a positive commitment to the existence of some kind of supreme being was required for use of their temple.

"FREEMASONRY — A SIMPLE RELIGIOUS FAITH" is the title of an article on the cover of the Royal Arch Mason, a monthly periodical, Vol. V, No. 9, March 1957, which says, "We have but one dogma, a belief in God, but this is so firmly established as the principal foundation stone of the brotherhood that no one can ever be admitted a member of an English-speaking lodge without a full and free acceptance thereof. In all reference to the Deity, God is reverently spoken of as the Great Architect of the Universe. . . . Upon this foundationstone we construct a simple religious faith — the Fatherhood of God, the Brotherhood of Man, and the Immortality of the Soul — simple, but all-efficient. By reason of this simple creed, Freemasonry has been able to attract and accept as members of the Fraternity adherents of every religious faith in the world — Christians, Jews, Hindoos, Mohammedans, Pharisees, Buddhists, and others — atheists alone being excluded."

In the experience of this writer most Christians who are members of the lodge do not share our concern over the Masonic compromise of God, nor agree that they are worshiping an idol at the lodge. And this is the difficulty. They say that although they use the term "Supreme Architect of the Universe" they understand him to be their Triune God — especially in a lodge made up mostly of Christians. To them it is just another descriptive name for God, and they see nothing wrong about it — even though the Bible never limits God to these terms.

It is our claim that to avoid the revealed Scriptural names for God is a deliberate attempt to deceive by reducing Christianity to just another of the religions of the world. What is even worse, it is succeeding. By doing this, the lodge effectively de-emphasizes the person and work of Jesus Christ.[37]

Rev. Rongstad is surely right on target when he comes to the conclusion that the lodge is a religion (in spite of its vehement protests to the contrary) — a Christless religion — and thus a cult, a cult which regularly conducts funerals for its faithful adherents, a cult which is clearly and totally incompatible with Christianity and which surely should be avoided by every conscientious, confessional Lutheran Christian.

Scouting

In his excellent booklet, "Scouting in the Light of Holy Scripture," the Reverend Erhard C. Pankow pinpointed how the popular Scouting organization and its offspring or relatives (Girl Scouts, Brownies, Cub Scouts, Explorers, Camp Fire Girls, et al.) have compromised and perverted the clear teaching of Holy Scripture on the subject of God. Although Pankow's booklet was published in 1946, his indictment of Scouting's blatant idolatry is still pertinent and timely, even after the passing of more than three decades. Pankow stated:

> Scouting demands recognition of, and belief in, a Supreme Being. Its Constitution plainly states:
>
>> "The Boy Scouts of America maintain that no boy can grow into the best kind of citizenship without recognizing his obligation to God." (ART. III, p. 3)
>>
>> "The recognition of God as the ruling and leading power in the universe, and the grateful acknowledgment of His favors and blessings, are necessary to the best type of citizenship, and are wholesome things in the education of the growing boy." (CONSTITUTION, ART. II, p. 4)
>
> In the Scout Oath and Scout Law, which every Scout and Scouter must know and subscribe to and according to which he must order his life and daily conduct, the Scout promises to do his "duty to God" and to be "reverent toward God".
>
> Who this God is, however, is nowhere clearly defined in Scout literature. His identity is carefully veiled in such expressions as "the leading power in the universe" (CONSTITUTION, p. 3), "the Infinite Creator of the universe", "The Source of Life" (HANDBOOK FOR BOYS, p. 108), and, in a suggested benediction for Scout masters, "the Great Master of all good Scouts" (HANDBOOK FOR SCOUT-MASTERS, Vol. 1, p. 71). Scoutism, like lodgism, purposely refrains from making any clear-cut pronouncement on the person and nature of God, for the obvious reason that its doors may be kept open to boys and men of every race, every creed and every class. (HANDBOOK FOR BOYS, p. 10). Its Constitution declares:
>
>> "No matter what the boy may be — Catholic or Protestant or Jew — this fundamental need of good citizenship (the recognition of some deity) should be kept before him." (ART. III.)
>>
>> "The Boy Scouts of America recognizes the religious element in the training of a boy, but it is absolutely non-sectarian in its attitude toward that religious training. Its policy is that the organization or institution with which the Boy Scout is connected shall give definite attention to his religious life." (ART. III, p. 4)

In other words, the Christian Church is to teach its boys that the true and living God is the Triune God — Father, Son, and Holy Ghost. The Jew, Unitarians, and Universalists are to teach their boys that the true and living God is a deity in which Christ, the second Person in the Godhead, has no place. Boys who have no church affiliation at all are to picture "the leading power in the universe" to themselves in whatever form or fashion they choose.

Thus Scoutism gives recognition to any and all gods. In its Oath and Law it demands "reverence" toward any and all gods, irrespective of who or what they may be, and consequently finds itself under the thundering condemnation of the very first Commandment of the one and only true God, the Triune God: "I am the Lord thy God. Thou shalt have no other gods before me," Ex. 20:2-3. "There is none other God but one," admonishes the divinely inspired apostle. Again: "There is but one God, the Father, of whom are all things, and we in him; and one Lord Jesus Christ, by whom are all things, and we by him," I Cor. 8:4-6. "Look unto me, and be ye saved, all the ends of the earth: for I am God, and there is none else," Is. 45:22 (See also: Deut. 6:4; Matt. 4:10.)

Inasmuch as the religious pronouncements of Scoutism on the subject of "God", even at their best, refer only to the first Person in the Holy Trinity, the Father, with no reference whatever to His only-begotten Son, the Movement also very definitely, and by no means undeservedly, falls under the condemnation of John 5:23: "All men should honor the Son even as they honor the Father. He that honoreth not the Son, honoreth not the Father which hath sent him." "Every spirit that confesseth that Jesus Christ is come in the flesh is of God: and every spirit that confesseth not that Jesus Christ is come in the flesh is not of God," I John 4:2,3.[38]

A similar statement condemning the idolatry that is inherent in the Scouting movement was issued by the Conference of Presidents of the Evangelical Lutheran Joint Synod of Wisconsin and Other States in 1954:

Our Position Against Scouting

Scouting's "God" Not the Triune God

Scouting places emphasis upon the boy's relation to "God." It speaks of "God" in its Oath and Law and frequently in its official handbooks. But who is the "God" of Scouting? Is it the God of Scripture, the Triune God, the Savior-God revealed in Christ Jesus? The "God" of whom Scouting so often speaks is nowhere identified as the Triune God. Nowhere does it honor Jesus Christ as the Son of God, the Savior of sinners, although He says: "He that honoreth not the Son honoreth not the Father which hath sent him." (John 5:23)

The omission of the Son of God from the Scout Oath and Law is not unintentional oversight but deliberate policy, for Scouting welcomes into its rank also those who deny that Jesus is true God and Savior. The "God" of Scouting is, therefore, not acceptable to the Christian, who will give honor only to the Triune God and who regards the worship of any other "God" as a sin against the First Commandment. We want our children to have the Scriptural answer to the question, "Who is God?" Scouting does not supply that answer and confuses young minds on this all-important question.

No "Duty to God" without Faith

Scouting insists on the Scout Promise: "On my honor I will do my best to do my duty to God. . . ." It requires an oath or promise that goes far beyond the "Yea, yea; nay, nay" of Scripture, and is forbidden by God. It implies that the Scout can on his honor, by his ability, do his "duty to God." It tells the Scout while describing his "duty" to "God": "Above all you are faithful to Almighty God's Commandments." "It is something to be good but it is far better to do good." This conflicts with the Scripture doctrines of Original Sin, Faith, and Conversion. The Scriptures tell us that natural man is born in sin, that he is an enemy of God, that he cannot please God. They teach that our first duty is to repent of our sins and believe in Christ Jesus. They insist that only he who believes in Christ can do work acceptable to God. Scouting disagrees with the central teaching of Scripture when it leaves faith in Christ completely out of the picture and then supposes that Scouts can do their "duty to God."

122

Scouting's Unionistic Character

Because Scouting invites boys of different creeds to participate in a program which contains religious elements, it cannot but come into conflict with the Scripture's teaching on church fellowship. The Twelfth Scout Law maintains: "A Scout . . . respects the convictions of others in matters of custom and religion." We grant that every citizen has the right to hold his own religious beliefs, but we ourselves will not join in religious endeavors with those who persist in false beliefs. We cannot grant religious error equal status with religious truth. We cannot respect anyone's religious errors. We cannot agree with Scouting when it says: "Your . . . rabbi will teach you how to know God better." No one can be "faithful in his religious duties" unless he is faithful to the Triune God. We do not accept the modern theology that all churches are alike, that one is as good as the other. We remember what our Lord says: "If ye continue in my word, then are ye my disciples indeed." (John 8:31)[39]

Most of the points made above about the lodges and idolatry apply as well to the Scouting organization. Scouting might be described as a "baby" or "junior" lodge, for its nonsectarian principles and proclamations about an all-purpose god are nearly identical to those promulgated by the lodges. Some time ago I read the death notice of a prominent Boy Scout executive. The fact that Masonic services were conducted at his funeral would not surprise anyone who would make a careful comparison of the two groups and their very similar religious beliefs. It is also significant that many Scout troops are sponsored by lodges. In a telephone conversation with a Scouting official in my area on 11/15/79, I was given the following 1978 statistics listing the number of Scout troops sponsored by various lodges: Eagles-82, Elks-849, Masons-168, Moose-225, Odd Fellows-64. Many troops are sponsored by public school parent-teacher associations, the Jaycees (1,032) and about half by churches (Roman Catholics and Methodists sponsor the most among the churches).

Most Americans have a very positive attitude toward Scouting, putting the movement on a par with patriotism, the American flag, baseball and apple pie. Among the ranks of former Scouts are such popular and prominent celebrities as former President Gerald Ford, astronaut Neil Armstrong, the first man to set foot on the moon, and the all-time home run record holder, Hank Aaron. Thus it is not surprising that most people have difficulty seeing anything wrong with a group that so vigorously promotes values like loyalty to country, reverence to God and respect for family. Few would question the statement of congressman Clarence J. Brown (R-Ohio) who conducted a Scouting survey of the Congress in 1971 because "participation in Scouting can provide one measure of the quality of the legislative branch of government." Brown learned from his survey that 193 of the 534 senators and congressmen once were Scouts. When former President Gerald Ford was criticized for being too much of a Boy Scout, he stated that scouting ideals would be his guide in all his official duties. At a Scout dinner, Ford, himself an Eagle Scout "recited the scout laws and oath, which emphasize honesty, bravery and reverence, and said 'Well, if these are not the goals the people of the United States want their president to live up to, then I must draw this conclusion: Either you have the wrong man — or I have the wrong country. And I don't believe either is so.' "[40] When Dr. Arthur A. Schuck, chief executive of the Boy Scouts of America, was honored by the Freedoms Foundation in 1959, he was credited with making "scouting a beloved word in every home in America."[41] On May 23, 1963, Dr. Oswald Hoffmann, longtime preacher on the Lutheran

124

Hour radio service, expressed his conviction that "The Lutheran Committee on Scouting should stop being apologetic with regard to cooperation of the Lutheran church with the scouting movement. . . . It is high time for the churches to recognize an organization whose settled policy it is not to compete but to cooperate with the churches."

In the face of such glowing testimonials, it may seem almost un-American to question the spiritual value of scouting and to suggest that this organization promotes a modern form of idolatry. Yet scouting stubbornly insists that all scouts must promise to do their duty to God, but they offer no clear guidance or instruction as to which god is to be obeyed. In fact, the impression is given that all religions worship one and the same god, a very popular but completely unscriptural heresy.

Who is the "GOD" of Scouting? In my files I have a news clipping which tells of Roman Catholic scouts praying: "Dear Immaculate Mary, our mother and queen, be pleased to receive our veneration as Boy Scouts of America. . . . Look down, dear mother, upon us who kneel in love and devotion before you. Help us to be faithful to our promise: To do our duty to God and our country." My files tell of a religious award for Buddhist Cub Scouts, the "Metta" award medal designed to help Cub Scouts deepen their knowledge and practice of the Buddhist religion. Some years ago I clipped out an article and picture which showed Presbyterian and Jewish Boy Scouts exchanging the scout salute at the Boy Scout Sunday services at the Presbyterian church; on the following Friday the Protestant scouts were scheduled to attend services at the Jewish synagogue. In the 11/17/70 *Milwaukee Journal* I came across a news item and AP Wirephoto with the following heading and information:

"WILL BECOME EAGLE — James Clark, 16, of Foster, R.I., displays some of the Boy Scout merit badges (22 were shown) which in part make him eligible for Eagle Scout rank. Officials announced that the youth, who is an atheist, would be recommended for the rank despite an earlier refusal because his application lacked 'confirmation of duty to God.' " Who, indeed, is the GOD of Scouting? Apparently this god is some sort of shadowy, vague, nebulous deity who draws out equal reverence and worship from Presbyterians, Roman Catholics, Jews, Buddhists and even atheists. What an absurd and blasphemous caricature of the true God emerges when organizations like the lodges and Scouting stray from the Holy Scriptures and fashion an idol that will fit in with their fanciful conceptions of God!

If the atheist James Clark did attain the Eagle scout ranking in 1970 in Rhode Island, this may have made Scout officials reconsider their position and tighten up, at least to some extent, their view of what constitutes duty and reverence toward God. Consider what happened to 10-year-old Claude Taylor in Maine in 1973:

Scouts Put God Above Boy's Faith

Portland, Maine — AP — Boy scout officials have been upheld for refusing to allow a 10-year-old boy to join the Cub Scouts because he crossed the word "God" out of the Scout Promise.

The Executive Board of the Pine Tree Council, Boy Scouts of America, said the youth, Claude Taylor of Hanover, Maine, would not recognize duty to God that is required of every scout.

"The position of the Boy Scouts of America is quite clear," a statement by the board said. "The Boy Scouts of America maintains that no boy can grow into the best kind of citizen without recognizing his obligation to God."

The board said membership in the scouts was voluntary "and young men who do not believe that they can adhere to the principles of the organization need not join. Thus, they eliminate themselves for qualification to membership."[42]

A few months after 10-year-old Claude Taylor was excluded from the Cub Scouts in Maine, the national president of the Scouts made it clear that the organization considers a belief in God an indispensable key tenet of their philosophy. According to a 5/30/74 *Religious News Service* release:

> The president of the Boy Scouts of America has strongly reaffirmed the religious principle of Scouting and the right "to say that one must have a belief in a Supreme Being."
>
> "Let those who choose not to believe form their own organization and exclude us, because we do believe in a Supreme Being," said Robert W. Reneker of Chicago, newly re-elected president.
>
> He addressed the religious convocation which opened the 64th annual meeting in Honolulu of the National Council of Boy Scouts of America.
>
> Attending were some 2,500 delegates and members of executive boards from more than 400 Councils in the U.S. The Councils, with their thousands of units, represent nearly 5 million youth and adult members of the Boy Scout movement in the U.S. . . .
>
> In his address, Mr. Reneker said "we have the right to be individuals, to believe what we want to believe just so long as that right does not infringe on the rights of others."
>
> "We have a right, as an organization, to say that one must have a belief in a Supreme Being. We do not say that anyone who does not, must belong to the Boy Scouts of America."
>
> Mr. Reneker asserted that to make the belief in a Supreme Being a paramount requirement "for those who join us, is our right. We will oppose with all our might, any change in that policy."
>
> "The success of the Boy Scouts of America is rooted in our partnership with religious, civic, service, fraternal, educational, and other groups," he said. "I know of none who have entered into this partnership with us who do not, in some form, express a belief in a Supreme Being. This is required in order for our partnership to be effective and complete."
>
> Mr Reneker held that "together the Boy Scouts of America and all our partners are not defending our stand. We are proud

of it. We are not trying to make it conform to all ideologies in order to gain members and support. We don't have to."

"We are not going to change or weaken our strong position that belief in a Supreme Being is one of the very foundation-stones of our movement. To do so would be cowardly," the Boy Scouts' president said.[43]

Mr. Reneker describes the position of scouting regarding belief in a Supreme Being as strong. Surely it is not strong enough, according to scriptural standards, nor does it give the rightful honor and reverence to Jesus that this world's one and only Savior so richly deserves. Scouting stands condemned by these strong uncompromising words of Christ: "Whosoever therefore shall confess me before men, him will I confess also before my Father which is in heaven. But whosoever shall deny me before men, him will I also deny before my Father which is in heaven" (Matthew 10:32,33).

Scout officials stubbornly insist that belief in a Supreme Being is necessary for membership in their organization, but they just as adamantly refuse to take a solid, scriptural stand confessing Jesus Christ as the only one who can save young scouts and their leaders from sin and hell. The deliberate Christlessness of scouting is the factor that should cause conscientious Christians to keep their youth out of this organization. Scouting's intentional denial of Christ (by refusing to confess him before the world) and their failure to identify God as the true, Triune God of the Bible make them guilty of out and out idolatry, in spite of their good intentions and great zeal to make their youth well-prepared, constructive American citizens. Their program combining fun, field trips, training in camping skills, along with moral instruction and stress on good deeds, even when related to their version of god, contributes to man's opinion of self-righteousness and work righteousness. In addition it fosters a fuzzy, unscriptural conception of the true God because morality and theology are divorced from simple, basic faith in Jesus Christ.

WOMEN'S LIBERATION AND IDOLATRY

In 1776 Ann Lee founded the first Shaker (Shaking Quakers) community in the United States at Watervliet, New York. This small, strange sect, formally called "The United Society of Believers in Christ's Second Appearing" or "The Millenial Church" was popularly known as "Shakers" because of their movements during religious excitement. Ann Lee taught and her disciples dutifully believed that God is dual, male and female; they prayed to "Our Father and Mother which are in heaven." According to Shaker belief Christ is not God, but the highest spirit, and is also dual, incarnate in Jesus (male) and Ann Lee (female). Jesus and Ann Lee were to be loved, honored and respected, but not worshiped. The Bible's teaching of the Trinity was rejected.

About a century after Ann Lee's death, the Shaker's idolatrous ideas about deity resurfaced through the teachings and writings of Mary Baker Eddy, the founder of the Christian Science cult. Mrs. Eddy's "spritually interpreted" version of the Lord's Prayer begins: "Our Father-Mother God," and she declared: "Woman was a higher idea of God than man, insomuch as she was the final one in the scale of being; but because our beliefs reverse every portion of Truth, we named the supreme being masculine instead of feminine."[44] Like Ann Lee, Mrs. Eddy also had no use for the scriptural teaching of the Trinity. She used the term, but for her, God was a vague pantheistic being with a triune capacity of Life, Truth and Love.

The idolatrous ideas about God expressed by Ann Lee and Mary Baker Eddy, as misguided and blasphemous as they were, seem like tame heresies compared with the concepts and convictions promulgated by the leaders of the radical women's liberation movement of modern times. Mary Daly, an eloquent spokesperson for radical feminism, angrily advocated deicide, the killing of God the Father, because she believes that the Bible's description of God as male is the main reason for the subordinate and oppressed position of women through the centuries. Ms. Daly writes:

> The biblical and popular image of God as a great patriarch in heaven, rewarding and punishing according to his mysterious and seemingly arbitrary will, has dominated the imagination of millions over thousands of years. The symbol of the Father God, spawned in the human imagination and sustained as plausible by patriarchy, has in turn rendered service to this type of society by making the mechanisms for the oppression of women appear right and fitting. If God in "his" heaven is a father ruling "his" people, then it is in the "nature" of things and according to divine plan and the order of the universe that society be male-dominated.[45]

Like the prominent women's lib leader, Betty Friedan, who declared that "the church is the enemy," Ms. Daly rails against basic biblical truth and fundamental Christian principles in her book. She dismisses the story of Eve's birth (sic) in Genesis as absurd, insisting that it is blatantly silly to believe that a male (Adam) was the original mother. She labels Old Testament prophets "sexist" because they compared the idolatrous, spiritually unfaithful Israelites to a whore (cf. Isaiah 1:21, Jeremiah 2:20, Ezekiel, chapter 16, and others). She obviously rejects the Triune God as he reveals himself in the Scriptures, but it is not entirely clear what deity she would put in his place. Daly's deity is "the Verb who transcends anthropomorphic symbolization, the Final Cause, the Good Who is self-communication Be-ing, Who is the

Verb from whom, in whom, and with whom all true movements move."[46]

Christian women who feel the pull and attraction of the women's liberation movement should be well aware of what is at stake. Not all the proponents of women's lib may be as radical and irreligious, as blasphemous and idolatrous as Daly and Friedan, but increasingly the Christian faith and the Holy Bible are seen as the enemy, as ancient superstitions which have oppressed women for centuries. Daly demands that the God of the Holy Scriptures must be castrated, that the divine patriarch who castrates women must not be allowed to live on in the human imagination, that what she calls the Supreme Phallus must be cut away, that women must free themselves from the bondage of Christolatry.[47]

For those who might dismiss Ms. Daly as too weird or far-out to have much influence on many women, the following article by John Dart distributed by the *Los Angeles Times Service* shows that Daly's ideas and even more blatant and patently pagan forms of idolatry are being promoted and inculcated by radical feminists on various university campuses as part of women's studies programs. Under the title, "Those Ancient Goddesses Aren't Ancient Anymore," Dart describes how women in search of freedom from domination by men are returning to ancient idolatrous religions, like the ones mentioned in Chapter Two, simply because they feature female goddesses rather than male. Dart writes, dateline, Santa Cruz, California, as follows:

> Nearly 400 women picked different notes and held them, catching their breaths at different times so that sound droned unabated for five minutes.
>
> The eerie monotones reverberated against the outside walls of the Theater of Performing Arts and filtered through clumps of tall pines on the University of California Santa Cruz campus.

The hymnic call was to the "Goddess."

Later in the day, encouraged by the beat of bongo drums, spontaneous groups of circling women danced bare breasted in scenes suggestive of frolicking wood nymphs.

The occasion was a university extension course, "The Great Goddess Re-emerging," a three day program. Surprised sponsors had to turn away potential registrants after the 450 spaces were filled.

Although the lectures were mostly academic, the gathering had the spirit of a feminist rally and the body contact of an encounter weekend.

Cheers and whoops went up for the goddesses of yore — Isis, Astara, Demeter, Artemis, etc. Likewise, there was applause for articulate or artistic use of divine female imagery to support contemporary woman's self-esteem.

More than a successful university extension course, however, the event was indicative of a growing spiritual dimension to the women's liberation movement in America.

A religious phenomenon virtually unknown outside feminist circles, "goddess consciousness," will be known widely in three to five years, predicted Carol Christ (rhymes with mist) of San Jose State University's women's studies program.

The official instructor for the UC Santa Cruz course and holder of a Ph.D. in religious studies from Yale, Ms. Christ described the rationale for new attention to goddess images:

"Religions centered on the worship of a male God keep women in a childish state of psychological dependence on men and male authority," she said, "while at the same time legitimizing the political and social authority of fathers and sons in the institutions of society."

Even people who say they no longer believe in God or participate in Christian or Jewish groups "still may not be free of the power of the symbolism of God the Father," Ms. Christ said. "Symbol systems cannot simply be rejected, they must be replaced."

Christine Downing, head of San Diego State University's religious studies department, estimates that many — if not most — spiritually sensitive women in the women's movement are willing to replace the biblical God with a frankly pagan and polytheistic approach.

"Maybe somebody will find a way of ducking those loaded words, but most people involved in this are not afraid ot the terms 'pagan' and 'polytheistic,' " Ms. Downing said.

Many Christian feminists, including growing numbers in seminaries, portray God as embodying both the male and female. Jesus is regarded favorably by them because of his sympathetic treatment of women.

But an influential book claiming that such theology is fruitless was Mary Daly's "Beyond God the Father," published in 1973. The Boston College theologian said Biblical materials were still basically patriarchal. Her book pointed to a spiritual vacuum for many women, Ms. Downing said.

The departure by some feminists from the Judeo-Christian heritage in the mid-1970's appears to have been fed partly by renewed interest in mythology by both men and women.

Witchcraft is used by some women in their search for roots and rituals — without the connotations of evil usually associated with witchcraft.

A Santa Cruz woman, Ebony of the Mountain, 38, said, "Some of the women think of themselves as witches, but not all."

A number of participants here said they used some rites, but they tend to be individualistic interpretations.

Using herself as a photographic model, then retouching slides with artistic designs, Mary Beth Edelson of New York creates representations of goddess power and potential.

"I used to paint concentric circles on myself," she said, "but I don't do it so much now because I can get energy without it." She closed her conference talk by having the class alternate in chanting, "The goddess is us, the goddess is here."

A brief appearance was made by Z Budapest, a self-described witch, who was an unsuccessful advocate of repeal of a Los Angeles' ordinance outlawing fortune telling as a business.

The goddess movement knows her as a leader of the Susan B. Anthony Coven No. 1 in Los Angeles and a spokeswoman for a feminist brand of Wicca, an ancient women's religion.

"I have been earning my living for seven years writing and speaking about the goddess," she said. She said she had initiated 300 women and ordained 10 priestesses.

The Wicca purposes are moral, according to Z Budapest,

who spoke of the goals of eliminating diseases and war.

The goddess movement is also called the womenspirit movement. What is considered its first major gathering was a conference attended by about 1,200 women at the University of Massachusetts in late 1975.

The absence of national organization is accompanied by a lack of uniform theology or doctrines.

Ms. Christ said the goddess, for most women, means one of three things:

The divine female who can be invoked in prayer and ritual.

Life, death and rebirth energy in nature and culture, and in personal and communal life.

The symbol of legitimacy and beauty of female power as realized in the women's liberation movement.

Ms. Christ said one woman told her that the symbol of the goddess had different meanings acording to how she felt: "When I feel weak, she is someone who can help and protect me. When I feel strong, she is the symbol of my own power. At other times I feel her as the natural energy in my body and the world."

The female registrants at this conference were reminded more than once that their 28 day menstrual cycles match the waning and waxing of the moon. There were also a dozen male students in the course.

The ancient Mediterranean world, pagan Europe, Native America and Hindu tradition are all sources for goddess imagery, Ms. Christ said. For many women, knowing about the goddesses is more important than believing in them.

Another conference lecturer, Merlin Stone, author of "When God was a Woman," urged women to learn ancient languages, such as Akkadian and Hittite. The translations and studies have been done primarily by men and sometimes, she said, their biases are evident.

One of the openly lesbian students in the course challenged the emphasis by speakers on heterosexuality. Ms. Stone responded that she had no objections to findings that might reveal a positive image of lesbianism in myths and ancient worship, but to date she had found no written evidence.

There were no indications that the goddess movement is an overly solemn religion.

> Four course participants who were once cheerleaders led an exuberant cheer for the Moon Goddess — "Give me an M . . . give me an O . . ."[48]

Talk about history repeating itself! How astounding that Satan has succeeded in seducing thousands of American women of high intelligence to worship primitive, pagan goddesses like Isis, Astara, Demeter and Artemis and to dabble in witchcraft, all in the name of liberation. In an article on the so-called neopaganist movement *Time* magazine reveals a definite connection between the beliefs of ancient pagan religions, the teachings of Ann Lee and Mary Baker Eddy, and the "spiritual" side of modern feminism. *Time* observed:

> Modern pagan groups tend to be small (at most 20 members) and eclectic, drawing their beliefs from such diverse sources as ancient Egypt, the Druids, Greek and Roman antiquity and the American Indian religions. But the groups share some tenets. Most believe in reincarnation and in a universe ruled by a supreme godhead comprising two parts: a male half, which includes the sun, and a female half, which includes the moon. The distaff side is frequently considered to have more status, which makes neopaganism especially attractive to some feminists.[49]

THE "GOD" OF MODERN MAN'S IMAGINATION

When people stray from the revelation of himself which the Triune God graciously supplies in the Holy Scriptures and give free rein to their imaginations, they come up with a wide variety of idols. Some are very simple, like "the Man upstairs" or, in the words of a popular song, the "Someone in the great somewhere (who) hears every word"; others are very sophisticated and complex as conceived by learned theologians and philosophers, like "the eternal Thou" of Martin Buber or Teilhard De Chardin's "Omega Point."

But what is the average man on the street's view of God, the average Joe who is unchurched, but who would feel like a fool talking about a god who is "the Wholly Other" or "the Ground of all being"? How does such a person see God if he has lost sight of the Bible's doctrine of God? I believe that the Hollywood movie and T.V. producer-director Carl Reiner was very much in tune with the thoughts of millions in his 1977 film, "Oh, God!"

Reiner recruited the veteran comedian George Burns to play God, who reveals himself to an atheistic grocery store manager, Jerry Landers, a part portrayed by the popular singer, John Denver. Most of the plot and particulars of this movie must be classified as blatant blasphemy, but it does reveal much about how modern men would imagine or want God to be. God, as conceived by Reiner and acted out by Burns, is very humanistic, a "real nice guy" god with a dry humor and a sharp wit, a funny deity who performs card tricks and triggers a rainstorm inside an A.M.C. Pacer automobile to demonstrate his supernatural power. The Reiner-Burns god is limited in his knowledge, for he says: "I only know the future as it becomes the present." His message for mankind, as Jerry Landers was to relay it, is that everything will work out all right if everyone gets together and does his/her share to help matters.

The moviemakers' Jewish background and bias are revealed by their statement about Christ. In response to the question, "Is Jesus Christ the Son of God?" Burns replies: "Jesus was my son, Buddha was my son, Mohammed, Moses, You (Jerry Landers), the man who said, 'there is no room in the inn' was my son." The script writer who came up with that syncretistic put down of our Savior either did not know about or — more likely — rejected what Scripture tells us about Jesus in John 14:6

and Acts 4:12, that salvation and access to the Father in heaven is available only through faith in Jesus.

In a very perceptive article, "Taking God's Name in Fun," Dominique Paul Noth, the movie critic for the *Milwaukee Journal*, put his finger on the average modern man's image of God, as it is revealed in recent theatrical and film productions. Noth wrote:

> These Gods (in plays and movies) are pleasant creatures (sic) — in part because the mass American audience still has enough of a religious ethic to make harsh attacks on the Lord unprofitable. Patrons clearly are not interested in rampant atheism, nor in subtleties about religious creeds. . . .
>
> The culture has gone through a transition — and not just in comedy. Jesus wailed his agonies to a rock beat in "Jesus Christ Superstar." He is a Clown in "Godspell." Franco Zeffirelli's TV miniseries, "Jesus of Nazareth", very deliberately sought a humanistic tone, as opposed to the beatific tiptoeing of the past.
>
> The treatment of God in modern entertainment reflects a change in the social pressure applied to religious beliefs, a basic adjustment in the general meaning of "keeping the faith." It is not the kind of treatment that could exist for long in a rabidly puritan climate, nor in a society where open professions of faith were normal, routine expectations.
>
> The movies and plays lean to a "one man, one God" philosophy. Though there is sympathy for God, there is more sympathy for man — a creature most comfortable with a nonsermonized, personable, sentimental approach to the Ultimate Being.
>
> The jokes about God are, underneath, jokes about man, who needs to feel he is special and yet is cynical about holding anything in reverence without rational, scientific basis. These works push God out of the closet, put makeup on Him and wryly manipulate His uneasy relationship with, and meaning for, mankind.
>
> The plot humor sometimes stems from the disbelief of the citizenry — they won't accept that John Denver saw God. . . . But the very use for this disbelief device reflects how much God has become a private thing in our society, a bogeyman for children who is forgotten, ignored or only quietly thought upon

after the age of puberty. He can be shaped as you wish, and He changes with the times.

The movies and plays are addressing that audience — and finding considerable response.[50]

Movie critic Noth pinpoints what is perhaps the most common form of contemporary idolatry, modern man's audacious manipulation of God, shaping him according to his mind, making him over into the kind of deity George Burns dreamed up and described in a letter to his agent: "He should be kind, wise, witty, sympathetic, and he could use more humorous epigrams. He shouldn't be ethnic and use words like schtick and schlock."[51] It's obvious that the god according to George Burns' imagination is totally out of touch with tough, scriptural truths like sin, death, damnation, hell and Satan. Burns' kind, wise, witty and sympathetic deity, lacking any plan for the salvation of sinners, would be powerless against the forces of evil which daily rear their ugly heads in human society.

The advice column of Ann Landers is carried in nearly 1,000 American newspapers with an estimated 60,000,000 readers; Phil Donahue has a popular T.V. talk show that attracts millions of viewers every week-day. Donahue and Landers achieved their success, at least in part, because they are very much in tune with modern society. It is also obvious that the opinions, ideas, advice and philosophy of life which they express with clarity and eloquence exert tremendous influence on their readers and hearers. Several years ago Landers appeared on Donahue's program where she reassured her host that he should not be concerned about his status as a lapsed and divorced Roman Catholic. She described God as a loving and forgiving deity who would not deal harshly with nice, kind and intelligent people like Donahue.

Her appearance and remarks on Donahue's program

prompted Professor Carleton Toppe to write as follows in a *Northwestern Lutheran* editorial:

> ... Her (Ann Landers') conception of a God who is loving and forgiving is the typical, deluded representation of God that is a caricature of the God of the Old Testament as well as the New. Indeed, God is loving and forgiving — but without insisting that His Ten Commandments are just as much in force today as they were on Mt. Sinai? without being in deadly earnest about sin? without requiring the sinner to acknowledge his guilt and to repent of it? without insisting that the only way the transgressor has to experience that love and forgiveness is through Christ crucified? Her representation of Christianity or even of the Judaeo-Christian religion is a spiritual fraud.
>
> Ann Landers' column makes some contribution to civic righteousness. It also distorts the morality and reality of God.[52]

MISCELLANEOUS MODERN DAY IDOLS

Communism

At the time of this writing a decade-long detente or diminishing of the Cold War between the United States and the Soviet Union has been severely damaged, if not destroyed, by the Russian invasion of Afghanistan. The majority of the Afghan people in that mostly Moslem country classify the Russian invaders as pagan, as heathen infidels who not only do not believe in Allah but also are citizens of a nation that is officially atheistic.

Sad to say, those Afghan Moslems are themselves idolaters, worshipers of a deity, Allah, who apparently originated in the mind of Islam's master prophet, Muhammed (d. A.D. 632). But what about the religious beliefs of citizens in the Soviet Union, in China and other Communist countries? In spite of rigorous religious persecution in those countries and much propaganda promoting atheism, religion has not been totally eradicated. There are, for example, 11,000 Russian Orthodox churches in the U.S.S.R. — only a fraction of the 53,000 in Russia before the 1917 revolution. It is estimated that there are about 400,000 Baptists in the Soviet Union as well. But most of the clergy seem to be puppet spokesmen for the Communist Party line. Russian Orthodox Metropolitan Filaret of Kiev claims that "the Soviet state is not an atheistic state. It consists of believers and non-believers. There are periods of strong antireligious propaganda and others of less." Another Russian Orthodox clergyman maintains that "the main principle of Christianity and Marxism is the same. Believers try to enter the kingdom of God, and Marxists strive for true Communism. The bright future for man and the kingdom of God — aren't they the same?"[53]

In addition to a bias favoring atheism and several thousand churches clearly subservient to the State, idolatry also is widely practiced in Communist countries. Every day there are long lines of people outside a crypt in Moscow waiting to file past the mummified corpse of Lenin. Their adulation of that mastermind of the revolution and his teachings seems to go beyond patriotism, such as the admiration and respect Americans accord leaders like Washington, Jefferson and Lincoln, to out and out idolatry.

In a tract, "Why Christians Must Fight Communism," a fervent anti-communist Lutheran minister, Paul C. Neipp has stated:

> Always remember that communism is not a mere political party. Communism is a religion! It is a powerful religion. Above all, it is a false religion.
>
> Communism should not be called a religion in the sense that we Christians or even the heathen use the term, for even the heathen in their religion have a system of ethical values and a code of morals. COMMUNISM IS A PERVERSION OF RELIGION. It is a system of beliefs that are rotten, amoral, blasphemous, devilish to the core and soul-damning! Commun-

ism is a distorted, twisted, deformed perversion of everything we hold sacred.

Communism has its own sacred writings — the books of Marx, Engles, Lenin and Stalin. These contain their false doctrines. Some of these false doctrines are: "In our revolutionary conception of the universe there is absolutely no room either for a Creator or a Ruler;" "Thou shalt not love the Lord thy God will all thy might, because man is the highest being for men;" "Thou shalt kill, if the resistance of the owners of property makes it necessary" — these and other doctrines must be believed by communists and will also be forced upon those whom they conquer by means of mass indoctrination and brainwashing.

On January 4, 1960, radio Moscow blared over the airwaves, "Science long ago established that Jesus Christ never existed!"

How godless! — Yet the bolsheviks have their gods: Marx is likened to God the Father, Stalin to Jesus Christ, the Savior, and Lenin to the Holy Spirit. For example, since Stalin fathered the Soviet industrial revolution, bringing Russian production ever closer to ours, he is referred to as their "savior."[54]

Stalin's status as a Communist idol was relatively short-lived, but Marx and Lenin continue to receive god-like honors and devotion from the Communist party comrades. In China, Mao Tse-Tung seems to be suffering a fate similar to Stalin's. For many years before and after his death at 82 in 1976, Mao was deified as China's "Great Helmsman" and the little red book containing his thoughts was obviously given reverence as the kind of divine revelation that Moslems give to their Koran and that Christians give to the Holy Bible. More recently China's leaders have attempted to dismantle the myth of Mao's infallibility. In a speech before 11,000 people packed into Peking's Great Hall of the People on Oct. 1, 1979, the 30th anniversary of the founding of the People's Republic of China, one of Mao's own colleagues, 81-year-old Ye Jianying, clearly was referring to Mao when he said: "Leaders are not gods; they are not infallible and therefore should not be deified."[55] A few weeks later, the Chinese Communist's party newspaper, *People's Daily*, flatly rejected the long-standing portrayal of Mao as a godlike, deified superman who singlehandedly pulled together a weak and divided China by describing him as "a man, not a god."[56] Still, idolatry dies hard, also in Communist circles. Garry Trudeau, creator of the controversial comic strip feature, Doonsebury, had one of his comic strip characters sum up the career of Mao as follows: "Dead? You think Mao Tse-Tung is dead! Listen, honey, for Mao, dying was strictly academic! He left behind a legacy and iconography that Muhammed, Buddha and Christ could envy! Mao dead? Don't believe it! His portrait is in every home, his sayings on every building, his name kept burning in the hearts of millions! Would that you and I could be half as alive now as Mao is in death!"[57]

There's no denying that during their lifetimes Josef Stalin and Mao Tse-Tung wielded tremendous power and were idolized, as well as feared, by millions of people all over the world. But where are they now? Historians will never ignore them, it is true, but when they face the Lord Jesus as their Judge on the Last Day the god-like power and status they enjoyed for a few decades on this earth will do them no good. On that day they will have to answer to Christ for their fierce persecution of his faithful followers, for the spread of atheistic philosophy in their countries and for the self-deification which they promoted.

Santa Claus

What could those idols of Communism, sadistic Stalin of the Soviet Union and the ruthless, egomaniacal Mao possibly have in common with Santa Claus, that roly-poly, jolly old St. Nick, who offers his ample lap and patient ear to millions of American youngsters for a month or so every year? Many people surely would classify it as sacri-

142

lege to suggest that there is an element of idolatry in the attention that is given to the owner of Rudolph the Red-nosed Reindeer. Others would dismiss such a suggestion as silly or the brainstorm of some sort of sour spoilsport like Scrooge in Dickens' "A Christmas Carol."

We took all five of our children to visit Santa Claus when he came to town to do his thing in department stores, helping merchants to go to sleep during December with visions of dollar signs and record profits dancing in their heads. But not for one moment did we encourage our offspring to really "believe in Santa." In the 12/19/77 edition of *Christian News*, Pastor Bruce Ray of the Juanita Community Church, Kirkland, Washington, wrote a thought-provoking article about the need to demytholo-gize Christmas with the title, "I Believe in . . . Santa Claus?" In his article Ray made the following observa-tions about the danger of Satan using Santa as a substi-tute for the Triune God:

Santa Claus a God-substitute? Listen again to the popular song that children sing each Christmas:

You better watch out, you better not cry,
Better not pout, I'm telling you why —
Santa Claus is coming to town!

He's making a list and checking it twice,
Gonna find out who's naughty and nice
Santa Claus is coming to town!

He sees you when you're sleeping,
He knows when you're awake,
He knows if you've been bad or good
So be good for goodness' sake!

Oh! You better watch out, you better not cry,
Better not pout, I'm telling you why —
Santa Claus is coming to town!

Now think about the Santa myth in general and this song in particular in the light of the attributes of God. Here is a partial listing:

1. GOD IS HOLY — This means that God is distinct from all of

143

His creatures. He is a unique being; there is nothing in heaven, on the earth, or under the earth that is like God. So is the imaginary Santa Claus. There is no other being in the universe like him. He may go by different names in different countries, but there are no other Santa Clauses — only one. He is unique.

2. GOD IS ETERNAL — So is the imaginary Santa Claus. He has no beginning (Who were his parents? Where was he born?), and he will presumably have no end.

3. GOD IS UNCHANGEABLE — Santa Claus hasn't aged a day since I was a child. He still looks the same and he still does the same things he has always done. He appears to be a changeless being, like God.

4. GOD IS OMNISCIENT — So is the imaginary Santa. "He sees you when you're sleeping, He knows when you're awake' He knows if you've been bad or good . . ." That sounds a lot like what David says about Jehovah in Psalm 139: "O Lord, Thou hast searched me and known me. Thou dost know when I sit down and when I rise up; Thou dost understand my thought from afar."

5. GOD IS OMNIPOTENT — Is there anything that Santa Claus can't do at Christmas? The parents who maintain the myth may not be able to afford the expensive toy their child wanted, but that's no defect in Santa.

6. GOD IS OMNIPRESENT — Santa is not exactly omnipresent — everywhere at the same time. We all know that he spends most of his time at the North Pole. But somehow from that vantage point his eyes peer out over the whole earth watching children day and night without any rest. As Christmas approaches, he can be found in every department store in the city, and on Christmas Eve he manages to travel the whole world over, leaving presents at every house. Even with our space-age technology, that's quite an accomplishment. While that's not quite the same as being omnipresent, it certainly is close.

7. GOD IS SOVEREIGN — So is Santa Claus. To whom is Santa responsible? Is there anyone who has authority over him?

8. GOD IS GOOD — Santa also reveals his character by doing good unto others. His whole purpose is to give gifts unto men.

9. GOD IS JUST — So is His mythical substitute. "You better watch out, you better not cry, Better not pout, I'm telling you

why — "Santa Claus is coming to town, and he's coming in the character of a judge. Children who have been good during the year will receive presents as their reward. But children who have been bad can expect stockings filled with cinders and ashes. Santa Claus, then, is the judge over boys and girls, and they had better live their lives in a way that is pleasing to him.

10. GOD IS RIGHTEOUS — Has anybody ever found fault with Santa Claus? Are there any moral imperfections in his character or conduct? Has he ever needed to confess his sins to anybody else?

Well, perhaps the Santa myth is not so innocuous after all. In all of these things Santa Claus is a children's substitute for the living God. But can it really be harmful to let our children believe in a myth? INDEED IT CAN! And in several ways. Let me explain.

First, if Santa Claus is a God-substitute for the pre-school generation, then what do young boys and girls learn about Deity during the highly impressionable years of early childhood? In an excellent article published some years ago (December 3, 1971) in "Christianity Today" Samuel Mateer argued convincingly that Santa Claus is a reflection of the secular man's concept of God. As a child accepts Santa to be his judge, he will also accept all or some of the following ideas:

1. Acceptance with God — "He's making a list and checking it twice, Gonna find out who's naughty and nice. . ." The child soon learns that he can be acceptable to Santa by being "nice". Being nice guarantees rewards; being naughty means cinders and ashes. The way to be acceptable in God's sight is to do your very best. Sound familiar?

2. God's Word — The child knows that Santa has promised blessing upon niceness and cursing upon naughtiness. As Christmas approaches he is continually reminded of his own behavior. He has not been perfect throughout the past year, and he knows it. In fact, he has had some spells of nastiness while out shopping with his parents. But, he reasons within himself, everything will be OK. He's never known a kid yet who got cinders and ashes from Santa Claus. Nothing that he's done is bad enough for that. And Christmas morning, just as he expects, his faith in his own goodness is rewarded again. He's OK just as he is — his behavior though not perfect, is acceptable.

And all this talk about cinders and ashes is just talk. Whatever God says, and whatever the child does, in the end God will reward everybody anyway.

3. God's interest and involvement — Santa watches his people from a distance 364 days a year, but he only visits them once —and then only when they're asleep. They can write to him at the North Pole, but he never answers their letters. Though he has a host of "angels" (elves) who assist him in his work, they generally stay at the North Pole and have little contact with children. Santa is not really interested in the whole life of the child, and certainly is not in a position to help him with his problems. God is seen as a friendly old man with a long white beard who generally stays aloof from the world but occasionally checks on it to make sure it's still running.

4. The child's faith — Belief in Santa Claus is not something that has a dominant, life-forming influence on the child. He only needs to be concerned with Santa as the day of judgment (Christmas) approaches. So God is not One with whom we have to be concerned every day of our lives. We only need to worry about God when the Day of Judgment is approaching, when we know that soon we will die. And then we don't need to be overly concerned, as long as we can say we've done our best. No one has ever yet got cinders and ashes in their stockings have they?

Secondly, playing the Santa Claus game can have a harmful effect upon the child's relationship to his parents. The child looks to his parents to furnish everything that he needs — food when he's hungry, love when he's lonely, comfort when he's hurt, courage when he's afraid, and truth when he asks questions. When his bright eyes look up at you and he says with all seriousness, "Can Santa's reindeer really fly" what will you say? If you answer, "Yes, Rudolph and the others really can fly," then you are no longer playing a game. You are lending your personal authority to the myth, giving it the ring of reality. He who has always trusted you for the truth, now believes you. The lie becomes truth for the child. And children will actually fight their playmates to defend the credibility of their parents. "My daddy says. . ." can be a fierce battle-cry in the small world of children. Time moves on, and the child begins to see that his parents have been pulling the wool over his eyes and laughing behind his back all these years. It begins to dawn on him that he made a fool out of himself fighting for what Mom and Dad said was true. What happens to their credibility now? Why should he believe what they say, let alone stick his neck out to defend them? Sadder, but wiser, he asks himself how he can ever be sure that they aren't fooling him again. That relationship that was characterized by trust and confidence is now shot full of holes; doubt and suspicion linger long in the child's mind.

Thirdly, the Santa Claus myth can have a harmful effect upon the child's faith-relationship with the true and living God. He once believed in a man with God-like qualities who turned out to be a fake. Why should he commit himself again to belief in a man who claimed to be God manifested in the flesh? If you get burned once, it's pretty silly to put your hand back on the stove, isn't it? Mom & Dad and even the television newsmen told him about Santa Claus, and it was just a trick. How can he be sure that Mom and Dad and the pastor aren't all trying to pull the wool over his eyes now? If Santa was just for little kids, maybe Jesus is just for older kids. But still just for kids. The gospel may turn out to be only another God-game, after all.[58]

For those who might classify our condemnation of Santa Claus as an example of far-fetched fanaticism in the name of the Christian faith, we mention an incident that occurred on the streets of New York City several years ago. During the Christmas shopping season members of the Hare Krishnas, the American Hindu sect referred to earlier in this chapter, traded their saffron robes for Santa suits and started to compete for holiday donations with the traditional street Santas from the Volunteers of America. In the battle of the Santas, the Volunteers of America charged the Krishna Kringles harassed them and potential contributors by insistently demanding: "Ho, Ho, Ho. Don't you have anything for Santa?" The Krishna Santas also were accused of violating the unwritten code of Christmas collectors by poaching on the other people's more lucrative territory. In response to the complaint Roma Pada, a Hare Krishna spokesman, claimed that wearing Santa suits fit in perfectly with their overall purpose and philosophy. He insisted that "the essence of our preaching mission is to have people remember God. Santa being the contemporary emblem of Christmas, when people see Santa we want them to think of God."[59]

Svetlana's God

When the daughter of the Russian dictator, Josef Stalin, sought asylum in the United States in April, 1967, her coming to America created a sensation. Her picture appeared in hundreds of magazines and newspapers and reporters eagerly passed along to a fascinated public her every word. An especially responsive chord was struck by Svetlana Alliluyeva when she told the press that "religion has done a great change to me." Although she was baptized into the Communist-controlled Russian Orthodox Church in 1962, she quickly made it clear that her religious beliefs were right in line with the faith of millions of Americans, the Common American Religious Creed (CARC), which was mentioned in chapter one. Stalin's daughter described her faith as a "generalized belief in God" and she asserted that "all religions are true . . . different religions are different ways to the same God." That is a classic example of CARC, but it also happens to be out and out 20th century idolatry, for Svetlana's god, as well as the god of the Hare Krishna Santa Clauses, will save no souls from sin, death, Satan and hell, since there is no salvation apart from the name of the Lord Jesus Christ (Acts 4:12).[60]

NOTES FOR CHAPTER THREE

[1] Kenneth Hamilton, *To Turn from Idols*, pp. 39, 41, 59, 123.

[2] *The Milwaukee Journal*, 22 June 1979.

[3] Ibid., 21 Aug. 1979.

[4] Ibid., 6 Dec. 1977.

[5] Ibid., 17 Apr. 1966.

[6] Material for the Dalai Lama section taken from these sources: *Time* Magazine, 17 Sept. 1979; *The Milwaukee Sentinel*, 18 July 1976; *The Milwaukee Journal*, 4 Sept. 1979 and 17 Sept. 1979.

[7] Paul N. Benware, *Ambassadors of Armstrongism*, (Nutley, New Jersey: Presbyterian and Reformed Publishing Company, 1975), pp. 42, 43, 48-50.

[8] Material for the Bahai section taken from *The Milwaukee Journal* articles of 20 Mar. 1962 and 13 Jan. 1968.

[9] Ibid., 19 Sept. 1979.

[10] Ibid., 29 June 1974.

[11] Ibid., 5 July 1975.

[12] *Time* Magazine, 12 Dec. 1977.

[13] *The Milwaukee Journal*, 15 May 1979.

[14] *Time* Magazine, 14 June 1976.

[15] *Time* Magazine, 7 Aug. 1968.

[16] Quoted from *Truth and the Mormons*, printed by Concordia Tract Missions, St. Louis, Missouri; no date.

[17] William J. Peterson, *Those Curious New Cults*, (New Canaan, Connecticut: Keats Publishing, Inc., 1973), pp. 146, 147.

[18] Joel C. Gerlach, *The Northwestern Lutheran*, 25 Dec. 1977, p. 434 in his regular column, "Looking at the Religious World."

[19] *The Milwaukee Journal*, 21 Oct. 1973.

[20] Ibid., 22 June 1977.

[21] Some of the information about Hare Krishna and TM in the section on Eastern religions was taken from Peterson's *Those Curious New Cults* cited in footnote #17.

[22] *The Milwaukee Journal*, 19 Aug. 1961.

[23] *Time* Magazine, 12 Jan. 1962.

[24] *Time* Magazine, 11 Sept. 1964.

[25] *The Milwaukee Journal*, 18 Nov. 1972.

[26] Ibid., 16 June 1973.

[27] Ibid., 23 Aug. 1969.

[28] Ibid., 4 Dec. 1970.

[29] Ibid., 17 June 1964.

[30] Ibid., 10 Feb. 1979.

[31] Ibid., 9 Sept. 1967.

[32] John Ferguson, *The Religions of the Roman Empire*, (Ithaca, New York: Cornell University Press, 1970), pp. 13, 31.

[33] No author given, *Was Mary Born Without Sin?* (St. Louis: Concordia Publishing House, no date given), p. 7.

[34] Roy D. Linhart, *The Evil of Lodgery*, (Columbus, Ohio: Lutheran Book Concern, 1923), pp. 13-16.

[35] Walter A. Maier Jr., *Should I Join a Fraternal Society?* (St. Louis: Concordia Publishing House, 1961), pp. 9, 10.

[36] *The Milwaukee Journal*, 8 Aug. 1976.

[37] L. James Rongstad, *How To Respond To . . . The Lodge*, (St. Louis: Concordia Publishing House, 1977), pp. 23, 24.

[38] Erhard C. Pankow, *Scouting in the Light of Holy Scripture*, (Milwaukee, Wisconsin: Northwestern Publishing House, 1946), pp. 15-17. The booklet contains Pankow's essay adopted by, and published at the request of, the Wisconsin Synod's Milwaukee City Pastoral Conference.

[39] No author given, *Our Position Against Scouting*, Tract #7 in a series, "Continuing in His Word" issued by the Conference of Presidents of the Evangelical Lutheran Joint Synod of Wisconsin and Other States in 1954, pp. 5, 6.

[40] *The Milwaukee Journal*, 3 Dec. 1974.

[41] Ibid., 23 Feb. 1959.

[42] Ibid., 5 Dec. 1973.

[43] *Religious News Service*, 30 May 1974.

[44] Georgine Milmine, *The Life of Mary Baker G. Eddy*, (Grand Rapids: Baker Book House, 1971 reprint of original 1909 Doubleday, Page & Co. Book), p. 188.

[45] Mary Daly, *Beyond God the Father*, (Boston: Beacon Press, 1973), p. 13.

[46] Ibid., pp. 97, 198.

[47] Ibid., pp. 19, 96.

[48] *The Milwaukee Journal*, 30 Apr. 1978.

[49] *Time* Magazine, 6 Aug. 1979.

[50] Dominique Paul Noth, excerpts from "Taking God's Name in Fun," a review of plays and movies like "God's Favorite," "Oh, God," and "The Best of God" in *The Milwaukee Journal*, 4 Dec. 1977.

[51] *Time* Magazine, 6 Aug. 1979.

[52] Carleton Toppe, *The Northwestern Lutheran* editorial, "Ann Landers Doesn't Speak for God," 15 May 1977, p. 147.

[53] *Time* Magazine, 3 Dec. 1979.

[54] Paul C. Neipp, *Why Christians Must Fight Communism*, undated tract available from Through to Victory, 731 N. Sanders Ave., Ridgecrest, Calif., 93555.

[55] *Time* Magazine, 15 Oct. 1979.

[56] *The Milwaukee Journal*, 29 Nov. 1979.

[57] Ibid., 21 Nov. 1976.

[58] Bruce Ray, "I Believe in . . . Santa Claus?" article subtitled (Demythologizing Christmas) in the 19 Dec. 1977 *Christian News*, p. 6.

[59] *The Milwaukee Journal*, 10 Dec. 1976.

[60] Item in *Lutheran News*, (now *Christian News*), 15 May 1967.

CHAPTER FOUR

IDOLS IN GOVERNMENT

. . . Then he (Jesus) said to them, "Give to Caesar what is Caesar's, and to God what is God's." (Matthew 22:21 NIV)

In her first news conference in September, 1979, after being chosen as Miss America at the annual Atlantic City pageant, Cheryl Prewitt, a born-again Christian, told of her plans to take every opportunity to tell about her Christian faith. She promised not to proselytize, but she insisted: ". . . America would be hard to represent without mentioning God. This is a God country."[1] It seems obvious that Miss Prewitt believes that her "Christian" God, the Triune God of the Holy Bible, is the God of all America. In a certain sense, of course, it is true that America's God is the Father, the Son, and the Holy Spirit as the Scriptures reveal him, three persons in One. But unfortunately millions of Americans, who express their faith in a god, do not have the Triune God in mind when they refer to their deity or supreme being. Indeed, much idolatry is practiced by citizens of the United States of America, when they make casual, careless or ill-conceived statements and proposals concerning God as they imagine him to be.

THE AMERICAN GOVERNMENT'S GOD

Which God was President Lyndon B. Johnson referring to in his 1965 Memorial Day Proclamation when he described his countrymen as "a people with an abiding faith in a merciful God and in His goodness. It is not only fitting but necessary that we seek His guidance and help ... I designate the hour beginning in each locality at 11 o'clock in the morning of that day as the time for all Americans to join in prayer"? Obviously Johnson assumed that Buddhists in Hawaii, Lutheran Christians in Minnesota and Jews in Miami would all be praying to the same merciful God. Many Americans, possibly a sizeable majority, seem to have no problem identifying with the "god" whose name appears on U.S. currency and who is referred to, since 1954, in the pledge of allegiance. They see God as an all-encompassing nondenominational deity big enough to cover Buddhism, Islam, Mormonism, Judaism, Christianity, etc.

Mrs. Helen Nencka undoubtedly was voicing the sentiments of millions of Americans when she expressed the following opinion:

> I write in defense of God, to keep In God We Trust on our coins and God's name in the Pledge of Allegiance ... God is not a church. God is the Universe ... the breath in our bodies. His name may be Creator, Jehovah, Brahma, Allah, Buddha, Supreme Being, Nature, Love, The Great Spirit, the Unknown, ... even Nothing ...[3]

The idolatrous, pantheistic and patently non-Christian nonsense expressed above by Mrs. Nencka ought to appall every Christian who has even just a basic knowledge of the Bible and the First Commandment. Yet such vague and sentimental false ideas about God are widely held in our country.

Many Americans are alarmed by the actions of Madalyn Murray O'Hair, the notorious atheist who in 1963 successfully argued before the U.S. Supreme Court against prescribed prayers in public schools. More recently Mrs. O'Hair and her American Atheists organization have been seeking to remove the phrase "In God We Trust" from all

U.S. currency and have it ruled as an improper national motto. She also has been seeking relief from the necessity of pledging allegiance to our country as one which is "under God."

Mrs. O'Hair is a fool. The Bible's description of an atheist, "The fool hath said in his heart, there is no God," (Psalm 14:1) fits Mrs. O'Hair perfectly. Yet, fool that she is, Mrs. O'Hair raises some legitimate issues and conscientious Christians, who are sensitive to the prevalence of the sin of idolatry in modern American society, may find themselves on the same side with Mrs. O'Hair and her fellow atheists, but for diametrically different reasons. Mrs. O'Hair is opposed to prayer in the public schools, the pledge of allegiance, and the "In God We Trust" motto on our U.S. currency because of her obnoxious, militantly atheistic beliefs. Concerned Christians, on the other hand, may take the same stands because of their Bible-based conviction that the only true God is the Tri-une God of the Holy Bible and that all other gods-in-general are dead idols.

In 1977 Mrs. O'Hair asked President Carter to decline the honorary presidency of the Boy Scouts of America because the organization requires a belief in God for membership.[4] Again, it was her stubborn, all-consuming atheism that motivated Mrs. O'Hair to make that demand. As we pointed out in the previous chapter we also reject the god of Scouting, not because of any atheistic bias, but because we must identify Scouting's umbrella deity as a Christless idol.

THE FAITH OF AMERICA'S FOUNDING FATHERS

Many Americans believe and promote a popular myth. Motivated by the spirit of patriotism they ignore history and idealize founding fathers like Franklin, Washington, Jefferson, et al., describing them as devout, orthodox Christians. Nothing could be further from the truth. While we should be grateful for the freedom of religion and separation of church and state which we owe in large measure to the thoughts and actions of the founding fathers, it would be a mistake, a dishonest distortion of history, to describe men like Washington and Jefferson as devout Christians. Most of America's early leaders were, in fact, deists who belonged to no orthodox Christian denominations and repeatedly disavowed basic doctrines of the Christian faith. The deists saw god as a prime mover who set the universe in motion according to strict laws and then went on to more important matters, leaving mankind more or less on its own. Now, by no stretch of the imagination can the idol of the deists be equated with the compassionate Triune God of the Bible who has numbered and is vitally concerned about the very hairs on our heads (Matthew 10:30).

In our early years, especially the last quarter of the 18th century, only a small fraction of Americans were affiliated with organized religion. None of our first seven presidents was, at the time of his election, a member of any church. The two basic documents of American freedom, the Declaration of Independence and the Bill of Rights, while they have been used by our Triune God to provide us Christians with precious blessings like freedom of worship and religion, are more deist in spirit than Christian. In the Constitution even vague references to "Divine Providence" were deliberately avoided by the founding fathers.[5]

In "The Rise of American Civilization" historians Charles and Mary Beard insisted that ". . . Jefferson, Paine, John Adams, Washington, Franklin, Madison, and many lesser lights were to be reckoned among either the Unitarians or the Deists." In his book on Washington and religion Paul F. Boller, Jr. gave this revealing picture of Washington's religious convictions and practices:

> If to be a member of a Christian church (Episcopalian), to attend with a fair degree of regularity, to insist on the importance of organized religion for society and to believe in an overruling Providence in human affairs is to be a Christian, then Washington can assuredly be regarded as a Christian. . . .
>
> On the other hand, if to believe in the divinity and Resurrection of Christ and His atonement for the sins of man and to participate in the sacrament of the Lord's Supper are requisites for the Christian faith, then Washington . . . can hardly be considered a Christian, except in the most nominal sense.[6]

There are many apocryphal legends about Washington devoutly kneeling in prayer in the snow at Valley Forge, but they probably are no more factual than the stories of his chopping down the cherry tree or tossing a silver dollar across the Potomac River. Washington's god was a deistic impersonal force and the fact that the name of Jesus does not appear anywhere in his letters to friends and associates speaks for itself. Washington's membership in the Masonic Lodge also forces one to describe the god of the father of our country as an idol.

We owe a great debt to the God-given genius of Thomas Jefferson and the sound principle of the separation of church and state for which he was largely responsible. Thanks to Jefferson it has been extremely difficult for a state church or government-sponsored religion to gain control in our country to the detriment of non-establishment, minority faiths. There are some notable exceptions, like the military and congressional chaplaincy programs, but for the most part a healthy separation of church and state spirit prevails in America and Jefferson played a key role in formulating and establishing that principle.

However, while we should give full credit to Jefferson as an American hero and patriot, it is impossible to escape the conclusion drawn from his own writings, that Thomas Jefferson was a non-Christian idolater, who repeatedly rejected and even heaped ridicule upon the Triune God of the Bible. He scrupulously avoided formal identification with any denomination, but he was most sympathetic toward the Quakers and Unitarians and fully expected that Unitarianism, a religion which denies the deity of Christ, would become the general religion of the United States either during or soon after his lifetime.[7]

Jefferson made the claim, "I am a Christian;"[8] he saw Jesus as "the most innocent, the most benevolent, the most eloquent and sublime character that ever has been exhibited to man,"[9] and he even wrote a book, "The Life and Morals of Jesus of Nazareth."[10] But Jefferson's admiration of Jesus was limited to his humanity. No miracles performed by Christ are included in his book; it closes, most significantly, with the stone being rolled in front of the sepulchre with a dead Jesus inside. It's obvious that Jefferson's immense intellect and proud reason would not permit him to believe in Jesus as the living, risen God-man and Savior of sinners. While he praised so-called "primitive Christianity," he expressed again and again contempt for "the incomprehensible jargon of the Trinitarian arithmetic."[11] He blamed "the fanatic Athanasius" for introducing "the hocus-pocus phantasm of a God like another Cerberus, with one body and three heads..."[12] The fundamental Christian truth of the Holy Trinity especially aroused the angry contempt of Jefferson, prompting him to express his scorn as follows: "I should as soon undertake to bring the crazy skulls of Bedlam (a notorious insane asylum) to sound understanding, as inculcate reason into that of an Athanasian."[13]

Abraham Lincoln was a student of the Scriptures and memorized long passages from the Bible. He prayed daily and called prayer "talking with God." It would be difficult to prove, however, that Lincoln's faith in God was directed to the Triune God, the only true God. Lincoln was married by an Episcopalian minister and attended Presbyterian services in Springfield, Illinois, and in Washington. When he ran for president for the first time, in 1860, detractors claimed that since he was not a member of any church (he rented pew No. 20 at the First Presbyterian Church of Springfield), had never been baptized or made a normal profession of faith, he could not be considered religious. His outright enemies called him an infidel. On the other hand, the Rev. Phineas D. Gurley, pastor of the Presbyterian Church in Washington which Lincoln attended regularly, considered Lincoln a practicing Christian.

Lincoln surely never made a clear statement of belief in the orthodox, Trinitarian Christian faith. He refused to become enmeshed in the interpretations of Christianity that were correct in his day, but he did say this: "I cannot without mental reservations assent to long and complicated creeds and catechisms. If the church would ask simply for acceptance of the commands, 'Thou shalt love the Lord thy God with all thy heart and with all thy soul and thy neighbor as thyself'— that church I would gladly join with."[14] If Lincoln's credibility as a devout Christian rested on the foregoing confession of faith, it would be impossible to separate him from the work-righteous, Unitarian, or deistic beliefs of Washington or Jefferson.

St. Paul wrote to the Romans: ". . . if you confess with your mouth, 'Jesus is Lord,' and believe in your heart that God raised him from the dead, you will be saved. For it is with your heart that you believe and are justified, and it is with your mouth that you confess and are saved" (Romans 10:9,10). Jesus, the Judge of the quick and the dead, will know on the Last Day what went on in the hearts of Lincoln, Washington, Jefferson and the other founding fathers of our country. His judgment will be just on the basis of his words in St. John 3:36, "Whoever believes in the Son has eternal life, but whoever rejects the Son will not see life, for God's wrath remains on him." No, mere human beings cannot judge hearts, but when we read the record of history relative to the confessions of faith made by America's founding fathers, it is almost impossible to avoid the conviction that those brilliant leaders were victims of idolatry, that their conceptions of God were woefully deficient and not at all faithful to the revelation of himself which God graciously supplies in the Scriptures.

THE FAITH OF 20TH CENTURY POLITICAL LEADERS

At his Presidential Prayer Breakfast on February 5, 1964, President Lyndon B. Johnson proposed that "a fitting memorial to the God who made us all" be erected in Washington. Nothing ever came of his misguided proposal, but that idea did typify the religious stance of most modern-day American politicians. They do not hesitate to invoke the name of God in their speeches and public pronouncements, especially in times of crisis, but they refuse to be pinned down as to God's exact identity. They seem to be satisfied that all Americans agree that there is a vague god-in-general somewhere out there, an all-American supreme being who has no trouble uniting Christians, atheists, Hindus, Moslems and Jews into one body and one super-faith that rises above all petty doctrinal disputes and insignificant denominational differences.

President Johnson joined the Christian Church (Disciples of Christ) at 14 and was baptized in the Pedernales River in Texas, but throughout his life he was the epitome of ecumenism and religious open-mindedness. One Sunday he would attend his wife's Episcopal church, the next week he would worship at a Baptist, Methodist, Lutheran or Presbyterian church. His younger daughter Luci's decision to leave her mother's Episcopalian faith and to convert to Catholicism, including a second baptism, was well within President Johnson's elastic understanding of God and religious practice. On the morning of his inauguration Johnson arranged for a private service at the Disciples' big National City Christian Church in Washington with the Baptist Billy Graham, a rabbi, an Episcopal priest and a Catholic monsignor taking part.

We do not question the sincerity of Johnson's faith. His open-minded attitude toward doctrine and wide-angled approach to churchgoing are fully in harmony with the stance of the Christian Church he joined at 14 and undoubtedly millions of Americans hold to the same Common American Religious Creed (CARC), which we described in Chapter One and which President Johnson espoused so exuberantly: it doesn't really matter whom or what a person believes in, as long as he believes something and tries to do his best. We do contend, however, that the CARC, for which President Johnson was such an enthusiastic spokesman and propagandist, is out and out non-Christian idolatry when it is looked at in the light of the Holy Scriptures.

We must agree with the editorial reaction in *Christianity Today* to Johnson's proposal that a "memorial to God" be erected in Washington. The editor made the following astute observation:

> Can a joint endeavor of the kind proposed by Mr. Johnson be carried out without the assumption that the various religions

are but different roads to God? While Christian Americans recognize the inalienable right of their fellow citizens to worship God according to conscience, they cannot go beyond the words of their Lord, "I am the way, the truth, and the life: no man cometh unto the Father but by me." . . . Christ's arms which were stretched out on the Cross for the redemption of the world are still beckoning all who labor and are heavy laden to come to him. But his invitation is unique; "for there is none other name under heaven given among men whereby we must be saved."[15]

In 1972 when Richard Nixon and Sen. George McGovern were seeking the presidency, Louis Cassels wrote the following article on the respective religious positions of the two contenders:

President Nixon is a Quaker. Sen. George McGovern is a Methodist. That's what their official labels say.

But both labels are highly misleading.

Nixon's Quakerism is so dilute — especially on the key doctrine of pacifism — that it would not be recognizable to George Fox, founder of the Society of Friends.

McGovern's brand of Methodism would be equally baffling to John Wesley, founder of the Methodist movement.

Nixon and McGovern have been described as "profoundly religious." This description was applied to Nixon by his unofficial White House pastor, the Rev. Billy Graham. It was applied to McGovern by Bishop James K. Armstrong of Aberdeen, S.D., head of the United Methodist Church in McGovern's home state.

Under questioning by this reporter, both Graham and Armstrong acknowledged that they were using the term religious in somewhat elastic fashion. They were thinking, they said, of conscientious effort to apply Christian ethical precepts to practical problems of public life, rather than to any pronounced personal godliness.

Actually, neither Nixon nor McGovern is religious in the traditional sense of being keenly interested in religious doctrines and faithful in worship.

Although his much publicized Sunday services in the East Room of the White House have created a widespread impression that Nixon is a regular churchgoer, the truth is that he attended church quite rarely before he was elected president. And since his election, his attendance at public worship (including the semiprivate White House services) has averaged less than once a month.

Although McGovern's father was a Wesleyan Methodist minister of rigorously fundamentalist faith, his son is a free thinker in religion, and persons close to him say he could not properly be described as a believer in orthodox Christian doctrine.

McGovern gave corroboration to this appraisal of his religious stance in a recent interview with Rev. Charles P. Henderson Jr., assistant dean of the chapel of Princeton University, published in *Commonweal* magazine.

Henderson reported that "despite the intense indoctrination" he received as a child, McGovern began to doubt many of the fundamentalist doctrines of his father's religion.

"Even before he left home to fight in World War II he rejected the literal inerrancy of Scripture. . . . He began to view the Bible as a work of great literature."

Henderson said McGovern told him "that he very seldom attended church and that he rarely prays 'at least in any conscious sense.' " His main interest, he said, is in "the social applications of Christianity" rather than the personal relationship of an individual to God.

Judging from the things he says, the kind of services he likes to have at the White House, and his choice of Baptist evangelist Graham as a spiritual counselor, Nixon probably would be more accurately described as an evangelical Protestant than as a Quaker.

On the basis of his interview with Henderson and similar things he has said to others, McGovern might be more at home in the Unitarian than in the Methodist fold.[16]

With few exceptions, modern American politicians and national leaders are unreliable guides in religion. A willingness to compromise and to avoid dogmatic assertions are much admired in the political arena and are essential in the legislative process. But when such attitudes carry over to religion, the biblical revelation of God becomes blurred and the spirit of idolatry intrudes on the scene as it surely did during the administrations of presidents like Johnson and Nixon.

THE PLEDGE, OATHS, STAMPS, CAROLS, COINS, CURRENCY — WHAT DO THEY HAVE TO SAY ABOUT GOD?

Many people probably have the idea that our country's pledge of allegiance goes back to 1776, and that the founding fathers drew it up and adopted it right along with the Declaration of Independence and the Constitution. In reality the pledge is less than a century old, dating back to 1892. In that year Francis Bellamy, a minister and an editor of *Youth's Companion* magazine, felt that patriotism was at a low ebb in the nation and so his magazine promoted the placing of an American flag in every schoolhouse. At that time there was an older form of flag salute, "I give my heart and my hand to my country — one country, one language, one flag." But Bellamy and his colleague, James Upham, felt a better pledge could be written. After considerable creative struggle and discarded phrasing experiments Bellamy offered the following version of the pledge in connection with the celebration of the 400th anniversary of the discovery of America:

> I pledge allegiance to my flag and (to) the republic for which it stands — one nation indivisible — with liberty and justice for all.

In the national flag conferences of the American Legion in 1923 and 1924 "*to* the republic" and "the flag of the United States of America" were inserted instead of Bellamy's optional "to" and the simple "my flag." This revised pledge became official in 1942 when the federal flag code was enacted by congress. In 1954, a religion revision was made when congress, following the suggestion of President Dwight D. Eisenhower, insisted on adding the words "under God" between "one nation" and "indivisible," although that insertion destroyed the meter.[17] Thus at the time of this writing, and since 1954, the pledge goes as follows:

> I pledge allegiance to the flag of the United States of America and to the republic for which it stands, one nation, under God, indivisible, with liberty and justice for all.

Over the years there have been scattered protests against the pledge because of the added phrase, "under God." For example, in June of 1963 a Los Angeles high school history teacher, Haswell Parker, a member of no church, objected to being required to take part in a pledge which included the reference to God. In 1959, the Los Angeles board of education had made a daily recitation of the pledge mandatory in its schools. The American Civil Liberties Union filed suit on Parker's behalf, declaring that the "under God" phrase made the pledge unconstitutional and violated the first and 14th amendments to the Constitution.[18] In 1964, two agnostics sued New York State's Education Commissioner James E. Allen on the ground that the amended pledge imposed "compulsion on the young children of nonbelievers" and violated the first amendment.[19] Not too surprisingly, the U.S. Supreme Court, which opens its own sessions with the cry: "God save the United States and this honorable court" has refused to abolish or call in question the addition, "under God."

In 1970, James E. Allen, mentioned above, at the invitation of *Look* magazine, suggested a revised pledge in order to remove from it "unsupportable claims to national virtues that we have not yet attained." Allen's pledge:

> I pledge allegiance to the flag of the United States of America and dedicate myself to the principle that the republic for which it stands shall be in truth one nation, under God, indivisible, dedicated to liberty and justice for all.[20]

164

About the same time that Allen offered his revision, a White House conference on children proposed a very similar revision to President Richard Nixon, seeking to make the pledge an "act of personal dedication." Their suggested pledge:

> I pledge allegiance to the flag of the United States of America, and to the republic for which it stands, and dedicate myself to the task of making it one nation, under God, indivisible, with liberty and justice for all.[21]

Either of the two above revised versions of the pledge have been favored especially by minority groups, such as blacks and Hispanics, who feel that the United States has not delivered to them the liberty and justice promised in the pledge.

In protest against the bloody slaughter of millions of unborn babies by means of abortion that began in the 1970's, the Knights of Columbus of Ohio and an eighth grade class in St. Mary's Catholic School, Martin's Ferry, Ohio, began a nationwide campaign in 1978 to add the words, "born and unborn," at the end of the pledge to make the point that abortion on demand denies liberty and justice to the millions of unborn infants whose lives are summarily snuffed out by that barbaric act. More than 10,000 letters were sent out to Catholic grade schools and high schools asking them to add the words "born and unborn" at the conclusion of the pledge.[22]

The several efforts described above to revise the pledge have met with no success. The pledge remains unchanged since the "under God" addition in 1954. Although it seems to put me in the company of agnostics, atheists and Jehovah's Witnesses who for various reasons have protested against the pledge's "under God" phrase, I must agree that addition was ill-advised. Who is the God that President Eisenhower and the U.S. Congress in 1954 were convinced our nation is under? Is there a true consensus in our country about this God's identity? Are American Jews, Christians, Hindus, Moslems, etc. supposed to project their own ideas about the deity into the pledge? Doesn't the pledge promote the popular heresy that people of all religions really worship the same God? Is the God referred to in the pledge in reality a non-existent, non-Christian, non-Trinitarian idol? I believe that those are very pertinent questions that Christians ignore or dodge only at great spiritual peril.

I would much prefer returning either to Bellamy's original 1892 pledge or its slightly revised form in the 1920s, which did not mix God or religion into that simple expression of patriotism. But perhaps the time has come for concerned Christians, sensitive to what Scripture says in St. John 5:23 and I John 2:23 about the importance of honoring and confessing Christ, as well as the consequences of denying him, to set forth a pledge that clearly gives due honor to the one true, Triune God. How about the following:

> I pledge allegiance to the flag of the United States of America and to the republic for which it stands, one nation, under the Triune God, Father, Son and Holy Ghost, indivisible, with liberty and justice for all.

It's obvious that the U.S. Congress would never approve such a pledge; non-Christians would vehemently object and find it offensive. However, the point is that the present pledge, including the reference to God, while deliberately omitting the name of Jesus, ought to be even more offensive to conscientious Christians, who recognize the pervasiveness of idolatry.

On two occasions I have been placed under oath in the course of official government proceedings. I have been asked: "Do you swear to tell the truth, the whole truth, and nothing but the truth, so help you God?" The first time I was asked the question was at a commitment proceedings for someone who was mentally incompetent. It was early in my ministry and due to nervousness and unfamiliarity with such official proceedings, I simply replied as I was expected to, with a routine "Yes". Several years later, when I appeared before a judge in connection with the adoption of one of my children, I was better prepared. I welcomed the opportunity to confess my faith in the true, Triune God of the Bible when I was placed under oath. When I was asked if I would tell the truth, "so help you God," I responded that I would do so in the name of the God I believe in and worship, the Father, the Son and the Holy Spirit as the Holy Scriptures describe our Creator, Redeemer and Sanctifier. The judge and his clerk seemed to be somewhat puzzled and surprised by that Christian, Trinitarian oath, but it was accepted by them without any challenge or problem. God's name should never be taken in vain; reference to God should never degenerate into meaningless routine or pietistic ritual. If the courts of our land choose to place us Christians under oath, as was done with our Savior during his Passion, we ought to make the most of that situation by confessing our Christian faith in the Triune God with conviction, courage and unmistakable clarity.

Back in 1964, when a 5¢ stamp was sufficient postage for a letter, a controversy arose about the annual Christmas stamps issued by the post office. That year four types of stamp designs were offered — a sprig of holly, mistletoe, pine cones and poinsettia. Representative Melvin R. Laird, then a Wisconsin congressman, vehemently objected to the deliberately non-religious designs. He did not agree with the post office department's special stamp committee that had turned down the traditional nativity scene on the basis that it would commemorate a religious holiday. Laird complained as follows:

> ... Again this year the post office has issued a highly commer-
> cialized stamp which purports to convey the "spirit" of Christ-
> mas, but which in no way symbolizes the true meaning of
> Christmas. ... Christmas is celebrated each year to honor the
> birthday of Jesus Christ. Even those who do not acknowledge
> him as the Son of God recognize that he was a great figure in
> history. A Christmas stamp commemorating His birthday
> should in some way convey that fact and not the commercialized
> symbol of a Christmas tree or Santa Claus.[23]

The celebration of Christmas often stirs up controversy
and conflict in our country, especially in public schools
where no religious worship or indoctrination is allowed.
For example, in Ithaca, New York, a superintendent of
schools ruled in 1973 that pupils would be permitted to
sing about Frosty the Snowman and Rudolph the Red-
Nosed Reindeer, but not about Jesus Christ, because the
parent of a non-Christian child had protested that Christian carols were out of place in public schools.[24]

The following report that appeared in the Religion section of *Time* magazine sums up the problem that pops up
periodically in connection with Christmas celebrations in
public schools:

Caroling Crisis
1st Noel vs. 1st Amendment

> While the number of languid non-believers in America is
> legion, the number of aggressive atheists is small, probably no
> larger than the 65,000 claimed for Archatheist Madalyn Murray
> O'Hair's mailing list. The number of atheists willing to go to
> court about religion is smaller still. One of these is a South
> Dakota laborer named Roger Florey.
>
> Imagine Atheist Florey's dismay, two years ago, when he
> walked into the holiday assembly program in the Hayward
> Elementary School in Sioux Falls, S. Dakota, and found
> youngsters, including his kindergarten-age son Justin, giving
> out with O Come All Ye Faithful and Silent Night. Then a
> teacher quizzed them on the religious theme. "They had just

gone overboard," Florey recalls. The result is the first federal court test of whether performance of religious Christmas music, a perennial issue in many cities, should be banished from public schools on grounds of church-state separation.

Florey decided to sue the Sioux Falls school board, but earlier this year a South Dakota federal judge rejected the Florey case, declaring that religious music and art have "become integrated into our national culture and heritage." The school board, meanwhile, had worked out a guideline policy, permitting the use of religious music, Jewish as well as Christian, in "a prudent and objective manner" in programs balancing religious and secular aspects of any holiday.

Florey was not appeased. He took his case to the Eighth Circuit Court of Appeals in St. Louis, where it is awaiting judgment. But on the way to St. Louis the suit acquired a major new supporter. The American Civil Liberties Union, national Jewish organizations and the Unitarian Universalists were joined last June by Lawyer William P. Thompson, chief executive of the 2.6 million-member United Presbyterian Church and former president of the National Council of Churches. The Presbyterian brief seeks to banish the singing of Christmas music in public schools, not because it is too religious (Florey's view) but because it is not religious enough. Such music used under the secular auspices, except formal music classes, Thompson feels, "debases" and "perverts" the religious significance of Christmas. Why mix Away in a Manger with Rudolph the Red-Nosed Reindeer? Thompson asks.

If approved by the high courts, Thompson's policy would further secularize American life. In Sioux Falls this Christmas, pending the forthcoming federal ruling from St. Louis, youngsters in some assemblies will be singing Christmas music as usual, perhaps for the last time. But for Justin Florey and his classmates it will be Suzy Snowflake and Santa Claus is Comin' to Town.[25]

The above report is very thought-provoking. It's apparent that many public school officials do not hesitate to include Christmas carols in their curricula, along with Jewish Hanukkah songs, because they see those songs as cultural rather than religious in nature. Such people argue that the lines between religious and cultural meanings of Christmas customs have been blurred. They contend that even "Silent Night" with its reference to the birth of "Christ the Savior" is more nostalgic and sentimental than religious. It's hard to dispute that leader of the United Presbyterian Church, Lawyer William P. Thompson, who contends in the *Time* article above that most public school Christmas programs debase and pervert the real religious significance of the season and that they are not religious enough.

What is worse? To have no references to Christ or God in public schools as well as a ban on singing Christmas carols? Or to have a cheapened and perverted holiday observance that mixes a veneer of Christianity with idolatry? The former choice seems preferable to the following Christmas program that was presented in a Milwaukee public school in 1978:

> The program will include two plays, "A Star Crossed Santa," a parody on the movie "Star Wars," and "A Christmas Gift." The school choir will sing a Christmas carol about a baby born in a stable and a lullaby about a mother and a little baby.
>
> The choir also will sing a Hebrew tune, "Any Time of the Year." In addition, a Jewish teacher at the school will conduct a ceremony, including a reading on the meaning of Hanukkah and the lighting of the menorah.[26]

On the surface, such a holiday program may seem to be a perfect solution, since it affords equal time to Christians and Jews. In reality, however, it cheapens and perverts the unique gospel message of the Savior's birth by putting it on a par with a non-Christian festival. Surely, it would be better to omit any and all religious songs and programs from public schools rather than to dilute or trivialize the matchless gospel of Jesus Christ.

William F. Buckley, Jr., the eloquent spokesman for political conservatism, does not agree with the above conclusion. In a column which attacks the American Civil Liberties Union for opposing the singing of Christmas carols in a South Dakota public high school, Buckley facetiously suggests that

> . . . the abolition of "Silent Night" is just plain temporizing. The ACLU should go to court and insist that the feast day on Dec. 25 be officially designated as Mas·Day (to omit any reference to Christ) . . .

In that same column Buckley commented on other controversial church-state areas that tie in with the singing of Christmas carols in public schools.

> No Christmas carols. The next step would be to forbid the invocations that precede every session of congress, which as a matter of fact are the most unheeded invocations in the history of prayer. Then there is the sticky matter of our coinage, bearing the legend, "In God We Trust": that is a rank affront on the atheist community, whose religion is no religion, and therefore violates the separation clause. So, by extension, does the Pledge of Allegiance, which includes the phrase, "under God."[27]

What Buckley states above with tongue in cheek makes sense. In our pluralistic society, made up of every shade of religious belief, misbelief, and outright unbelief, vague references to an unspecified god on our coins and currency, at the beginning of Congressional sessions, or in the pledge of allegiance are as bad or even worse than no references at all and surely have not transformed the United States into a devout Christian country. A federal appellate court in 1970, in response to a suit that called for the removal of the phrase "In God We Trust" from our coins and currency, denied the suit and ruled that the phrase "is of a patriotic or ceremonial character and bears no true resemblance to a governmental sponsorship of a religious exercise."[28] In other words, that court saw no connection between the God referred to on our coins or currency and religion. We agree. That vague, intentionally Christless "god" is in no way connected with true Christianity and serves as a readily available and highly visible example of modern-day idolatry.

GOVERNMENT CHAPLAINS — MILITARY AND LEGISLATIVE

Military

In 1937 President John Brenner of the Evangelical Lutheran Joint Synod of Wisconsin and other States (now called the Wisconsin Evangelical Lutheran Synod) stated in his convention report that "requests have come to District Presidents and to me to recommend ministers for chaplaincies in the service of the Government." In response to those requests, a special committee was assigned to study the matter and to give attention to three questions: 1. Is there need for this work? 2. Is such service in the employ of the Government compatible with Scripture principles? 3. Would it not be more expedient to pay the salaries of such missionaries (chaplains) ourselves?

The committee carried out its assignment and reported to the 1939 synod convention its negative recommendation. It was the committee's conviction that "to appoint or call ordained pastors as commissioned chaplains in accordance with the rules and regulations of the government, which includes remuneration by the government for their services, as well as the final choice by the government of the man so commissioned, is not in harmony with Scripture, because the fundamental principle of the separation of Church and state is thereby violated." That conviction prevailed in 1939 and was maintained through World War II, the Korean conflict, and the Vietnam War, although the Synod set up a system of camp pastors adjacent to military bases in the United States and sought

172

to keep in touch with Wisconsin Synod military personnel through an extensive mailing program. During the Vietnam War our synod was given permission to send a series of chaplains, at our expense, to Southeast Asia to seek out and minister to our servicemen. These non-military chaplains were able to utilize military transport and base chapels for their work through a special arrangement with the government. The Synod has also made use of civilian chaplains for several years in Germany to meet the spiritual needs of Wisconsin Synod servicemen assigned to Europe.

Why has the Wisconsin Synod refused to take part in the government sponsored military chaplaincy program, especially in the face of considerable criticism and controversy in the form of charges that we were unconcerned about the spiritual needs of our men in uniform? Prof. Edward C. Fredrich summed up the objections of our Synod to the military chaplaincy in an essay prepared for the 1954 Synodical Conference Convention by quoting the Synod's 1941 chaplaincy resolutions as follows:

> The Commissioning of Army and Navy Chaplains by our Synod would conflict with Scriptural principles and established Lutheran practice because 1. The application and appointment to chaplaincy conflicts with our doctrinal stand on the divinity of the pastoral call. Also, the training Manual of the War Department entitled "The Chaplain" specifies duties to the chaplain which are in direct violation of the divine call of a Lutheran pastor. 2. The appointment to chaplaincy and the regulation of the chaplain's duties by the War Department are a violation of the principle of separation of Church and State. 3. The spirit of doctrinal indifferentism pervades the regulations of the War Department pertaining to the office of chaplaincy and fosters unionism.[29]

Advocates and supporters of the U.S. military chaplaincy system look to it for much more than mere spiritual values for servicemen. They see it as a program to improve general morale and to promote military efficiency. They contend that if the Government did not provide chaplains, it would be open to the charge of violating the first amendment. They maintain that when men are lawfully removed from their homes and deprived of their right to worship in the churches of their choice, the Government must provide a substitute if it is to avoid restricting freedom to worship.

Unfortunately, the substitute offered by Uncle Sam smacks of idolatry. A 1954 Wisconsin Synod tract on "The Chaplaincy Question" pointed out the compromising, idolatrous nature of the chaplaincy as follows: " 'The religious programs and services of the Armed Forces' are obviously Christless (and therefore idolatrous) in character, since the Government sees helpful 'spiritual values' also in the chaplaincies of the Unitarians, Mormons, Jews, and Universalists, who deny Christ or His redemptive work."[30]

A *Milwaukee Journal* editorial some years ago described the military mindset that makes the chaplaincy what it is, a classic example of reprehensible, idolatrous, religious compromise and the determination to agree to disagree in the face of denominational differences:

> . . . The military has long had its own mysterious ways of dealing with religion. Take the true story of a group going through basic training recently. The company was lined up and the sergeant ordered that all Catholics "step forward." They did and were marched off to a Catholic lecture. Then all Protestants were ordered to step forward. They, too, were marched away. A small group remained, to the consternation of the sergeant.
>
> "What are you?" he asked recruits, one after another. One was a Mohammedan, one a Seventh-day Adventist, one a declared atheist. There were a few Jews, several agnostics and several who had no religious affiliation or interest.
>
> The sergeant was baffled. Then he settled the problem with

typical military precision: "Look, in the army we got Romans and we got Protestants, one or the other." He ticked off the group into two equal squads and marched them off, one to the Catholic lecture and the other to the Protestant. That's about as ecumenical as you can get.[31]

Although every chaplain is supposedly permitted, with the specific protection of military regulations, to teach and practice according to the requirements of his own denomination (in 1965 about ¼ of the Navy chaplains supported by public taxes were Roman Catholic), there are many pressures applied to ignore doctrinal differences. For example, all Protestant chaplains must first conduct an inoffensive, non-controversial general Protestant service, deliberately devoid of any denominational distinctives. Only after that are they free to give a particular service of their own sect. It is contended that one of the main principles of the chaplaincy is that the good of the serviceman is paramount, with no room for dedication only to one's own religious denomination.[32]

For many years the Wisconsin Evangelical Lutheran Synod was a lonely voice in the wilderness protesting against and refusing to participate in the military chaplaincy program. The unpopular Vietnam War led other groups to take a closer look at the military chaplaincy and to call out for changes. In 1968 the American Jewish Congress urged that military chaplains be replaced with civilian religious counselors receiving no pay from the Government and possessing no military rank.[33] In 1969 the San Francisco Conference on Religion and Peace, contending that chaplains do not have freedom of movement or of conscience, called for the abolition of the military clergy. About the same time liberal Lutheran anti-war critic, Pastor Richard John Neuhaus charged that clerics in military service expose themselves to "spiritual prostitution" and suggested that they be replaced by civilian clergy accredited to the armed forces like Red Cross personnel.[34] A similar proposal was made in 1972 by the unofficial National Association of Laymen in the Catholic Church; they urged the creation of a civilian chaplains corps with rights of access to troops similar to those accorded journalists and Red Cross workers.[35]

At the time of this writing, no significant changes have been made in the military chaplaincy system. Military leaders continue to support the customary chaplaincy status quo, mostly for non-religious reasons, because chaplains have been available for educational lectures to new recruits, for counseling on problems such as drug addiction and for assisting general morale by offering a channel for personnel with petty grievances, which commanders don't want to be bothered with. "Tell it to the chaplain" remains a common, familiar expression, most often used facetiously or mockingly, among servicemen.

In the previous chapter we posed the questions: Who is the god of Scouting? Who is the god of the fraternal lodges? We had to conclude that their god is a non-existent idol, the kind of man-devised deity the Triune God warned against and condemned in the First Commandment: "Thou shalt have no other gods." We can't avoid coming to the same conclusion when we consider the military chaplaincy. It too promotes a god-in-general that is idolatrous to the core. It can't be denied that such a god is popular, especially in critical periods like the heat of battle. For example, on D-Day, June 6, 1944, on a jam-packed landing craft crossing the English Channel, a Jewish officer called on a military chaplain, Captain Lewis Koon, to lead his company in prayer "to the God in whom we all believe, whether Protestant, Roman Catholic or Jew, that our mission may be accomplished and that, if possible, we may be brought safely home again."

Chaplain Koon gladly obliged and most Americans probably would agree that in life-threatening emergencies like that, fine points of theology, such as the fact that Jews worship an idol instead of the true God of the Bible, should be overlooked in the interests of American patriotism and broadminded brotherhood.

A military chaplain, of all people, has pointed out the perils of believing in a vague, god-in-general and refusing to confess Christ when it might offend non-Christians. Lt. William P. Dillon, a Roman Catholic Atonement Friar wrote as follows:

> Americans generally believe in God, but God has no face . . . the nation is apparently secure in the half-remembered, hardly-digested religious ideas of its Judaeo-Christian origins. . . . Extreme circumstances require God; from the ordinary, let him be distant. . . . Certainly an ecumenism of respectful silence about areas of religious disagreement or vague ecumenical documents that seek overarching agreement can only further strengthen popular feeling for a god powerful enough to be respected, but vague enough to be ignored . . . ecumenical dialogues have produced a feeling of vagueness and uncertainty among the churches. Many Christians no longer seem sure about the specific characteristics of their communities, doctrines, and ethical living . . . A church which follows a god who can be so vague about the shape of his own institution will quickly become as distant from specific human concerns as the god of that uncertitude. Neither one can be taken too seriously. . . . Ecumenism must become apologetic if it is to lead "a nation of believers" in they-know-not-what to at least some responsibility to the god in whom they trust.[36]

Apparently that Roman Catholic military chaplain fails to see that the chaplaincy system itself bears much of the responsibility for the problems he pinpoints: Americans believing in a faceless god (idol), that America's general god is vague enough to be ignored and is widely perceived to be distant from the ordinary details of daily life. Only a clear uncompromising confession of faith in the true, Triune God of the Holy Scriptures will lead our nation of believers in they-know-not-what out of their vague idolatry to the knowledge of the precious truth of the gospel, salvation for sinners through God-given faith in the Father, Son, and Holy Ghost.

Legislative

In 1972, John H. Averill wrote as follows in a *Los Angeles Times Service* article:

> Every two years Congress elects two officials whose only prescribed duties require no more than two minutes of work a day — and sometimes less.
>
> They are the chaplains of the Senate and the House of Representatives. The standing rules of both chambers require that the daily session begin with a chaplain's prayer. Unofficial rules stipulate that the prayers last no longer than two minutes.
>
> For this, and ancillary duties, the House chaplain receives $19,768.80 a year and the Senate chaplain $10,086 (remember, that was back in 1972 and that those plush salaries are provided by tax-payers). The Senate salary is less because the Senate traditionally selects as its chaplain a clergyman who is a pastor of a District of Columbia Church (in other words, the Senate chaplain receives in excess of $10,000 a year for a part-time job! Talk about extravagant government spending!).[37]

Who is the god these House and Senate chaplains petition in prayer prior to congressional sessions? Since an overwhelming majority of these chaplains have been Protestant, it might be argued that it is the Triune God that is being addressed in those prayers which William F. Buckley Jr. described above as "the most unheeded invocations in the history of prayer." However, in 1975, the U.S. Senate heard Chief Frank Fools Crow, an Oglala Sioux holy man from Kyle, South Dakota, pray to "Grandfather, the Great Spirit," and "Grandmother, the Earth who Hears Everything." Part of that pagan prayer: "I come to you on this day to tell you to love the red men and watch over them and give these young men (the senators) understanding, because, Grandmother, from you comes the good things."[38] So much for the possibility that the Congress prays to the Triune God!

There must be a better way. Would our country really be any worse off if those overpaid congressional chaplains were taken off the government payroll and the Senators and Congressmen prayed on their own? On June 29, 1972, the Senate chaplain was not on time. Senator Hart (D.-Mich.) was perplexed for a moment as the acting presiding officer that morning. Then he came up with an excellent and perfectly simple solution as he announced to his colleagues: "This morning we shall open with a moment of silent prayer." According to the Congressional Record for that day "the Senate stood in silence."[39] Silence is golden, so the saying goes. And silence for a few moments before the sessions of Congress would seem to be a simple solution to the problem of idolatrous prayers in public places and it would give the American taxpayer some relief by not having to pay the inflated salaries of those legislative chaplains.

In 1975, there was some controversy when the California State Senate appointed the Rev. Shoko Masunaga, a Buddhist minister, to serve as their chaplain. Buddhism clearly rejects the Christian concept of a supernatural divinity, yet the Interreligious Council of Southern California at Los Angeles, including Protestants, Jews, Catholics, Hindus, Buddhists and Moslems, backed the appointment of Masunaga. On the face of it, it may seem fair and part of the American way to give non-Christians a turn as legislative chaplains. But Christians, who are sensitive to the fundamental sin of idolatry, ought to offer a better answer: the elimination of all prescribed prayers and chaplains from all legislative chambers and let a few moments of silence afford an opportunity for our leaders to pray (or not to pray) to whomever or whatever they choose.

PUBLIC SCHOOL PRAYERS

In June, 1962, the U.S. Supreme Court declared unconstitutional the following brief prayer written and recommended by the Board of Regents for use in New York State public schools: "Almighty God, we acknowledge our dependence upon Thee, and we beg Thy blessings upon us, our parents, our teachers and our country." That decision brought cries of protest, outrage and dismay from many Americans. Since 1962 there have been numerous attempts to erase the court's decision by constitutional amendments of one sort or another.

That 22 word prayer seems innocuous enough, but it is another classic example of the subtle idolatry that permeates our society and many of our governmental institutions. That prayer fits perfectly the description of idolatrous prayers given by Prof. Martin H. Franzmann more than two decades ago. Franzmann pointed out that:

> A compromise prayer, in which Moslem, Hindu and pious agnostic may join, is always and everywhere an abomination on the lips of a Christian. . . . A prayer which is the product of a blind, sentimental enthusiasm and therefore conceals or smoothes over differences in themselves divisive is indefensible.[40]

Shortly after the Supreme Court's decision was announced, the dean of the Marquette university law school expressed the opinion that only atheists would object to the prayer that had been prescribed in New York State public schools. His statement prompted me to write the following letter to the editor which was printed in the *Milwaukee Journal*:

The Christless Prayer
To the Journal: According to the dean of the Marquette university law school, Reynolds C. Seitz, only atheists could reasonably

object to the official New York state public school prayer that was recently ruled unconstitutional by the United States supreme court.

Dean Seitz should be corrected, for not only atheists but also sincere Christians have found that prayer objectionable and extremely offensive.

The prayer in question, hopefully designed to please people of all religions, failed in its purpose because it studiously avoided any reference to God's Son, Jesus Christ. Christians were displeased by that crucial omission and could not conscientiously recite such a prayer that intentionally snubs and thus insults their divine Savior.

We Christians believe that only prayers offered in the name of Jesus Christ will be heard and heeded by our Heavenly Father. In John 16:23 Christ Himself clearly instructed His followers to pray in His name: "Whatsoever ye shall ask the Father in My name, He will give it you."

Another Scripture passage which we Christians find pertinent in this public school prayer controversy is John 5:23: "All men should honor the Son, even as they honor the Father. He that honoreth not the Son honoreth not the Father which hath sent Him."

Because of its vague reference to "Almighty God" and the intentional omission of Christ's name, the New York public school prayer had to be condemned and avoided by sincere Christians.[41]

At the time of this writing, proponents of public school prayer stubbornly continue to seek out ways to get God and prayer back into the classroom. In early 1980 a Massachusetts law went into effect which required public school teachers to invite students to say prayers if they wanted to. Teachers also were required to ask if anyone wanted to leave the room during the prayer. According to *Time* magazine (3/24/80) students seemed confused or embarrassed by the new law and the results were mixed. Some children chose to recite the Lord's Prayer, a few chose to say Hail Mary; after a few weeks the Massachusetts Supreme Court ruled that the new law was unconstitutional.

Surely the true, Triune God is not pleased with perfunctory prayers addressed in a diluted nondenominational form "to whom it may concern." Surely the true God is not honored by posturing politicians who seem to promote a constitutional amendment to permit public school prayer, more to please fundamentalist voters than to promote real Christian piety. The true God is not glorified by prayers that are a rote exercise, so vague that they can't possibly arouse any real religious conviction or supply any solid Christian comfort. Window dressing prayers or prayers that function like parsley on a plate in a restaurant, more for appearance than nourishment, are a perversion of prayer, as well as an insulting abomination in the sight of the true God.

STATEMENTS FROM THE TWO SIDES

The subject of this chapter, "Idols in Government," impinges on many parts of our daily life. This is not surprising. What the government does sooner or later touches every citizen, and every Christian needs to be on guard against the sin of idolatry, which Satan so subtly seeks to insinuate into every facet of our life. If he cannot persuade people to worship him directly or to join the ranks of militant atheists, he will settle for people worshiping and praying to a god-in-general or any kind of amorphous deity, as long as it is an idol. It is this writer's contention that many well-meaning Americans have stumbled into idol worship by making crucial compromises, by promoting prayer and worship at any cost. Even when such prayer and worship include no references to Christ and the Triune God, they apparently fail to see the sinful, Satanic folly of such critical omissions.

In my study of this subject over the years I have come across many statements on both sides of the issue. As a fitting summary to conclude this section I herewith present the two statements which I feel best describe the two sides.

The first is from an editorial that appeared in "Christian Economics" in 1963, in which the unnamed editor contends that the removal of references to God in government would actually violate the constitution:

The next step in the movement to remove any reference to God from our schools has now been taken. New York State Commissioner of Education, Dr. James E. Allen, Jr., ruled recently that the singing or recitation of the fourth stanza of "America" had "deliberately set out to evade the constitutional prohibition against any daily religious exercises in the public school."

Where can we find nobler words:

> Our fathers' God to Thee,
> Author of liberty,
> To Thee we sing.
> Long may our land be bright
> With freedom's Holy Light.
> Protect us by Thy might,
> Great God, our King!

But now for millions of children, "America" will have no fourth stanza. In addition, Dr. Allen has ruled the words, "In God is our trust," in the fourth stanza of "The Star Spangled Banner," invalidate its use in opening exercises in the schools. The tide is rising; the dam has been broken. What next? Probably new coins minted without "In God We Trust," a pledge of allegiance without "under God," oaths without the Bible and the removal of Chaplains from Congress and the Armed Forces.

Of course there is no "Constitutional prohibition against any daily religious exercises in the public school." The Constitution specifically prohibits Congress from passing any law "prohibiting the free exercise" of religion. Apparently, Dr. Allen and the Supreme Court think they can do what Congress cannot constitutionally do. The ruling of the Supreme Court did not change the Constitution.

For nearly a century and a half the children of America have sung this beautiful hymn with delight and reverence. Now, because eight people have protested, the rights and wishes of more than 180 million are to be set aside. We protest and we insist that majorities, especially when as overwhelming as in this case, have some rights.[42]

What that "Christian Economics" editor wrote in 1963 has been repeated many times by those who favor the reintroduction of prayers into public schools. Some of the more zealous proponents maintain that the rising tide of rape and robbery, of drug abuse and drunkenness, would be dramatically reduced if only public school teachers were permitted or directed to begin the school day with a brief non-denominational prayer. The second statement I've chosen, an essay on the public school prayer issue by Smith Hempstone, exposes the absurdity of the above position and eloquently argues that more energy ought to be expended to get children to pray where no constitutional prohibition interferes, namely, in the home and church, rather than the public school where religion can only be diluted, cheapened, or offered as an inoffensive conglomeration of Christless mush. In his essay, "Why Pray in School? Try Home, Church," Hempstone wrote:

Washington, D.C. — Despite the Supreme Court's 1962 and 1963 rulings, the school prayer issue is, like the poor, always with us.

And school prayer, like abortion, gun control and the Panama Canal, is for rightwing pundits one of the bloodyshirt issues. Forgive me if, as a card carrying conservative, I decline to wave.

Before the rail is selected, the feather gathered and tar put on to boil, permit me a couple of observations:

There are those, and I number myself among them, who hold that Shakespeare, Milton, the Book of Common Prayer and the King James Version of the Bible are the four great pillars upon which the English language rests.

There are those, and, again, I count myself in their company, who believe that the last of these contains not only great poetry but a message of divinely inspired truth. I know, if Madalyn Murray O'Hair does not, that my Redeemer liveth.

But a person's religious beliefs are — or ought to be — among his most prized and private possessions. And just as I would resist the imposition of another man's beliefs on me, so I would not foist mine on him.

Proponents of organized school prayer, citing the strength of tradition, point out it was 170 years after passage of the Bill of Rights before the Supreme Court — the hated "Warren Court," of course — discovered that the practice violated the First Amendment rights of school-children. It also took the court nearly a century — and then only by the amendment route — to learn that slavery deprived blacks of their constitutional rights. Better late than never, as they say.

A puzzlement is why Jesse Helms and others washed in the blood of the Lamb feel prayer is most efficacious when muttered in Home Room. God, unlike some unionized teachers, does not work a 40 hour week. He invariably is available when and where His children — including senators from North Carolina — seek Him.

The Bible thumpers have contributed more heat than light to this emotive issue. Little Johnny will not be sent home with a note from Miss Prim for muttering a heart-felt prayer — which of us has not done so? — before the geometry test. He will not be severely disciplined if caught reading Deuteronomy behind a cover of Playboy during study hall.

What the court has ruled is that Johnny cannot participate in a worship service conducted on public school property, even if attendance is voluntary. Neither teachers, principals nor elected school boards may tell him what, how or when to pray — nor how not to do so.

This is so even when, as in New York state, Catholic, Protestant and Jewish leaders have agreed on a common form of worship. The constitutional principle remains the same: The power to prescribe prayer implies the right to proscribe it, to promote one form of worship over another.

In any case, to lay upon educators and schoolboards the burden of promoting religion is to risk theological illiteracy.

Associate Justice Potter Stewart, the lone dissenter in the 1962 school prayer case, Engel vs. Vitale, held that to forbid schoolchildren from reciting together a themeless pudding of a prayer was "to deny them the opportunity of sharing in the spiritual heritage of our nation." With respect to Justice Stewart, an otherwise sensible man, that is nonsense.

There is a place to pray. It is called church, and there is one within walking distance of Justice Stewart's home at 5136

Palisade La. There are services there every Sunday, and on certain weekdays. Where the crime level permits, churches are left unlocked so those who wish to do so may pray at any time of day or night.

Another place where prayer is both constitutional and altogether pleasing in the sight of the Lord is called home. No policeman will knock if Sen. Helms gets down on his knees by his bed to seek divine guidance. Neither will the courts intervene should my conservative colleagues wish to say grace before breaking bread.

There was a time when church and state were, for all practical (and many impractical) purposes, indistinguishable from one another, when kings ruled by divine right as God's lieutenants on earth.

But those days are gone and, in the main, good republican riddance to them. To attempt now to marry church and state is to strengthen neither and demean both.[43]

When the government moves into the realm of religion, even with the best of intentions, and makes pronouncements about God, it is inevitable in our pluralistic society that the least-common-denominator kind of deity and religion will prevail. When the god, who is promoted by the military chaplaincy, whose name appears on our American coins and currency and in the pledge of allegiance, and whom public school prayer advocates would have us worship, when that god is looked at in the light of the Scriptures, one cannot escape the conclusion that such a god is in reality a Christless idol.

NOTES FOR CHAPTER FOUR

[1] *The Milwaukee Journal,* 10 Sept. 1979.

[2] *The Milwaukee Journal,* 27 May 1965.

[3] *The Milwaukee Journal,* 10 Nov. 1977.

[4] *The Milwaukee Journal,* 17 Feb. 1977.

[5] Excerpted from *The Milwaukee Journal,* 3 Oct. 1977.

[6] The Boller Quotation was taken from an article by Alicia Armstrong, "Washington Was Quiet Concerning His Beliefs," in a series on the *Religion of the Presidents,* in *The Milwaukee Journal,* 11 Jan. 1964. The other information about Washington's religion was also taken from this article.

[7] Norman Cousins, *'In God We Trust'* — The Religious Beliefs and Ideas of the American Founding Fathers, (New York: Harper & Brothers Publishers, 1958), p. 159.

[8] Cousins, *'In God We Trust',* p. 168.

[9] Ibid., p. 166.

[10] Ibid., pp. 173-216.

[11] Ibid., p. 157.

[12] Ibid., p. 159.

[13] Ibid., p. 162.

[14] Herman Blum, "Deeds Showed Lincoln's Faith," article in *The Milwaukee Journal,* 6 Feb. 1971. My information about Lincoln's religion was also taken from this article.

[15] Editorial excerpt in *Christianity Today,* 28 Feb. 1964, "Another Memorial in Washington".

[16] *The Milwaukee Journal,* 14 Oct. 1972.

[17] *The Milwaukee Journal,* 3 July 1966 and 28 Sept. 1967.

[18] *The Milwaukee Journal,* June 1963.

[19] *Time* magazine, 4 Dec. 1964.

[20] *The Milwaukee Journal,* 16 Nov. 1970 and 23 Nov. 1970.

[21] *The Milwaukee Journal,* 23 Jan. 1971 and 11 Jan. 1977.

[22] *The Milwaukee Journal,* 11 Mar. 1978.

[23] *The Milwaukee Journal,* 7 Dec. 1964.

[24] *The Milwaukee Journal,* 17 Dec. 1973.

[25] *Time* magazine, 17 Dec. 1979.

[26] *The Milwaukee Journal,* 10 Dec. 1978.

[27] *The Milwaukee Sentinel,* 16 Dec. 1978.

[28] *The Milwaukee Journal,* Oct. 1970.

[29] *The Wisconsin Synod Convention Proceedings,* 1941, p. 43f.

[30] *The Chaplaincy Question*, Tract Number 11 in the series, *Continuing in His Word*, issued by the Conference of Presidents, The Evangelical Lutheran Joint Synod of Wisconsin and Other States, 1954, p. 1.

[31] *The Milwaukee Journal*, 4 Apr. 1969.

[32] *The Milwaukee Journal*, 17 Apr. 1965 and 27 Oct. 1968.

[33] *Time* magazine, 13 June 1969.

[34] *Time* magazine, 30 May 1969.

[35] *The Milwaukee Journal*, 5 Feb. 1972.

[36] Lt. William P. Dillon, CHC, USNR, — *Chaplaincy* magazine, Vol. I, No. 3 & 4, Third and Fourth Quarters, 1978.

[37] *The Milwaukee Journal*, 28 Aug. 1972.

[38] *The Milwaukee Journal*, 1975. (The clipping in my file has no month or exact date.)

[39] *The Milwaukee Journal*, 28 Aug. 1972.

[40] *Time* magazine, 8 Aug. 1960.

[41] *The Milwaukee Journal*, 10 July 1962.

[42] *Christian Economics*, 29 Oct. 1963, Vol. XV, No. 20, p. 2.

[43] *The Milwaukee Sentinel*, 17 May 1979.

CHAPTER FIVE

IDOLS IN JUDAEO-CHRISTIANITY

Jesus answered, "I am the way and the truth and the life. No one comes to the Father except through me. . ." (John 14:6 NIV)

Do Christians and Jews believe in and worship the same God? To many Americans that question would sound foolish. "They certainly do!" would be the response of people who belong to or are in sympathy with the National Conference of Christians and Jews, an organization that promotes religious tolerance and union between the two groups and is quick to condemn any pronouncements or actions that would seem to smack of anti-Semitism. If the average American were asked the above question, it is likely that his reply also would be in the affirmative. In his essay in American religious sociology, *Protestant-Catholic-Jew*, Will Herberg astutely observes that Americans have a common religion which is the system familiarly known as the American Way of Life. Herberg contends, quite convincingly, that "by every realistic criterion the American Way of Life is the operative faith of the American people."[1]

Describing this American Way of Life faith in greater detail, Herberg quotes Reinhold Niebuhr and Daniel Poling as follows:

"The 'unknown God' of Americans seems to be faith itself." What Americans believe in when they are religious is . . . religion itself. Of course, religious Americans speak of God and Christ, but what they seem to regard as really redemptive is primarily religion, the "positive" attitude of *believing*. It is this faith in faith, this religion that makes religion its own object, that is the outstanding characteristic of contemporary American religiosity. Daniel Poling's formula: "I began saying in the morning two words, 'I believe'— those two words with nothing added. . ." may be taken as the classic expression of this aspect of American faith.[2]

If Herberg is correct, and I think he is, in his assessment of most Americans' religious convictions, then anyone who would describe the Jewish faith as idolatrous, as I do in this chapter, must expect to receive criticism and opposition, if not vituperation and bitter invective, from most Americans. Although St. John repeatedly states that the rejection of Jesus, which is the fatal flaw in the Jewish faith, inevitably involves the loss and rejection of the Father as well, still many who claim themselves Christians consider the Jewish religion a bona fide, saving faith. Consider the following inspired words of St. John:

> No one who denies the Son has the Father (I John 2:23). Anyone who believes in the Son of God has this testimony in his heart. Anyone who does not believe God has made him out to be a liar, because he has not believed the testimony God has given about his Son. And this is the testimony: God has given us eternal life, and this life is in his Son. He who has the Son has life; he who does not have the Son of God does not have life. (I John 5:10-12). We know also that the Son of God has come and has given us understanding, so that we may know him who is true and we are in him who is true — even in his Son Jesus Christ. He is the true God and eternal life. Dear children, keep yourselves from idols (I John 5:20,21). Anyone who runs ahead and does not continue in the teaching of Christ does not have God; whoever continues in the teaching has both the Father and the Son (II John 9).

Now compare those crystal-clear, inspired words of Scripture with the answer which a Roman Catholic Monsignor, Raymond Bosler, gave to the following question: "Christ said there is no way to the Father except through him. To me 'no way' means no way. So how are the Jews and others who do not accept Christ to be saved?" To that question, which appeared in the Question Box column of the 9/19/79 issue of the *Denver Catholic Register*, Msgr. Bosler offered the following incredible Scripture-distorting answer:

> That God wants all men and women to be saved and that Christ's redeeming death and resurrection make this possible for all is now an established belief of the Catholic Church. Vatican Council II teaches that even "those who, without blame on their part, have not yet arrived at an explicit knowledge of God, but who strive to live a good life, thanks to His grace" can be saved (Constitution on The Church No. 16).
>
> Note the "thanks to His grace." This is a way of saying that even those who do not believe in God depend upon the grace that comes through Jesus Christ for their ability to live the kind of good life necessary for salvation. In other words, the church teaches that even for the atheist who does not know him, Jesus is the only way to the Father.[3]

Roman Catholic spokesmen and leaders like Msgr. Bosler find that they have much in common religiously with the people of the Jewish faith, whether they are Orthodox, Reform, or Conservative Jews. They believe that the way to salvation is by living a good life. Even though Catholics like Bosler, and many Protestants too, use terms like grace and frequently refer to Jesus Christ, the real foundation of their faith is right in line with Judaism, reliance on good deeds and a good life as the way to salvation. That fact helps one to understand how about 100 Protestant clergymen and Reform rabbis could come together for joint worship at St. Peter's Lutheran Church (LCA) in New York City on June 6, 1979. The service was sponsored by the Office on Christian-Jewish relations of the National Council of Churches (NCC) and the Department of Interreligious Affairs of the Union of American Hebrew Congregations (UAHC). After the service and an all-day symposium organized to develop guidelines for joint worship of Christians and Jews, a statement of principles was issued. The guidelines suggested that the Lord's Prayer was unsuitable for such joint services and that Jews should not be expected to use a cross or crucifix in such worship. The statement of principles declared: "We dare to come together because we share a sacred Scripture and worship the same God. ..."4

The above statement is at best, misleading, and at worst, a blatant falsehood. Jews and Christians, at least those Christians who are faithful to their Savior and his revealed Word, do not share a sacred Scripture. Jews do not accept the teachings of the New Testament and they reject the main message of the Old Testament: the hundreds of prophecies which foretold the coming of the Messiah, the Christ, which were fulfilled by the coming of Jesus of Nazareth. Nor do Jews and genuine Christians worship the same God. The adamant denial by all strands of the Jewish religion that Jesus is the Messiah and is true God with the Father and the Holy Spirit constrains us to classify the "god" of the Jews as an idol.

Compromise is commendable and, indeed, indispensable in many areas of life. In politics, in labor-management disputes, in marital conflict, compromise is frequently the only solution. However, when compromise is introduced into the Christian religion for the sake of Jewish-Christian worship, it brings down dishonor upon him who insisted: "He that is not with me is against me" (St. Luke 11:23). To identify Judaism as an anti-Christian religion is not being unfair to Jews. The Jews themselves have made it abundantly clear that they do not and will not recognize Jesus as the Christ. It should not be considered anything but honest and Christian to identify Jews and Judaism as opposed to Christianity. We show our Christian concern and love for our Jewish fellow Americans best by seeking to share with them the gospel of free salvation through God-given faith in Christ Jesus. Such efforts to evangelize or convert Jewish people often are resented, resisted, and even ridiculed. When the Evangelism Department of the Lutheran Church-Missouri Synod launched a campaign in 1978 to convert "Mr. Average Jew" to Christianity, it ran into a hornet's nest of stinging criticism. Rabbi A. James Rudin of the American Jewish Committee described the Missouri Synod's efforts to convert Jews "a moral affront to the Jewish people" and declared that "the Missouri Synod has sadly revived the medieval image of the Jews as a theologically deficient people."[5]

Are Jews "theologically deficient"? Indeed, they are, from the perspective of Bible-based, historic Christianity. Their reliance on leading a good life as the way to salvation and their rejection of Jesus as the promised Messiah and Son of God reveal a fundamental theological deficiency. A survey conducted among the readers of *McCalls* magazine also suggests an alarming moral deficiency among Jews, undoubtedly due to their denial of Christ who insisted: "Without me ye can do nothing" (truly good and God-pleasing) — St. John 15:5. According to that *McCalls'* survey:

> . . . a great difference was shown between Christians and Jews on several moral issues. While 50% of Christians said premarital sex is sinful, only 16% of the Jews believed this. On the subject of extramarital sex, 73% of the Christians called it a sin, while 48% of the Jews agreed. Concerning abortion, the opinion that it is wrong was 40% to 7% respectively. On homosexuality the difference was 62% to 27%, and on suicide it was 70% to 42%.[6]

Neither Christians nor Jews come off with very strong moral convictions according to that *McCalls'* survey of its readers in which 60,000 respondents reported on their religious/moral attitudes. However, the much lower percentages for Jews on key moral issues does demonstrate disastrous effects of failing to believe in and confess Christ. The much publicized and promoted Judaeo-Christian foundation for religion in our land is for the most part a popular myth that ought to be rejected and exposed by concerned Christians.

The sad truth must be told. Jews do not believe in Jesus; they do not recognize Jesus as God and as their Savior. Some Jews are still looking for a messianic era to arrive. In an article, "Passover Reflections," Jewish writer Alan J. Borsuk described his family's Seder customs, including his revealing, tragic and Christ-denying practice: "We have a cup of wine set aside for Elijah the Prophet, in hopes he will show up, a sign that the messianic era is at hand. We even open the door, just to make sure he knows he's welcome."[7]

When Bill Bright's Campus Crusade for Christ was pushing its "Here's Life, America" evangelistic campaign in 1977 and promoted the phrase "I found it" on billboards, buttons and bumper stickers, a Milwaukee rabbi advised his fellow Jews to respond to eager-beaver, overzealous Christian evangelists with the polite reply: "My dear young man, we Jews never lost it."[8] One can sympathize with Jews and other non-Christians who are badgered by well-intentioned Christians, who demand that they be "born again" and "make a decision for Christ" at the drop of a hat. Such "Brother (Sister), are you saved?" street corner evangelicals are no credit to our Christian faith, but their excesses and dubious evangelism tactics dare not divert our attention from a fundamental fact. Jews did lose it when they failed to recognize Jesus as the Messiah promised and foretold throughout the Old Testament and they will remain lost as long as they worship a god without Christ and look to themselves and the works they do as the way to please their Christless idol. How ironic that modern religious Jews who regularly read and hear God's repeated warnings (in the Old Testament) against the practice of idolatry, some of which were pointed out in Chapter Two, now must be classified as idolaters due to their stubborn refusal to believe that God is Triune, Father, Son, and Holy Ghost.

We are not motivated by bias, bigotry or anti-Semitism when we insist that the god Jews worship is in reality an idol. Our love for the truth and also love and Christian concern for our Jewish fellow human beings compel us to speak the truth in love. Without faith in Christ people, whether they are Jews or Gentiles, are lost and whatever or whomever they worship must be classified as idols. Jesus, the Jew from Nazareth, surely could not be considered anti-Semitic or bigoted against his fellow-Jews. Yet he insisted that many of the Jews of his day did not know God because they rejected him as their Messiah. He once said to some of his Jewish countrymen:

> . . . If I glorify myself, my glory means nothing. My Father, whom you claim as your God, is the one who glorifies me. Though you do not know him, I know him. If I said I did not, I would be a liar like you, but I do know him and keep his word. Your father Abraham rejoiced at the thought of seeing my day; he saw it and was glad (St. John 8:54-56).

After that encounter the angry Jews picked up stones to stone Jesus. They were infuriated by Jesus' claims and his statement that they did not really know God. On another occasion Jesus warned his disciples about the hostility and murderous hatred they would encounter from their fellow Jews and why this would happen to them:

> They (the Jews) will put you out of the synagogue; in fact, a time is coming when anyone who kills you will think he is

offering a service to God. They will do such things because they have not known the Father or me (St. John 16:1-3).

The great Apostle Paul, who was reared as a Jewish Pharisee, fit the above description prior to his conversion to Christianity. He presided over the slaying of Stephen, the first Christian martyr, and subsequently persecuted scores of other Christians because he thought he was serving God. Only after he was brought to faith in Christ did he realize how wrong he had been and that it had been a Satan-inspired idol, rather than the heavenly Father, who motivated him to persecute and stone to death sincere, courageous Christians like Stephen. St. Paul never forgot his tragic error and devoted the rest of his life to telling his fellow-Jews and the Gentiles the truth about the Triune God by his tireless preaching and his many epistles. In his second letter to the Thessalonians Paul issued the following warning which all people, Jews and Gentiles alike, need to heed to this day:

> . . . when the Lord Jesus is revealed from heaven in blazing fire with his powerful angels . . . he will punish those who do not know God and do not obey the gospel of our Lord Jesus. They will be punished with everlasting destruction and shut out from the presence of the Lord and from the majesty of his power on the day he comes to be glorified in his holy people and to be marveled at among all those who have believed (2 Thessalonians 1:7-10).

Note how Paul equates those who do not obey (believe) the gospel of our Lord Jesus with those who do not know God. It is scriptural statements like those above, inspired by God the Holy Spirit, which compel us to come to the conclusion that the god of the Jews or even a Judeo-Christian deity devised by the mind of man must be labeled and rejected as an idol. Following the lead of the Lord Jesus and the Apostle Paul, Dr. Martin Luther also insisted that any worship apart from Christianity is idolatrous and that any deity that excludes Christ is an idol. Luther declared:

Here Christ would indicate the principle reason why the Scripture was given by God. Men are to study and search in it and to learn that He, Mary's Son, is the One who is able to give eternal life to all who come to Him and believe on Him. Therefore he who would correctly and profitably read Scripture should see to it that he finds Christ in it; then he finds life eternal without fail. On the other hand, if I do not so study and understand Moses and the prophets as to find that Christ came from heaven for the sake of my salvation, became man, suffered, died, was buried, rose, and ascended to heaven so that through him I enjoy reconciliation with God, forgiveness of all my sins, grace, righteousness, and life eternal, then my reading in Scripture is of no help whatsoever to my salvation. I may, of course, become a learned man by reading and studying Scripture and may preach what I have acquired; yet all this would do me no good whatever. For if I do not know and do not find the Christ, neither do I find salvation and life eternal. In fact, I actually find bitter death; for our good God has decreed that no other name is given among men whereby they may be saved except the name of Jesus (Acts 4:12). . . . I have often said that whoever would study well in the Bible, especially the spiritual significance of the histories, should refer everything to the Lord Christ. . . . It is beyond a doubt that the entire Scripture points to Christ alone. . . . Whatsoever people pray, teach, and live apart from Christ is idolatry and sin before God.[9]

During his campaign for the presidency in 1976 Jimmy Carter spoke to about 2,000 people at the Jewish Educational Institute in Elizabeth, New Jersey. On that occasion Carter, a Southern Baptist, expressed what could be described as a basic tenet of Judeo-Christian religion in the U.S. He stated: "I worship the same God you (Jews) do. . . . We study the same Bible you do."[10] Carter's statement prompted me to write the following essay which appeared in the "In My Opinion" column of the *Milwaukee Journal* on August 20, 1976:

Candidate Carter Proved Unconvincing as a Confessor of Christianity — The Journal reports that Jimmy Carter's brand of religion worries some people, especially Roman Catholics, because of his permissive, even approving, approach to abortion on demand (The Journal, July 16).

As an evangelical Lutheran Christian I suppose I should be delighted that a "born again true believer" may be headed for the White House, especially after a series of presidents who seemed to be lukewarm at best in their religious convictions, or at worst appeared to exploit religion for crass political purposes by inviting big name religious leaders to a weekly game of musical chairs in services at the White House during the Nixon years.

However, I, too, am troubled by the Carter brand of religion, over and above his stand on abortion. On the campaign trail, candidate Carter sought to reassure a predominantly Jewish audience in New Jersey by saying: "I worship the same God you do." Surely the sincerity of a man who contends that he never lies should not be questioned, but it should be pointed out that Carter's statement in New Jersey is completely at odds with a basic truth of the Christian faith. It is apparent that the Plains, Ga., Sunday school teacher still has a big gap to close in his knowledge of the Bible.

In the Scriptures Jesus insists: "I am the Way, the Truth, and the Life: No man cometh unto the Father but by me" (John 14:6) . . . "all men should honor the Son, even as they honor the Father. He that honoreth not the Son, honoreth not the Father which hath sent him" (John 5:23). Christians and non-Christians alike must recognize those exclusive claims of Christ.

To many modern day Americans with a bent toward broadmindedness in religion, Jesus' words surely sound too narrow and restrictive, but it can't be denied that the Bible teaches: "Neither is there salvation in any other: For there is none other name (Jesus Christ) under heaven, given among men, whereby we must be saved" (Acts 4:12). Probably a big majority of Americans hold to the popular belief that it really doesn't matter which god a person worships as long as he tries to do his best and is sincere, but that doesn't make it true or scripturally correct.

Most Jews do not believe that Jesus is the savior of sinners and is the true God, one with the Father and the Holy Spirit. With the precious freedom of religion we enjoy in this land, Jews have the right to believe what they wish. But this Christian also enjoys the right to tell Jews as humbly, lovingly and tactfully as possible that they are dead wrong in rejecting Jesus as their Lord and Savior.

Since the Bible states that "Whosoever denieth the Son, the same hath not the Father" (I John 2:23), concerned Christians, who care about the eternal fate of their fellowmen, will warn their Jewish fellow Americans that the god of 20th century Jewry, in the light of the exclusive claim of Christ, is an idol, i.e., no god at all. They will do this even at the risk of being branded anti-Semitic, a label that seems to be immediately attached to anyone who says anything critical of Judaism.

Because of his fuzzy stand on the God issue and his failure to grasp a golden opportunity to confess before a group of non-Christians, the competence of Carter as a reliable spokesman for evangelical Christians must be called into question.

Compromise plays a key role in political maneuvering, but it is completely uncalled for when it comes to confessing Christ. Jesus said: "He that is not with me is against me." In New Jersey, at least, Carter was caught straddling the fence and was unconvincing as a confessor of Jesus Christ.[11]

The printing of my essay in the *Milwaukee Journal* triggered a series of letters to the editor, essays, and personal letters, many of which took issue with my opinion of Jimmy Carter's compromising theological position and confession. A reading of a representative sample of these letters and essays provides, I believe, a good insight into the thinking of those who support and promote a Judeo-Christian concept of religion and see no appreciable difference between the Triune God of the Christian faith and the Christless, non-Trinitarian supreme being worshiped by Orthodox, Reform, or Conservative Jews.

A prominent Milwaukee insurance agency president wrote to me as follows:

This letter is being written in reference to your "Opinion" in the Milwaukee Journal, Friday, August 20, 1976. This is the article where you start talking about Carter and end up talking about Jews, whom you say have no God. In fact, you claim that the god that the Jews worship is an "idol, i.e. no God at all," because they do not agree that Jesus is the Son of God, and then you quote scripture wherein you state, "whosoever denieth the Son, the same have not the Father."

This may come as a surprise to you, Mr. Schulz, but according to the 1975 Encyclopedia Brittanica Book of the Year and taken from the 1976 World Almanac, there are a total of 944,065,450 Christians in the world and over 1 billion, 600 million non-Christians in the world. These non-Christians in addition to including a paltry 14 million plus Jews include Muslims, Zoroastrians, Shinto, Taoist, Confucians, Buddhists, and Hindus. So what you are saying is that 1,600,000,000 plus people have no god or have not the true god, and only the Christians do.

This is a pretty sad commentary, Mr. Schulz, and if I recall properly, Muslims and many others consider Christians infidels because they do not believe in Allah.

I suppose you will find it difficult to believe, but the Jewish Bible and the New Testament and the Koran were written by people and printed by people, and of the three, probably the New Testament has changed the most to adapt to the times.

To suggest that because you or anyone with your type of thinking feels like you do about Jews makes you anti-Semitic is utter nonsense. There aren't enough Jews in this world to make much difference any more, but for what there are, if it hadn't been for the One God theory of the Jews, there would have been no Allah and no Jesus. In the New Testament there are numerous Gospels generally telling the same story in a different way and with different conclusions as, for example, the Christmas story. It's sort of take your pick, if you will, and this is true throughout the New Testament.

If you, who I assume consider yourself an intelligent man, would sit down and just think about this for a while and try to imagine 1,600,000,000 people wrong and 900,000,000 right, it sort of doesn't really ring true.

There is but one God, sir, and he is the same to all faiths. You are right, you have every right to believe in Christianity, but not at the expense of telling other people they are wrong, any more than they have a right to tell you that you are wrong.

Forget quoting the Scriptures, but use the brains that God gave you to see things in a clear light, and pray to him to give you the strength to realize that in all religions, including the Great Spirit the American Indians prayed to, there is but one God.

The Bible is made up of many stories, many fantasies, probably most of them being told around campfires from the beginning of time and long before the printed word from the so-called Gutenberg Bible, and if one has the spirit of God in him as you supposedly have, you take the Bible for what it is worth, but certainly not claiming that almost double the amount of non-Christians have no God because they do not believe as you do.

It is sheer hypocrisy to believe like that, as it is hypocrisy for the Muslims and the Christians to be fighting each other in Lebanon, and the Irish and Protestants fighting each other as they have in the past in the Middle East.

The Ten Commandments were given to the Western world, supposedly by God through Moses, and for sheer hypocrisy, the Commandment that says, "Thou shall not kill," has become just a bunch of words.

I believe that it was Voltaire that supposedly said, "If there had been no God, man would have invented Him."

We all need God, but we need God without bigotry and intolerance and immaturity. After reading your article, assuming you believe exactly what you said, religious tolerance is a long way off.

Let the 1,600,000,000 non-Christians in this world have their God, and you have yours, and leave it just like that. Don't start trying to tell other people that because they don't believe the way you do, their God is an idol, regardless of what religion you are talking about.[12]

The preceding letter advances what might be called the "mathematical" argument in support of a Judeo-Christian concept of deity. Since there are so many millions of non-Christians on this earth, how can they all be wrong?

Followed to its logical conclusion, that argument would either make majority rule the test of truth in religion or, as the letter writer-insurance man implies, there is no such sin as idolatry. That evil, warned against repeatedly in the Holy Scriptures, can be dismissed as one of the Bible's "fantasies."

A self-styled evangelical Lutheran, a Lutheran Church in America clergyman, was also critical of my criticism of Carter's theological stance. In a letter to the *Milwaukee Journal* he made the following points:

> *Unfounded Presumption* — To The Journal: As I read the article in the "In My Opinion" column written by a minister (Rev. Reuel J. Schulz) on Aug. 20, I became aware of certain passages of Scripture the pastor had omitted in his unfounded criticism of Jimmy Carter. We cannot so neatly exclude our Jewish brothers and sisters from God's plan and grace.
>
> Throughout the Old Testament the Jews are promised salvation by God, and nowhere does He take the promise back. I, also, would like to quote first a hymn from Paul's letter to the Romans in regard to the Jews and secondly a passage attributed to Jesus.
>
> In Romans 11:33-36, Paul exclaims over his concern and love for the Jews: "O the depth of the riches and wisdom and knowledge of God! How unsearchable are His judgments and how inscrutable His ways! For who has known the mind of the Lord, or who has been His counselor? or who has given a gift to Him that He might be repaid? For from Him and through Him and to Him are all things. To Him be glory forever."
>
> In other words, it is God's decision, not our decision, as to their salvation.
>
> And then in Mark 10:26, as Jesus speaks to his disciples: "They said to Him, 'Then who can be saved?' Jesus looked at them and said, 'With men it is impossible, but not with God; for all things are possible with God.'"
>
> Schulz should seriously consider such passages before he purports to make his opinion a dogma of the evangelical tradition. As a Lutheran who is evangelical, I find such personal and private decisions about who is saved offensive and carrying

with them an unsound presumption about the will of God. Carter appears the wiser and better informed.

Rudy Hokanson Pastor, Evangelical Lutheran Church of Good Shepherd, Houghton, Michigan.[13]

The Reverend Hokanson insists quite correctly that "throughout the Old Testament the Jews are promised salvation by God, and nowhere does He take the promise back." What Hokanson fails to point out is that the promise of salvation for Jews as well as Gentiles is inseparably connected with faith in the Messiah, the "seed of the woman" mentioned already in Genesis 3:15. There was no salvation for Jews of the Old Testament who refused to believe in the promised Messiah, nor is there salvation for Jews, or Gentiles, today who reject Jesus of Nazareth as the one and only Savior of sinners (Acts 4:12 and John 14:6).

Elmer O. Hochkammer, a retired businessman and truck driver from Manitowoc, Wisconsin, was the next essay writer to express his displeasure with my criticism of Carter. Hochkammer's humanistic, anti-Biblical bias needs no refutation; it stands self-condemned. But it does reveal the kind of people who are attracted to a watered-down, unionistic, compromising Judeo-Christian kind of religious expression. Hochkammer wrote as follows:

> *Carter's Grade on Theological Test Has No Relevance in Election* — The Rev. Reuel J. Schulz nailed Jimmy Carter to a carefully constructed theological cross in his discussion of the Democratic presidential candidate's religious convictions in The Journal of Aug. 20.
>
> His "In My Opinion" article was critical of Carter's remarks to a Jewish audience in New Jersey to the effect that he worshiped the same god as they. The thrust of Pastor Schulz's article was that Jimmy Carter couldn't possibly worship the same god as members of his audience, since Jews do not acknowledge the divinity of Christ. According to Pastor Schulz, since Jews do not worship Christ as God, they worship an idol,

no god at all. Ergo Jimmy Carter is an idol worshiper, a worshiper of no god at all.

If one accepts pastor Schulz's unstated premise that what he calls the Bible is inspired truth from a supernatural force, his logic is unassailable and Jews become idol worshipers and Jimmy Carter comes through as a muddled theological thinker, but a decent human being nevertheless.

The problem is that Pastor Schulz quotes from a book that is not universally regarded as the Bible or Scriptures, the New Testament, to convince Jews of the authenticity of his claim that Christ is God along with the other components of the Christian trinitarian deity makes about as much sense as an adherent of Islam quoting the Koran to prove his theological arguments to a person who rejects that book as divine in its origins.

Would Pastor Schulz be impressed with that kind of an intellectual approach being directed at him? Then why should Jews, or anyone else for that matter, be impressed with his quotations from a book that is to many people singularly lacking in divine credentials?

The truth of the matter is that Pastor Schulz and the Evangelical Lutherans who believe as he does could be the ones who are the worshipers of an idol, a false god, therefore no god at all. Who can really say for sure, in the absence of any empirical evidence that could settle the question once and for all?

Viewing the problem from strictly a neutral or humanist perspective, this writer might be tempted to say that the Jews had more reason and logic on their side, since Christians do accept the Jewish Scriptures, the Old Testament, however wretchedly interpreted, as part of their Bible.

This writer is pleased to learn that Jimmy Carter is not a theological fossil, an uncompromising dogmatist, as the press notices on his religiosity seemed to indicate. His acceptance of the Jewish deity as his own tells us that even in religious matters he is not an uncompromising, mindless dogmatist ready to accept a god that condemns a portion of humanity to eternal suffering simply because these human beings do not accept a deity acknowledged by Christians to be supreme.

Although Jimmy Carter may have flunked Rev. Schulz's theological test, it should be noted that Jimmy Carter is running

204

for the presidency of the United States — he is not applying for a professorship on a theological faculty. Moreover, the constitution forbids any religious test to be made for people who are to hold office under it.

This writer doesn't know if he is going to vote for Carter or not. In any event, he will make up his mind on the issues, not on whether the Pastor Schulzes of this world award him an A for "cool" theological thinking. Elmer O. Hochkammèr.[14]

Martin Linwood Whitmer, the minister of the Roundy Memorial Baptist Church of Whitefish Bay, Wisconsin, offered the following opinion of my charge that Jews are idol worshipers due to their denial of the deity and Messiahship of Jesus:

> *Criticism of Jimmy Carter's Christianity is Shortsighted and Inaccurate* — In an Aug. 20 "In My Opinion" article, the Rev. Reuel J. Schulz found fault with Jimmy Carter as a confessor of Christianity because Carter said to the Jews, "I worship the same God as you do." Schulz saw this position as representing a "big gap" in Carter's knowledge of the Bible, and contended that his position "is completely at odds with a basic truth of the Christian faith," the centrality of Christ. He went on to support his view by quoting various isolated verses from the Bible.
>
> To dimiss Carter as a serious Christian because he believes he worships the same God as do the Jews is unfair to Carter, the Jews and the Bible.
>
> There may well be big gaps in Carter's knowledge of the Bible, but his affirmation of one universal God is certainly not one of them. After all, Jesus didn't have faith in himself, but in God, and he taught that love of God and neighbor is the heart of Biblical faith.
>
> Carter's position would seem to be Biblical and universal, Schulz's, institutional and sectarian. The former lets God be God, the latter creates idols. The one is conciliatory, the other divisive.
>
> While each one is free to be his or her own interpreter of scripture, there are ground rules necessary if the Bible is to have meaning other than that which is read into it by whoever used it to support his or her own position.
>
> Appealing to the Bible in support of his position, as Schulz

does, can be very misleading. For one, it implies literal acceptance of the Bible and seems to grant it an accuracy and inerrancy of authority that is usually in the needs of the reader, but not in the Bible itself.

There are statements in the Bible with which no caring person could agree. The Bible says "Blessed is the man who takes your little ones and dashes their heads against the rock" (Psalm 137:9). While war and child abuse bring this to pass, certainly no one would want to insist that this must be believed as true and good for all people because it is in the Bible.

When we appeal to the Bible we should also remember that the people of the original Biblical experience were just as prone as we are to misunderstand and abuse power. Jesus' disciples often fought among themselves as to who was the greatest. They still do. Fearful things are done to the gospel in the hands of insecure followers. The verse Schulz quoted — "I am the way, the truth, the life" (John 14:6) — should not be heard as the words of Jesus about himself, but as the words of the church about Jesus. Jesus claimed love to be the hallmark of the worshiper of God. To say that Jesus is the way is to say that love is the way. Too frequently, the church wants to make Jesus its disciple.

The position for which Schulz argues has all the appearances of hubris, pride. The insistence that one alone knows who God is, or knows who truly worships him, or that only one particular community knows, is not only a dangerous form of pride, but may also be a form of unbelief, demonstrating not an abundance of faith, but a lack of it. To make God in one's own image is Biblical idolatry. Said Dietrich Bonhoeffer, the martyred German Lutheran pastor of World War II, "I can never know in advance how God's image should appear in others."

Surely God is larger than my concept of Him, and He may even choose to make Himself known at the place and in the person where I least expect Him, for the sport of it, or so as not to leave Himself without a witness while the church is busy building idols.

As to the religious beliefs of a president, I would feel much more secure and hopeful with one who allows God to be God of the Jews as well as of himself, than the one who believes that God is his own exclusive property.

While I like what President Ford has done, and believe that he deserves to be elected in his own right, I would feel safe with Carter if his only shortcoming is believing in a God larger than the one Pastor Schulz would have him believe in.[15]

It is obvious that Whitmer belongs to the school of theology that espouses the historical-critical approach to the Bible. He calls into question the "accuracy and inerrancy" of God's Word and tries to undermine the claims of Christ in John 14:6 — "I am the way . . . no one comes to the Father except through me" by arbitrarily insisting that the passage "should not be heard as the words of Jesus about himself, but as the words of the church about Jesus." In other words, Whitmer denies that Jesus really said what St. John says he said, a typical modernist, historical-critical approach to those portions of God's Word with which they do not agree.

A Marquette University professor of theology, J. Coert Rylaarsdam, also joined the debate that was originally triggered by my essay. His contribution to the discussion follows:

'God' of Philosophers and Theologians Has Obviously Failed Us All — In this column on Aug. 20, the Rev. Reuel Schulz charged Jimmy Carter with being "fuzzy on the God issue" for having said that Jews and Christians "worship the same God." Schulz said they do not: "The God (sic!) of 20th century Jewry . . . is an idol; i.e., no god (sic) at all." Schulz attempts to equate the Jew with the pagan. But if he really believed Jews were pagans, why would they be so much on his mind?

Century after century Jews have said, "No, thank you" to the formulae by which Christians express their understanding of the meaning of the career of Jesus. So Christians have called them disobedient and taught that they are blind to the deeds of God, often adding that this was due to Satanic possession or to a divine curse. And Jews suffered persecution and martyrdom.

Throughout this long history Christians have had alternating spasms of insecurity and guilt. They struck out at Jews because they smudged the Christian script; and then they periodically repented because they had consented to their humiliation and murder. Yet they could not leave them alone or simply dismiss them as pagans, though that would have spared the Jews much sorrow. Instinctively, it seems, Christianity has always known that to deny that God's covenant with Israel stands, jeopardizes its own gospel. In St. Paul's words, it remembered that "It is not you (Christians) who support the root (Judaism); the root supports you (Romans 11:18)."

Since Christians lacked the temerity to dismiss Judaism as paganism and scorned a critical review of their own formulations, they rationalized their dilemma by multiplying pictures of the curse that God has supposedly placed on his own people, blinding them to the truth of Christianity. Ironically, this curse was often appealed to most loudly by those who professed great "love" for the Jew and longed passionately for his eventual "homecoming." In our day Dietrich Bonhoeffer, a spokesman of the German "Confessing Church," epitomized this role in a tragic and poignant manner.

Now there are hopeful signs for a new beginning. "Nostra Aetate, 4," the Vatican II statement on Judaism, and similar Protestant statements do not provide a new understanding of the relationship between the faiths. But they do clear away much of the old debris; deicide, curse, demonic possession, and spiritual blindness. So they invite new openings.

For example, in a manifesto, "Christian und Juden," recently published by the German Evangelical Church, the first of six propositions reads, "Jews and Christians confess one God, the Creator and Redeemer." A vote for Carter! There is nothing new in it; but it is important that Christians say it officially.

On the God issue "fuzziness" is a virtue. Pastor Rudy Hokanson (" What our Readers Are Saying," Aug. 31) reminded us that "the ways of God are past finding out." Since the God of Israel is the living God who is always doing "a new thing," His ways for tomorrow can not be deduced from our imperfect understanding of His deeds yesterday. To understand the meaning of Israel, this is a time for Christians to ask new questions, and not answer them at once.

Is it possible, for example, that the separation of the two faiths from each other may signify both Jewish and Christian faithfulness? This is a time to wait, and to listen. On the subject of

Christian teachings about the Jews and Judaism, the "God" of the philosophers and theologians has obviously failed us; we must be prompted anew by the Spirit of the living God of Abraham, Isaac and Jacob.[16]

Rylaarsdam maintains that "on the God issue 'fuzziness' is a virtue." While it's true that many of "the ways of God are past finding out," the Triune God surely has not given mankind a "fuzzy" picture either of himself or of the way of salvation. In his Word, the Holy Bible, he has given a very clear picture of himself and his will. He insists: "I am the Lord; that is my name! I will not give my glory to another or my praise to idols" (Isaiah 42:8) and "I, even I, am the Lord, and apart from me there is no savior" (Isaiah 43:11). As a Christian, I believe that the God who revealed himself through his prophet Isaiah in the Old Testament is the same God who in the New Testament commissioned his followers to "make disciples of all nations, baptizing them in the name of the Father and of the Son and of the Holy Spirit" (St. Matthew 28:19). Those Scripture verses describe one and the same God. There's nothing "fuzzy" about them. However, when Jews, other non-Christians or even pseudo-Christians turn away from the God whose name is Father, Son, and Holy Ghost, they simultaneously forfeit any saving connection with the God who revealed himself through Isaiah in the verses above.

The God of Abraham, Isaac and Jacob is the same God who revealed himself at the Jordan River when Jesus was baptized (St. Matthew 3:16,17): the Father in the voice, the Son in his humanity, and the Holy Spirit in the form of a dove: three distinct persons and yet only one God, one almighty, eternal, divine essence (Luther). The fact is that God already clearly revealed himself as the Triune God in the Old Testament (the Aaronic blessing in Numbers 6:24-26 is just one example), but admittedly not as clearly as he did in the New Testament. Unfortunately, those who have been taken in by Judeo-Christian propaganda and idolatry reject that basic Biblical truth about God's identity.

NOTES FOR CHAPTER FIVE

[1] Will Herberg, *Protestant-Catholic-Jew* (Garden City, New York: Anchor Books, revised edition: 1960; originally published by Doubleday & Company, Inc. in 1955) p. 75.

[2] Ibid., p. 265.

[3] Msgr. Raymond Bosler, author of the Question Box column in the *Denver Catholic Register*, 19 Sept. 1979, reprinted in *Christian News*, 8 Oct. 1979, p. 2.

[4] The material for the Jewish-Christian joint worship in New York City was taken from a Religious News Service article reprinted in the 6 June 1979 issue of *Christian News*.

[5] *The Milwaukee Journal*, 7 Apr. 1978.

[6] The results of the *McCalls* magazine survey appeared in the Spring, 1979, issue of *The Milwaukee Lutheran*, No. 8, Vol. 31.

[7] *The Milwaukee Journal*, 8 Apr. 1979.

[8] Ibid., 5 Mar. 1977.

[9] Ewald M. Plass, compiler, *What Luther Says*, 3 vols., anthology (St. Louis: Concordia Publishing House, 1959), Vol. I, #206, #207, #208, and #599, pp. 69, 70 and 206.

[10] *The Milwaukee Journal*, 7 June 1976.

[11] Ibid., 20 Aug. 1976.

[12] This personal letter was written on Aug. 27, 1976.

[13] *The Milwaukee Journal*, 31 Aug. 1976.

[14] Ibid., 20 Sept. 1976.

[15] Ibid., 27 Sept. 1976.

[16] Ibid., 6 Oct. 1976.

IDOLS VERSUS CHRISTIAN MISSIONS — EVANGELISM

". . . you turned to God from idols to serve the living and true God, and to wait for his Son from heaven, whom he raised from the dead — Jesus, who rescues us from the coming wrath." (I Thessalonians 1:9,10 NIV)

In the previous chapter I included a letter from a Milwaukee insurance executive who criticized me for describing non-Christians as idol worshipers. He advised me to "let the 1,600,000,000 (his figure is too conservative, R.J.S.) non-Christians in this world have their God, and you have yours, and leave it just like that. Don't start trying to tell other people that because they don't believe the way you do, their God is an idol, regardless of what religion you are talking about."

We Christians, of course, cannot follow that advice. We cannot, in good conscience, "leave it just like that." We have been commissioned by Christ to be his witnesses and ambassadors, to preach the gospel to every creature, to make disciples of all nations, so that millions of non-Christian people, presently headed for hell, may be turned by the Holy Spirit "from idols to serve the living and true God." The eternal fate of precious, blood bought souls is at stake and conscientious Christians will make every effort to share the gift of eternal life through faith in Christ by means of mission work and evangelism.

MISSIONS — EVANGELISM AND CONVERSION UNDER ATTACK

Satan has stirred up many forces in recent decades to discredit the concept of converting pagan people to Christianity and to discourage Christian evangelism efforts and mission work. Donald McGavran, a veteran missionary and mission theorist, described the situation as follows:

> Fifteen years ago (about 1965) missions and world evangelization were in retreat. . . . Exposed to a mounting knowledge of other religions and to the guilt complex of Europe vis-a-vis the peoples of Asia and Africa, it seemed crude and triumphalistic to talk about conversion. The ecumenical movement kept insisting that all denominations, from Roman Catholic to Pentecostal, forget their exclusive claims and realize that they are all one. Many mission theorists kept urging that similar inclusiveness be applied to all religions. All were ways to God. World evangelization was consequently a relic of the old days when Christians had no knowledge of the great world religions. In short, *the basic reasons for Christian mission and world evangelization were disappearing one by one.* In 1963, a most prestigeful gathering in Mexico City declared that from now on sending missionaries would cease. Whatever was done would be done by each Church in its own land. World evangelization was in retreat. In places, the retreat turned into a disastrous rout. . . .[1]

Although McGavran contends that a more positive attitude toward Christian mission work is making a dramatic recovery, the negative forces which he refers to above and the basically idolatrous philosophy that all religions are ways to God are still very powerful and pervasive at the present time. In many circles Christian mission work and evangelization efforts are condemned and classified as "triumphalism," as arrogant "imperialism" running roughshod over the ancient, valuable cultures of non-Christian people. Feminist Mary Daly, for example, is scathingly sarcastic in her criticism of Christian mission efforts. She contends that

The imagery and the behavior implied in mission, then, is phallic. It is only necessary to think of the word in a very common contemporary military context — "bombing mission" — to perceive the direction implied by the word (outward, thrusting, exploding in many directions from one source). Moreover, the example conveys the burden of violence with which the history of the word is weighted down. Mission, then, is not communication but compulsion, whether this be understood as physical or psychological compulsion and coercion. (It is) . . . an imperialist expansion that pushes back the territory of others.[2]

More and more voices like Mary Daly are being heard, questioning the need for Christian missions, condemning the claim that Christianity is unique and clearly superior to other religions, asserting that the truth about God is divisible — that many people have parts of it, but no one is likely to have all of the truth. Eloquent experts on comparative religion maintain that there is truth in all religions and that God's saving revelation of himself can be other than Jesus Christ. In a letter to the editor in *Time* magazine, one Prabhat Acharya expresses an increasingly common opinion that calls all Christian mission efforts into question:

Evangelicals do harm in preaching in places like India. If faith in and fear of God are what they think Christianity preaches, I hasten to remind them that so too do all other religions. If the Bible is divine, then so too are the Gita and the Koran; any other conclusion would imply that God discriminates. He doesn't.[3]

Acharya certainly is correct when he insists that God is not guilty of discrimination. The Triune God we Christians worship wants all people on this planet to be saved and to come to know the truth of the gospel (I Timothy 2:4); he is not willing that any person should perish and suffer eternal punishment in hell, but that all should come to repentance (2 Peter 3:9, Acts 2:38). However, what

Acharya doesn't realize or believe is that the gods mentioned in the Gita of the Hindus and the Moslems' Koran are dead idols, the worship of whom is condemned as idolatry by the true God in his revelation to mankind, the Holy Bible. Any religion which fails to confess that Jesus, the God-man, is the way, the truth and life (John 14:6) is not preaching or teaching about faith in and fear of the true God, no matter how many millions of adherents it may attract and mislead.

MODERN ROMAN CATHOLICISM'S VIEW OF MISSIONS — EVANGELISM

In the Documents of Vatican II, the Roman Catholic Ecumenical Council, held between 1963-1965, the "Declaration on the Relationship of the Church to Non-Christian Religions" makes some startling statements in the light of the traditional, centuries-old Roman Catholic stand which contends that there is no salvation outside the Roman church. Ignoring the unpleasant fact that Hindus, Buddhists, Jews and Moslems worship and serve dead idols, the Vatican II participants heaped high praise on those false faiths with statements like the following: ". . . In Hinduism men . . . seek release from the anguish of our condition through ascetical practices or deep meditation or a loving, trusting flight toward God. . . . Buddhism . . . teaches a path by which men, in a devout and confident spirit, can either reach a state of absolute freedom or attain supreme enlightenment by their own efforts or by higher assistance. . . . Upon the Moslems, too, the church looks with esteem. They adore one God. . . . Though they do not acknowledge Jesus as God, they revere Him as a prophet . . . they prize the moral life, and give worship to God especially through prayer, almsgiving, and fasting."[4]

At first glance, the statements above seem incredible. How can a denomination claiming to be Christian so casually and cavalierly dismiss the Moslems' denial of Christ's deity and seem oblivious to the rank idolatry that permeates those non-Christian religions? However, upon some reflection one begins to realize why Roman Catholicism, which reeks of work-righteousness and injects the performance of good deeds into the doctrine of salvation, can describe these idolatrous religions in such flattering terms. They share the error of seeking salvation by human works. In addition, Catholic theologians like Karl Rahner contend that the devout disciples of the aforementioned non-Christian religions are in reality "anonymous" Christians. Although they do not consciously confess Christ as their Lord and Savior, their good works identify them as unwitting Christians, Christians in spite of themselves. With that elastic definition of Christianity, Catholics can keep right on claiming there is no salvation outside their church because they unilaterally push out their church's borders to take in Jews, Buddhists, Moslems, Hindus and most other religions as well, whether they want to be taken in or not.

In November, 1979, when Pope John Paul II visited Istanbul, Turkey, he stressed how much Moslems, who make up more than 98% of Turkey's population of 45 million, and Catholics have in common. He declared that both religions worship one God and that although Moslems "do not accept Christ as the Son of God, they accept him as one of the prophets. They also respect his mother in the Virgin, and they call to her for help. Besides, they also believe that there will be a last judgment and those who live a decent life will be rewarded. They have many similar values with Christians and Catholics."[5]

Statements and attitudes like those documented above,

coming from the Vatican II Council and the Pontiff himself, have to have a crippling effect on Roman Catholic evangelism zeal and mission work. The desire to preach Christ crucified has to suffer when prominent leaders of modern Roman Catholicism imply that pagan people and non-Christians, whether they are Moslem, Hindu, Buddhist or Jewish, can save themselves by leading outwardly decent lives and that their adamant refusal to accept Christ Jesus as God-man and Savior is not so serious and surely no reason for them to be damned. Increasingly, mission work by Roman Catholics is defined as social welfare activism and charitable endeavors like those carried out by Nobel prize-winning Mother Theresa in India or political liberation movements in Central and South America. More and more the idea of pagan people being converted from their heathen beliefs to saving faith in Jesus Christ by the forceful, persuasive proclamation of the gospel is condemned and classified as Western chauvinism and cultural genocide. If the Apostle Paul were to appear today and preach the uncompromising gospel as the New Testament describes him and his message, his missionary methods most likely would be considered too gauche, too ill-mannered and judgmental, too narrow, arrogant, self-righteous and triumphalistic.

Hans Küng, a controversial Swiss Roman Catholic theologian who has been censured and muzzled to some extent by his Vatican superiors, expresses an ultra-liberal Catholic stance toward non-Christian religions that totally fails to recognize the deadly, diabolical evil of idolatry. Küng contends that "every world religion is under God's grace and can be a way of salvation: whether it is primitive or highly evolved, mythological or enlightened, mystical or rational, theistic or non-theistic, a real or a quasi-religion. Every religion can be a way of salvation and we may hope that every one is."[6] Although Küng also speaks of the uniqueness of the Christian faith, his soft-headed universalistic theories, such as "the world religions do, though in error, proclaim the truth of the true God"[7] finally distort crystal clear statements of Scripture like John 14:6 and Acts 4:12 and pull the rug out from underneath traditional Christian mission endeavors which correctly emphasize the necessity of conversion from pagan error and idolatry to Christian faith and the Triune God as the obvious goal of all legitimate missionary activity.

WHAT ABOUT MISSION WORK AMONG AMERICAN INDIANS?

For nearly a century, since 1893, the Wisconsin Evangelical Lutheran Synod has been privileged to preach and teach the gospel of Jesus Christ among the Apache Indians of Arizona. This mission work has produced countless blessings both for the scores of Lutheran Christian missionaries who over the years eagerly shared their faith in the Savior and for the Apaches who were led from superstitious, idolatrous darkness into the bright and beautiful sunshine of the gospel and God's free grace.

However, as the 20th century is drawing to a close, one has to wonder whether our church body would be given a chance, as it was almost one hundred years ago, to preach Christ to modern-day American Indians, other than the Apaches of Arizona. Would Christian missionaries be welcomed with open arms by the average American Indian in the 1980's? There is plenty of evidence to suggest that Christian missionaries would encounter many obstacles and much resistance to the gospel of Christ from Indian militants who are seeking to revive native Indian customs and religion. It is claimed that the native religion of the American Indian is a gentle, powerful faith, rich in sym-

217

bolism and impressive in principle. More and more one hears Indians expressing resentment about the European Christians who invaded their land and attempted to convert every Indian to Christianity. Consider, for example, the complaint of 66-year-old Irene Mack Pyawasit:

> I was raised on the Menominee reservation and I remember well those do-gooder nuns trying to civilize us savages. They wanted to eliminate our religious beliefs, our history, our culture. We had to go to catechism class whether we liked it or not. We couldn't even use our own language.
>
> I remember this one nun. . . . She was 6 feet tall with feet this long, a big old ugly thing. I've never forgotten that old witch. She locked me in a closet all day, mice running all over; it was dark, and I was scared as ****. She was a lady of God teaching us savages about good.
>
> They said our religion was that of pagans, practices of the devil, and that we were supposed to embrace Christianity. Now they are more lenient to us, but they still don't want to acknowledge that we have the same God, that the same Creator is responsible for everything on this earth.[8]

Many of the early missionaries may well have been insensitive to the rich cultural heritage of the Indians and treated them as hopeless inferiors with contempt, instead of with Christian courtesy, kindness and compassion. There undoubtedly were many mistakes made by missionaries and some serious abuses which brought about the bitterness that is expressed toward the white man by many modern American Indian leaders. However, while we readily acknowledge the errors of some of our Christian predecessors, we should defend their good intentions, their courage and mission zeal, and we should not lose sight of the fact that the god or "Great Spirit" of the Indians is as much a pagan idol as any other we've exposed on these pages.

Harold Buchanon, a Winnebago Indian leader from Wisconsin, undoubtedly would challenge my statement above, that the native religion of the Indians is idolatrous. At a Winter Feast of the Winnebagos in 1978 Buchanon stated: "Some people say Indians are idol worshipers. We're not. We make offerings to recognize our God, like it is done in the Bible, along with praying for a better and a longer life."⁹ We have no intention of ridiculing the religion of the Winnebagos or of any other tribe, nor do we challenge the rights and freedom of the Indians to worship who, what, how, and in whatever way they wish. However, in the interest of simple truth and out of concern for the unique position of the true Triune God whom we Christians worship, we must maintain that native American Indian worship is idolatry that has only superficial similarities (like the offerings and praying Buchanon mentioned above) to our Christian faith.

Consider the following description of a sacred Indian sun dance ritual at Porcupine, South Dakota, which included the offering of human flesh:

> Human flesh is the only offering the Great Spirit will accept.
> "We cannot give back to the Great Spirit what is already his," explains Matthew Noble Red Man, a Sioux Indian. "We could not give him money or presents because they are his and he would not accept them.
> "Only our flesh is our own," he says, "so we offer that to him."
> And so, Indians wait their turn to kneel on a buffalo skin robe, clutch a ceremonial pipe, and offer a prayer and a donation at the annual Lakota Sun Dance on the Pine Ridge Reservation. . . .
> A medicine man makes an inch-long cut on the upper arm with a razor blade and begins extracting tiny hunks of flesh, placing them in a red ribbon for the Great Spirit.
> The devout might give 100 pieces of flesh a day without changing expression.
> Since the Sun Dance is one of the seven sacred Sioux Ceremonies, cameras and tape recorders are forbidden. Tribal police stop the few non-Indians attending the ceremony about 10

miles north of Wounded Knee and search cars to insure compliance.

Inside the pavilion is a confusion of old and new. Traditional buffalo teepees stand beside pup tents and campers, and Indian boys tie their ponies next to the cars in the parking lot.

The four-day dance is held in a circle about the size of a circus ring. Spectators sit around the edge under a sunshade made of pine logs and fresh-smelling balsam boughs.

Firmly implanted at the center of the ring is a tree bedecked with banners. Long colorful leather thongs hang from it.

Four eagles drift lazily across the sky overhead.

About 70 dancers, who eat and drink nothing for the four days, enter the ring and begin the dance by saluting the sun and blowing eagle wing whistles which make a pleasant peeping noise.

Then a brave is pierced in the center of the ring. Two slits are cut in his skin over each shoulder blade, a wooden peg is slid under the skin, and a leather thong is tied to the peg.

As the dancers peep their encouragement, he pulls four buffalo skulls around the ring until at last he lurches forward and breaks free.

"That is called the pull of ignorance," says James Gillihan, former director of cultural preservation of South Dakota. "It signifies that the empty skulls should always be behind you."

Later, nine dancers are pierced in the chest as the tribe watches. Like children dancing around a Maypole, they dance in and out and salute the sun with upraised arms until they fall back and break free, popping the pegs and the leather thong 30 or more feet back against the pole. Blood streams down their chests.

In 1881, the Sun Dance was outlawed as barbaric. It was permitted as a religious ceremony in 1928, but piercing did not slip back in until the early 1950's.

"Man must suffer," says Noble Red Man. "Piercing and constant pain keep our minds from wandering off our purpose. We are here to devote ourselves to the Great Spirit, every minute of the time."[10]

The above ritual reminds one of the ancient pagan mystery religions, described in Chapter Two, which also featured frenzied, fanatic devotees inflicting suffering and injuries upon themselves, but such rites surely have nothing in common with genuine Christianity.

According to Leonard Crowdog, a Sioux medicine man, Indian religion is deeply mystical. Little has been written about it because it is not systematized, and it has no single source, like the Bible. Their beliefs have been handed down through the generations by medicine men. Medicine man Crowdog claims he can communicate with deceased Indian leaders to receive guidance from his dead elders. Indians like Crowdog also use peyote in their ceremonies because that mind altering or hallucinogenic drug allows them to reach higher levels of consciousness. There is a pantheistic element in Crowdog's faith for he believes that everything is religious and sacred and all things are part of the whole. He contends that his "Great Spirit" is similar to the God of Judaeo-Christianity, but he does not believe in the devil. Crowdog declared: "White men have two things — God and devil, two masters. The devil only exists in man's mind. Same with hell. It's man's bad conscience that's hell. An Indian has only one master, the Great Spirit. What evil there is is man's doing and man can stop it."[11] Crowdog, of course, is correct when he traces the cause of evil to "man's doing" but he is tragically in error when he contends that "man can stop it (evil)." The heart and core of the Christian faith is that because man could not cope with evil, God sent his Son to rescue sinful mankind from the clutches of Satan, who originally had triggered the fall of mankind by his successful temptation of Adam and Eve. The coming of Christ and his all-sufficient sacrifice on Calvary's cross saved sinners from the fate all people deserve, eternal punishment in a very real, literal hell. How sad that Crowdog's idolatrous belief in a non-existent "Great Spirit" makes him deny the deadly, damning reality of Satan and hell and fills him with false confidence that he can overcome evil on his own. How delighted the devil must be when he succeeds in shackling many modern American Indians to primitive superstitions, peyote-induced visions, and alleged communication with dead ancestors, thereby diverting them from the gospel of Christ and the worship of the Triune God!

SWEET MEDICINE AND MOSES — MOUNT SINAI AND BEAR BUTTE

Several years ago I shared my plans to write this book with Pastor Gerhold Lemke, minister of Trinity Lutheran Church in Sturgis, South Dakota. Since that time Pastor Lemke has sent me considerable information about the religious beliefs of the Plains Indians and their association with a 1400 foot mini-mountain known as Bear Butte, located six miles northeast of Sturgis.

Bear Butte, a South Dakota state park (since 1961), was registered as a National Landmark in 1965 and subsequently was placed on the federal list of National Recreational Trails and in 1973 was included in the National Register of Historic Places. Undoubtedly the main reason for the prominence of this place is its striking physical appearance, a 4,422 foot high volcanic bubble rising abruptly 1400 feet above the surrounding flat prairie. It gained its name from its resemblance in profile to a sleeping bear with outstretched paws. Bear Butte has served as a landmark for centuries for a variety of travelers: early Indians, pioneers on their way across the continent, cattle drivers, and more recently, jet pilots. However, for the Plains Indians, Bear Butte is much more than a spectacular piece of scenery or a convenient geographic reference point. They see it as a sacred, mystical place, even the birthplace of their religion (especially for the Cheyenne), where Indians still come to pray, meditate and seek visions.

An article in the *Sturgis Tribune* summed up the spiritual and religious significance of Bear Butte as follows:

> The Butte has always gone by a variety of names. The Mandans know it as the resting place of Nu-mahk-much-a-nan. For the Cheyenne, it is Noavosse, home of the Four Sacred Arrows. The Sioux call it Mato Paha, mountain of the bear. But for each of these important Plains Indian tribes, Bear Butte is historically a natural ceremonial shrine, a symbol of religious power and spiritual energy.
>
> Mandan tradition makes Bear Butte the home of their festival, Settling of the Waters, which celebrates the end of a devastating flood. Like the Old Testament's Noah, Chief Nu-mahk-much-a-nan was warned of a coming flood and constructed a special canoe to save himself. As the rains began to subside, Nu-mahk-much-a-nan sent a turtle dove out to daily assess the depth of the flood waters. When the dove returned with a willow branch, the Mandan chief knew the dangers of the flood had finally passed. His canoe ultimately came to rest on Bear Butte.
>
> The Mandans celebrated Nu-mahk-much-a-nan's safe passage by offering tools as sacrifice to ward off another flood. Interestingly enough, Bear Butte's limestone bluffs, visible on the Ceremonial Trail in Bear Butte State Park, were once the floor of an ancient ocean that surfaced when molten rock formed the Butte itself. Hikers frequently find fossils of sea shells or petrified moss in this area.
>
> For the Cheyenne, however, Bear Butte is more than a legendary festival site. It is the birthplace of their religion.
>
> According to Cheyenne legend, Sweet Medicine, a young Cheyenne warrior, found a refuge on Bear Butte and confronted the great spirit of the mountain here. Banished from his tribe for murdering another warrior, Sweet Medicine spent four years in the limestone caves on the Butte. During this time, he married a young Cheyenne woman, another exile who had taken refuge on the sacred mountain. The gods summoned the two to one of the Butte's many caves and told Sweet Medicine

the Cheyenne people desperately needed religious instruction. They then entrusted the pair with the Four Sacred Arrows, which symbolized prohibitions against murder, theft, adultery and incest. Sweet Medicine and his wife consulted with the spirits for another four years and returned to the Cheyenne with the gods' message.

Other aspects of both the Cheyenne and Sioux religions have their origins on Bear Butte. For example, the Medicine Lodge Ceremony with its eight days of fasting and spiritual fellowship had its birth here. It began as a summer pilgrimage — a time for gathering food, fashioning clothing, and making shields.

A ritual of self-torture gradually evolved as warriors, confronted with personal crisis or a dangerous mission, sacrificed their bodies in return for the gods' favor. Known as the Sun Dance, this ritual requires participants to stare into the sun while performing the dance. After fasting and purification rites in a sweat lodge, warriors pierced their chests with rawhide thongs and danced around a cottonwood sun pole until they tore themselves free.

The traditional Indian campground, teepee ring and ceremonial mound still exist on Bear Butte today, and the Cheyenne and Sioux still come to Bear Butte State Park to pray, fast and seek visions. As recently as 1976, a Cheyenne delegation brought Sweet Medicine's Four Sacred Arrows to the Butte for a special religious ceremony and fast. And according to Tony Gullett, Bear Butte park manager, over 50 Indians visited the Butte during May of this year.

In a sense, Bear Butte remains unchanged by 20th Century advancements. Young men seek visions; young women dream dreams. Bear Butte remains Noavosse and Mato Paha — the ancient mountain of the bear.[12]

Many tribes and societies throughout the world have in their heritage a flood epic or legend and a Noah-like hero who was saved from a devastating deluge by his benevolent deity. Skeptics may cite those similar stories to discredit the Bible and the historical account of the universal flood which the true God revealed through his holy writer, the prophet Moses. Actually those numerous flood legends, whether they are Babylonian or American Indian, reveal that a very real disaster once did descend on this planet and that descriptions of it were passed along from generation to generation after the confusion of tongues at Babel. We are confident that Moses' account in Genesis is genuine, but it's not surprising that many imitations, with erroneous details, also developed among pagan people. A world-wide flood and its after-effects had to make a tremendous impression on the offspring of Shem, Ham and Japheth.

Not only Noah, but also Moses, has been associated with Bear Butte. The Cheyenne legend of Sweet Medicine corresponds in many details to the life and calling of Moses, the leader of Israel who rescued his people from bondage to Pharaoh in Egypt. Pastor Lemke theorizes that the Cheyenne were told about Moses, the Exodus and other incidents connected with the Israelites' forty years of wandering in the wilderness by French missionaries. Lemke offers the following 17 points of comparison between Sweet Medicine-Bear Butte and Moses-Mount Sinai to support his theory that the Cheyenne legend originated from Bible stories told to them by Christian missionaries:

HOW GREAT IS THE LIKELIHOOD THAT THE CHEYENNE *SWEET MEDICINE* MYTH CAME TO THE INDIANS BY WAY OF FRENCH EXPLORERS AND FURTRADERS OR PRIESTS TELLING THE STORY OF *MOSES* ON MOUNT SINAI?

Comparisons:

Sweet Medicine	*Moses*
1. Raised by foster parents.	1. Raised by the pharaoh's daughter.
2. Injured or killed a Cheyenne in argument over buffalo.	2. Killed an Egyptian taskmaster in defending a Hebrew slave.
3. Was banished from his home.	3. Fled the land of Egypt.

4. Ended up alone at Bear Butte.	4. Came to Midian, near Mt. Sinai.
5. Was joined by a Cheyenne girl.	5. Married a daughter of Reuel.
6. Stayed 4 years on the Butte.	6. Stayed 40 years in Midian.
7. Received a book-like rock from the mountain.	7. Received the Ten Commandments written by God on stone.
8. Was called by "the Gods" to be a prophet to his people who were forgetting their religion.	8. Was called by God at the burning bush to lead Israel out of Egypt. Gave Israel God's laws & promises.
9. Was offered two bundles of arrows, and took one.	9. Received the two-tablet Commandments a second time after smashing the first set in the Golden Calf story.
10. Received four commandments.	10. Received ten commandments.

(Moses' 5th, 6th, 7th, also one from the Israelite laws of marriage).

11. Was not at first accepted by his people.	11. Moses was afraid Israel would not believe he came from God.
12. Set up 4 tepees, 4 directions. Tepees for 4 wise men.	12. Oriented the Israelite camp NSEW, Levites on 4 sides of tabernacle.
13. Terrible drought, children ask for food.	13. Israel in wilderness, people complain to Moses, no food or water.
14. "White things" and buffalo meat supplied. "Have faith."	14. God supplies manna, meat of wild birds. God trained Israel to trust Him.
15. Lived to be very old man.	15. Lived to age of 120 years.
16. Foretold times to come when Indians would suffer.	16. Foretold blessing for faithfulness, chastisement for disobedience.
17. Climbed alone to top of Butte.	17. Climbed alone up Mt. Nebo, where he died, and God buried him.

(Historical note: The French Jesuit priest, Jacques Marquette, 1637-1675, explored part of the Mississippi River more than three hundred years ago, and met many native Americans.)

(Historical note: The Cheyenne originated in Minnesota.)

In 1979, Lemke shared his observations with a professor of anthropology from Wichita State University. This ethnohistorian, a visitor at Bear Butte and an expert on the Plains Indians, wrote to Lemke as follows:

In your comparison betweeen Moses and Sweet Medicine some details regarding the Cheyenne prophet are wrong. With your basic idea that the two persons, and events surrounding them, were similar, I would agree. And so would the Cheyenne.

You are wrong, however, thinking that Sweet Medicine and his achievement are fiction. There was a historical Sweet Medicine, and he died long before the first Europeans set foot on this continent. Sweet Medicine was at Bear Butte a number of times in his life. I must say this as an ethnohistorian.

Like you, Mr. Lemke, Cheyenne traditionalists believe in a central, mysterious power that permeates all of life. Only the *name* they call this great power by is different from the one you use: *it is the same God.*

God's ways are mysterious. When he revealed himself to a tribal man (Moses) on a mountain on Sinai Peninsula, why should he not reveal himself to another tribal man (Sweet Medicine) on a mountain in South Dakota? Who are we to question his reasons?

If you would correctly see what Bear Butte is: a sacred place of revelation where the one great mysterious power talked to a human, and where this power still can be listened to, you would also see what your obligation is. Your obligation as a minister is to take an active role alongside Cheyenne and Lakota religious people, to protect Bear Butte from abuse and destruction, to assist in keeping Bear Butte unchanged, in beauty, in the Lord's glory!

And do remember:

"The Lord also told him (Moses) . . . Set limits for the people all around the mountain, and tell them. Take care not to go up the mountain, or even touch its base. If anyone touches the mountain he must be put to death. No hand shall touch him; he must be stoned to death or killed with arrows." Exodus 19[14]

The professor of anthropology contends that "it is the same God" who revealed himself to Moses on Mount Sinai and to the mythical Cheyenne hero, Sweet Medicine, on Bear Butte. However, when one closely examines the religious system of the Israelites in comparison with the beliefs of the Cheyennes, some striking differences are immediately apparent which reveal that Moses was in contact with the true God while idolatry and superstition characterize the faith of the Cheyenne. Surely there are some superficial similarities. Animals, for example, play a key role both for the Children of Israel and the Cheyennes. But the many animal sacrifices described in the Old Testament all foreshadow the ultimate, all-sufficient, substitutionary sacrifice of the Lamb of God, the Messiah, on the altar of the cross. Such emphasis, which is the very heart of the unique gospel, is conspicuously absent in the Cheyenne religion.

E. Adamson Hoebel described the beliefs of the Cheyennes in their heyday (1840-1860) as follows:

> The Cheyennes have a small core of ancient beliefs about spirits other than the four groups of the spirits of the major directions. There is the all-knowing high god, "Heammawihio," The Wise One Above. . . . The sun is believed to represent "Heammawihio," although the deity is a good deal more than the sun; he is an abstraction, not just a super-brilliant, heat-radiating celestial sphere. The first offering of the (peace) pipe is made to him in all smoking."[15]

Hoebel's description of the Cheyennes' deity surely has little in common with the Triune God who reveals himself to us in the Holy Bible. We cannot escape the conclusion that their Heammawihio must be placed in the same category with Baal and Jupiter, another example of pagan people trying to describe the supreme being whose existence they cannot but acknowledge. The wonders of nature and the testimony of their conscience assert that they must answer to Someone who fashioned their world, but without the written revelation of the Bible their ideas about God will be distorted and inevitably idolatrous, with a good measure of work-righteousness mixed in.

Consider Hoebel's further description of the Cheyenne creed and note the element of do-it-yourself religion, which seems to be present in every false faith:

> For the Cheyenne there is no hell or punishment of any sort in after-life; no judgment or damnation. Although Cheyennes sin when they commit murder and they often do wrong, murder is expiated in the here and now, and wrongdoing builds up no burden of guilt to be borne beyond the grave. For the Cheyenne there is no problem of salvation; goodness is to be sought as rightness for its own sake and for the appreciative approval of one's fellow man. When at last it shakes free of its corporeal abode, the Cheyenne soul wafts free and lights up the Hanging Road (Milky Way in the sky) to dwell thereafter in benign proximity to the Great Wise One (Heammawihio) and the long-lost loved ones. Only the souls of those who have committed suicide are barred from this peace.[16]

Except for a few exotic details, such as souls soaring to the stars, the religion of the Cheyenne Indians in the 19th century does not seem much different from the religious beliefs of millions of modern Americans who ultimately trust in themselves and the decent lives they think they lead, to see them through any judgment they may face after death. Human beings have within themselves from birth a streak of self-righteousness which cuts across cultures and continents and can be spotted both among the Cheyennes and sophisticated, 20th century jet-setters. In chapter one we labeled it CARC, the Common American Religious Creed, which in the final analysis, makes an idol of self. People who embrace the CARC show little concern about the sin of idolatry; to them it doesn't matter what or in whom one believes as long as he sincerely tries to do his best. Hoebel's description above of the Cheyennes' faith in the mid-19th century reveals that the CARC is by no means a recent religious development in our country.

229

A WORLD WITHOUT CHRISTIAN MISSIONARIES?

Would the Cheyennes and other American Indian tribes be better off if white Christian missionaries had never contacted them and tried to convert them to Christianity? Although some anthropologists and militant Indian spokesmen would answer that question with a resounding yes, one cannot turn back the clock, rewrite history, or keep the idealized Indian culture uncontaminated by so-called Christian imperialism. A strong case can be made that contacts with white men brought mostly misery and disaster to the American Indian, and that the rug was rudely pulled out from under the culture which seemed to work well for them before the white man's invasion and arrogant occupation of the native Americans' territories. However, we dare not forget that the Cheyennes' Sweet Medicine legend or the superstitious myths of other American Indian religions never saved a single soul. The gods of the Indians were and are idols. Their codes of conduct and their culture, although commendable in many respects, were contaminated by an underlying paganism, a fatally-flawed view of God and man, which originated in the minds of primitive men rather than coming from the supernatural revelation of the Triune God in the Holy Scriptures.

In an article about the non-denominational Christian New Tribes Mission, Bryan Coupland, director of that organization, declared:

> Missionaries get a lot of flak about changing peoples' cultures. Most is predicated on the idea that savages live some kind of idyllic, Arcadian life and that outsiders spoil it.
>
> The thing our missionaries have found is that these people are not happy. They live in fear and sadness. They are frequently miserable physically and terrified by evil spirits. The Ayore of Bolivia bury their old people alive, because if they don't, the spirit

may escape and follow the tribe. They feel twins are bad, and kill both.

We don't go in on a crusade to change these practices, but as a people becomes Christian, God Himself begins to transform their lives.[17]

The words of Coupland describing the true, tragic condition of primitive, pagan people in the last quarter of the 20th century sound almost identical to what J. F. Gustave Harders stated as the 20th century began. Harders, a pioneer Wisconsin Synod Lutheran missionary to the Apaches of Arizona, insisted that "the Apache is a man who has lost all joy in being alive. He is a man without hope. He walks in darkness and in the shadow of death. . . ."[18]

No Christian missionary, who sincerely seeks to share the saving gospel message with heathen people, will ever have to apologize to God or to the pagans to whom he reaches out and preaches, for robbing them of their culture. Surely mistakes were made in the past and modern day missionaries should be very sensitive to respect customs which may seem wrong-headed and weird to Westerners, but which do not conflict with God's Word. But the inescapable fact remains that millions of pagan people in every corner of the globe still desperately need to have missionaries reach them with the good news of the crucified and risen Savior, the only message which can rescue them from Satanic, soul-destroying superstition and damning idolatry. Dedicated Christians dare not allow passionate arguments about alleged cultural deprivation of primitive people to distract them from their calling to preach the priceless gospel to every creature without exception. Every person in every culture, in every tribe, clan or nation desperately needs to hear the timeless truth that free salvation has been won for all people by Christ on Calvary, and that it is freely available to everyone by God's grace through God-given faith in

Jesus. That is the message that transcends and even trivializes all cultural differences among the peoples on this planet.

MISSIONS — EVANGELISM AND UNIVERSALISM

Sooner or later, every Christian is confronted by the nagging question: Will God really damn the millions of people on this earth who never heard of Jesus or who were born into false, idolatrous non-Christian faiths like Hinduism, Buddhism, or Islam? In spite of clear statements of Scripture like John 3:36; 8:24; 14:6 and Acts 4:12 we are tempted to hedge on the basic biblical principle that sinners can be saved only through faith in Christ. For no one likes to think of even one soul, no matter how wicked, suffering eternal punishment in a literal, fiery hell.

Universalism is a false doctrine that was devised by the devil to mislead well-intentioned people who understandably have been horrified by the thought of seemingly "innocent" non-Christians being damned. Several years ago Dr. Clark Pinnock, at one time a relatively conservative theologian, opted for the ancient idea of non-Christians who had "the desire for salvation" during their life on earth being offered a second chance after death to believe in Christ for salvation. That is one very common form of the heresy of universalism.

As a result of the Vatican Council II Roman Catholicism also has been deeply infected with unscriptural universalism that inevitably dampens mission zeal and the desire to evangelize the heathen. For example, Msgr. Raymond Bosler, in his *Denver Catholic Register* Question Box column, contends that:

> . . . the council (Vatican II) . . . made it clear that other Christians (non-Catholics), Jews, non-Christians and even atheists can be saved and are united to the Church as the People of

God in various degrees. For example: "Those also can attain to everlasting salvation who through no fault of their own do not know the gospel of Christ or His Church, yet sincerely seek God and, moved by grace, strive by their deeds to do His will as it is known to them through the dictates of conscience."

Catholic theologians are now busy discussing how or whether non-Christians can be in any way united with the Church. There is ambiguity in the present interpretation of the necessity of the Church for salvation. But the Church does clearly teach that Jews and other non-Christians can be saved.[19]

The universalism of the modern, post-Vatican II Roman Catholic Church is not a pure, blanket universalism. Seemingly some people could end up in hell due to their lack of desire, their insincerity, or their failure to produce the good deeds that are indispensable according to Rome's unscriptural concept of salvation. How ironic and tragic! Rome opens the gates of heaven to people who do not believe in Christ, as long as they sincerely seek salvation and do good works. Thus Rome reveals its true colors, placing top priority on human deeds and downgrading, or even eliminating, the role of faith in Jesus Christ.

The point is, such universalism or semi-universalism, has to have a very negative effect on Christian missions and evangelism. Why should missionaries travel to primitive, underdeveloped lands at considerable personal sacrifice to preach to savages, if it's true what Vatican II and theologians like Clark Pinnock theorize, that non-Christians may be given a second chance to convert after death or that they may be saved even if specific faith in Jesus Christ is absent? Why indeed? And, of course, underlying the errors of universalism is the evil of idolatry, the failure to recognize that any and every deity worshiped by non-Christians is a death-dealing idol. No matter how dutiful, devout and sincere such idol worship is, no matter how diligent such non-Christian idolaters may be in trying to do good deeds as their conscience guides them, they will not receive the gift of eternal life without God-given faith in Christ. Even their "good" deeds will be lacking God-pleasing goodness for Jesus insisted that "apart from me you can do nothing" (John 15:5).

MISSIONS — EVANGELISM AND SYNCRETISM

My *Living Webster Encyclopedia Dictionary* defines syncretism as follows: "The attempted blending of irreconcilable principles or parties, as in philosophy or religion." Originally the word was a political term. Plutarch described the unity of the usually quarrelsome Cretans against a common enemy as a *synkretismos*. Later the term was used of harmony or union in the sphere of philosophy and religion. In our day syncretism is another error or false belief that promotes the practice of idolatry or at least minimizes the evil of that common deadly sin against the First Commandment.

The renowned historian Arnold Toynbee was an avid syncretist who would have been horrified by the theme and message of this book, that the only true God is the Triune God who reveals himself to us in the Bible. Toynbee contended that Christianity must free itself from its spirit of arrogant exclusiveness and seek some sort of synthesis with other world religions in order to assure future unity and harmony of mankind. Obviously Toynbee would not classify Allah, Buddha or any other man-devised deities as idols.

Syncretists believe that every religion offers a valid way to God and salvation. They criticize "the parochialism of Christian theology," especially Christianity's doctrine of redemption exclusively through faith in Christ Jesus. To get out from under what they would see as the narrow-minded exclusivism of Christianity, syncretists have devised a vocabulary of double-talk that maintains that the "cosmic Christ" is present in non-Christian religions, that a so-called "Christ reality" can be discerned among men even where Jesus' name is not known. When one cuts through the pious phrases and double-talk, it finally boils down to this: According to the syncretists, one does not have to become a Christian to be saved and to be acceptable to God. They declare that their position is even biblical. They like to employ as a proof passage Acts 10:34,35 where one finds the following words of Peter during his encounter with the Gentile Cornelius: "I now realize how true it is that God does not show favoritism but accepts men from every nation who fear him and do what is right." The syncretists ignore, however, that Peter goes on to say in the very next verse, that peace and acceptance with God come only "through Jesus Christ, who is Lord of all" (Acts 10:36).

How does syncretism affect Christian missions and evangelism efforts? Consider the following statement of syncretist Timothy Miller of the University of Kansas:

> If we are to affirm a truly cosmological Christology . . . we should now openly question the validity of the missionary impulse in our time, for it is entirely possible that the proper era of the unrelenting call to "conversion" is past.[20]

Syncretist Miller rejects the idea that Christianity is incomparably greater than any other religion and offers the only way of salvation. He describes such a belief as a blatant example of religio-cultural chauvinism, proud provincialism, and part of the political and cultural imperialism of the West cloaked in the guise of missions. Miller maintains that in today's pluralistic world, we must separate the concepts of redemption and salvation from the Christian Church and the person of Jesus. We can present our Christian faith only *as our own choice*, as one among many possibilities. Other religions, according to Miller, offer satisfying values, valid insights into ultimate truth, and supporting hope, and have their own validity. Spokesmen for syncretism insist that Christians must not be so proud as to think they are called to evangelize the world by preaching the gospel to all nations in the hope of converting other people to the "Christian way." They claim that non-Christian religions may also be instruments of God to reveal his will and save his people.

Under the influence of syncretism and universalism, which was considered in the previous section, many Roman Catholics today no longer believe that members of other religions will go to hell unless they are converted. Syncretist-inclined Catholic leaders like Brother David Steindlrast of Graymoor, New York, are responsible for those easy-going attitudes toward the fate of non-Christians. Steindlrast advises missionaries to help the Buddhists develop the so-called "Christian dimension" of his faith and at the same time seek the Buddhist's help in developing the "Buddhist dimension" of his own faith. Equally incredible, unscriptural, and Christ-denying are the following statements of Brother David: "If you have the key intuition of the Buddhist, you are also a Christian and a Hindu whether you know it or not. . . . We are going to the Buddhist to learn the theology of the Spirit. And we are bringing something of the Word [the theology of the Son]."[21] What a perversion of the basic doctrine of the Holy Trinity.

A Southern Baptist scholar, A. Roy Eckhardt, reveals how syncretism has influenced him and colored his view of Christian mission-evangelism efforts, especially toward the Jews, with this statement: "Let me affirm, with a number of convincedly Christian colleagues, opposition to any avowed effort on the part of the church to missionize the Jewish community as such. . . . For if the Jewish people are not already amongst the family of God, we who are Gentiles remain lost without hope."[22] Eckhardt boggles the mind when he says that Christians should understand that "the Jewish non-acceptance of Jesus as the Christ is an act of faithfulness to the God of the covenant, and *not*, as in the historic Christian polemic, an act of faithlessness."[23]

The statements and teaching of the false prophets quoted in this chapter show how Satan seeks to put stumbling blocks in the path of Christian missionaries and evangelists. Why should we experience hardships in heathen lands or endure ridicule and rejection by non-Christians at home and abroad if such pagan people are going to be saved in some mysterious, non-Christian way, apart from faith in Jesus? But we dare not swallow or be taken in by such Satanic propaganda. Whether one calls it syncretism, universalism, "cosmological" Christianity, or native American Indian religion, it all boils down to pure and simple idolatry, the worship of something or someone other than the Father, the Son, and the Holy Spirit, the God whom we should fear, love and trust above all things. May the evil ideologies and false philosophies exposed in this chapter never succeed in diverting concerned Christians from our calling to preach the gospel to every creature and to be witnesses for Christ to the ends of the earth!

NOTES FOR CHAPTER SIX

[1]Donald McGavran, "The New Era in Missions: Debacle — Recovery-Advance"editorial in the *Global Church Growth Bulletin* Vol. XVII, No. 2 (March-April, 1980), p. 16.

[2]Mary Daly *Beyond God the Father*, (Boston: Beacon Press, 1973), p. 168.

[3]Prabhat Acharya, *Time* magazine, 16 Jan. 1978.

[4]cf. "Declaration on the Relationship of the Church to Non-Christian Religions" in the *Documents of Vatican II*, Walter M. Abbott, S.J., General Editor, an Angelus Book, (New York: Guild Press, America Press, Association Press, 1966), pp. 661-663.

[5]*The Milwaukee Journal*, 29 Nov. 1979.

[6]Hans Küng, *Freedom Today*, trans. by C. Hastings (New York: Sheed and Ward, 1966), p. 147.

[7]Küng, quoted by Hans Schwarz, *The Search for God*, (Minneapolis: Augsburg Publishing House, 1975), p. 141.

[8]*The Milwaukee Journal*, 27 Jan. 1980.

[9]Ibid., 27 Dec. 1978.

[10]Ibid., 28 Aug. 1978.

[11]Ibid., 21 Jan. 1978.

[12]The article on Bear Butte as a spiritual and religious sanctuary appeared in the 21 June 1978 issue of the Sturgis , S.D., *Tribune*.

[13]Comparisons provided by Pastor Gerhold Lemke, Sturgis, South Dakota.

[14]Letter supplied by and addressed to The Rev. Gerhold Lemke, Sturgis, South Dakota, from a Wichita State University Professor of Anthropology.

[15]E. Adamson Hoebel, The Cheyennes: *Indians of the Great Plains* (New York: Henry Holt & Co., 1960), A Holt-Dryden Book — University of Minnesota, p. 86.

[16]Ibid., p. 87.

[17]*The Milwaukee Journal*, 3 Feb. 1980.

[18]Harders' quotation from Erwin E. Kowalke, *You and Your Synod*, The Story of the Wisconsin Evangelical Lutheran Synod, (Milwaukee, Wisconsin, Northwestern Publishing House, 1961), p. 64.

[19]Msgr. Raymond Bosler, The Question Box column in *The Denver Catholic Register*, 16 Mar. 1977 reprinted in *Christian News*, 28 Mar. 1977.

[20]Timothy Miller, "Cosmological Christianity and the Missionary Impulse" in *The Christian Century*, 12 Jan. 1972, p. 42.

[21]Brother Steindlrast's statements quoted in Ralph E. Powell's article "Stumbling over Syncretism" in *Christianity Today*," 13 Apr. 1973, from which were gleaned other facts about modern manifestations of syncretism.

[22]Ibid. Eckhardt also quoted in Powell's article.

[23]Ibid.

CHAPTER SEVEN

IDOLS DEFINED BY DOCTOR MARTIN LUTHER

. . . the Father judges no one, but has entrusted all judgment to the Son, that all may honor the Son just as they honor the Father. He who does not honor the Son does not honor the Father, who sent him. (John 5:22,23 NIV)

I am a Christian, a Lutheran Christian, a Lutheran Christian pastor serving Woodlawn Evangelical Lutheran Church of West Allis, Wisconsin, a congregation affiliated with the Wisconsin Evangelical Lutheran Synod. The Wisconsin Synod is known as the most conservative of the four largest Lutheran church bodies in the United States because it holds to the conviction that the Bible is the inspired, inerrant Word of God. The Wisconsin Synod also has the reputation of being a staunch, ultra-conservative church body because of its confessional stance. It binds itself to the ancient creeds (Apostles', Nicene and Athanasian) and 16th century, Reformation-era confessions (Luther's Small and Large Catechisms, the Augsburg Confession and its Apology, the Smalcald Articles and the Formula of Concord) of the Evangelical Lutheran Church embodied in the Book of Concord of 1580 because they are a correct presentation and exposition of the pure doctrine of the Word of God.

I am deeply indebted to Dr. Martin Luther. Although I do not claim to be a learned Luther scholar, I have had regular contact with his ideas and writings for many years.

Nearly every week for more than two decades I have used one or more quotations from the great reformer's writing or off-the-cuff table talks to emphasize the Sunday service theme in our weekly church bulletin. I believe that a regular exposure to Luther's works has helped me to look at issues and to approach theological questions in Luther-like fashion.

The positions on various matters that I've taken in this book are not original with me. As a Christian I have tried to write what my Master, my Lord Jesus Christ, would want written by one of his disciples. My observations about idolatry have been made out of a deep concern for the honor which all people owe to God's Son (cf. John 5:22,23 at the beginning of this chapter). I have been greatly influenced by the Savior's uncompromising declaration in John 14:6 — "I am the way. . . . No one comes to the Father except through me." The courageous confession of Jesus' disciple, the Apostle Peter, when he was called before the hostile Jewish Sanhedrin, headed by the high priests Annas and Caiaphas, has permeated my consciousness as I've worked on this book. Indeed, how can any Christian escape the clear implications of Peter's inspired words in Acts 4:12 — "Salvation is found in no one else, for there is no other name (Jesus Christ of Nazareth, v.10) under heaven given to men by which we must be saved." To those who might be inclined to criticize what I've written about other religions and label this work anti-Roman Catholic, anti-Semitic, anti-Islam, or anti-every-religion-that's-not-Christian, I offer no apologies. With the Apostle Paul I must respond: "For no one can lay any foundation other than the one already laid, which is Jesus Christ" (I Corinthians 3:11).

My thoughts about idolatry have been triggered by what my Lord Jesus says about himself, his Father, and the Holy Spirit in the Holy Scriptures and by what Jesus' disciples, like Peter and Paul, have written by inspiration of the Holy Spirit in the Bible. In this I follow Martin Luther and proudly call myself Lutheran in the sense that Luther himself approved and used that label. At first, Luther was opposed to people identifying themselves as "Lutherans." In fact, the expressions "Lutheran" and "Lutheran Church" were first coined by Luther's enemies. Luther himself declared:

> "I ask that men make no reference to my name and call themselves not Lutherans but Christians. What is Luther? After all, the doctrine is not mine, nor have I been crucified for anyone. St. Paul in I Corinthians 3 would not allow Christians to call themselves Pauline or Petrine, but Christian. How, then, should I, a poor evil-smelling maggot sack have men give to the children of Christ my worthless name? Not so, dear friends. Let us cast out party names and be called Christians after Him whose doctrine we have. The papists justly have a party name because they are not satisfied with the doctrine and name of Christ but want also to be popish. Let them be popish, then, since the pope is their master. I neither am nor want to be any man's master. Christ alone is our Master. He teaches me and all believers one and the same doctrine. (Matthew 23:8)"[1]

Later, Luther modified his position against the use of his name and reluctantly permitted people who agreed with his teachings to identify themselves as Lutherans. He wrote in this connection:

> "It is true that you should never say: I am Lutherish or popish; for neither of them died for you; neither is your master. Only of Christ may this be said. Therefore you should profess to be Christian. But if you believe that Luther's doctrine is evangelical and the pope's unevangelical, you must not flatly disown Luther; otherwise you also disown his doctrine, which you admittedly recognize as the doctrine of Christ. Rather you must say: Whether Luther personally is a scoundrel or a saint means nothing to me. His doctrine, however, is not his but Christ's own. For you see that the object of the tyrants is not only to slay Luther but also to extirpate the doctrine. They lay hands on you

because of the doctrine, and for this reason they ask you whether you are Lutheran. Truly, here you should not speak in a weak whisper but should freely confess Christ, whether Luther, Nicholas, or George preached Him. Let the person go. But the doctrine you must confess. . . . Luther himself has no desire to be Lutheran except insofar as he teaches the Holy Scripture in purity."[2]

What precisely did Luther believe and teach from the Holy Scripture on the subject of idolatry? In this chapter I intend to allow Luther to give his Bible-based definitions and vivid descriptions of idolatry. Then I invite the reader to decide whether the previous chapters of this book are in harmony with Luther's views on idolatry and deserve to be called Lutheran, Christian, and faithful to the Word of God, as I want them to be and as I believe they are.

Luther did not consider idolatry an obscure or uncommon sin. He recognized how prevalent it was in ancient times, in his own day, and still is today. He observed that

It is very easy to fall into idolatry, for all of us are idolaters by nature. Since idolatry is born in us, it pleases us very much. . . . Human nature is idolatrous and superstitious; it flees from the true God, the true worship and fear of God, and promotes confidence in its own brand of worship and in its own works. . . .[3]

Luther did not hesitate to put the label of idolatry on other people, such as the papists, Jews, Turks and the ancient heathen, as we shall see farther on in this chapter; but he also recognized his own past guilt, prior to his spiritual awakening, and the ever-present danger of falling back into idolatry, especially the worship of self and trust in one's own works and merits. In that connection he wrote in his Large Catechism about two common forms of idolatry.

In reality the heathen make their own fictitious notions and dreams of God an idol and rely on what is altogether nothing. That is what all idolatry is. For it consists not merely in erecting an image and worshiping it. Its seat is the heart, which stupidly stares in other directions and seeks help and comfort from creatures, saints, or devils. It does not look to God, nor does it expect Him to be so good as to help; neither does it believe that whatever good it experiences comes from God. Besides this, there is a false worship, an extreme form of idolatry, which we have hitherto practiced and is still prevalent in the world. All ecclesiastical orders are based on it. This idolatry concerns only that conscience which seeks help, comfort, and salvation in its own works, presumes to wrest heaven from God, and counts how many bequests it has made, how often it has fasted, celebrated Mass, etc. On this it relies and of this it boasts, as if it were unwilling to take anything from God as a gift but desired to earn or richly merit it, just as though He were our servant and our debtor, while we are His liege lords. What is this but turning God into an idol, yea, a pseudo god, and regarding and elevating ourselves as God?[4]

Luther was well aware of the dangers of pride and self-righteousness. He equated those common sins with idolatry and pointed the finger of accusation at himself, as well as at others, when he said that "it (pride) is the worst kind of vice and the most demonic kind of pride for us to commend ourselves and pat ourselves on the back if we see or feel some special gift in ourselves. . . . We steal and rob God of His glory this way, and we make ourselves an idol. . . . This idol — presumption, pride, and arrogance — spoils all virtues."[5]

The reformation of the Christian church in the 16th century occurred when Luther was led by the Lord to see that the salvation of sinners is a free gift of God, not a human do-it-yourself project. When Luther recognized the full significance of scriptural statements such as Romans 3:28 — "For we maintain that a man is justified by faith apart from observing the law," he could no longer identify with the Roman Catholicism of his day, which was so deeply infected with deadly self-righteousness. Therefore it's not surprising to find Luther condemning self-righteousness in no uncertain terms and describing it as one of the most virulent, diabolical and deceitful forms of idolatry:

> Among all obstacles or offenses and idolatries none is greater or more harmful than the one called self-righteousness or holiness, whereby one relies on one's own work and merit. Yet this idol is not as coarse, as common, as the others which rule in the world among the common people. On the contrary, it is the most subtle, beautiful, and cunning devil, one who bewitches only the best, the finest people. Most of all, however, he plagues and assails true Christians, and he clings and sticks so tightly that no one can get rid of him as long as we have this flesh. . . . Some of the pious fathers in the desert have also complained about this, and one of them gave this illustration: He said that this idol reminded him of an onion; when one peeled off one skin, the onion always had another underneath as long as anything remained of it. This filth of self-righteousness is like that too. Even though it has been overcome once or twice in this or that particular so that God's grace retains its glory and honor, yet it forever returns; it so sticks and clings to all works that no one is able to keep himself untainted by it.[6]

Idolatry, as this book has demonstrated, is a multi-faceted evil, a subtle device of the devil which attacks people in many different ways. Luther was well aware of this characteristic of idolatry. He recognized that idolatry may be gross and readily recognizable as primitive pagans bow down before images of wood, stone and metal. But he also realized that there are many forms of idolatry which are not as easily identified and which accordingly pose very real and powerful temptations for the unwary, even among Christians. Self-righteousness and the love of money fit into this latter category of idols, as Luther declared:

> For not only the adoration of images is idolatry but also trust in one's own righteousness, works, and merits, and putting confidence in riches and human power. As the latter is the commonest, so it also is the most noxious idolatry. Therefore

Paul calls covetousness idolatry (Colossians 3:5). How godless do you think it is to rely on these things and to reject confidence in the eternal and omnipotent God?[7]

Preachers are often criticized today if they preach about money. Luther obviously was not concerned about such sentiments. He described money as the "most popular idol on earth," and preached many eloquent and hard-hitting sermons on the subject. In a sermon on Colossians 3:1-7, where St. Paul classified covetousness as a form of idolatry, Luther described greed or covetousness as "a thing that turns a man away entirely from faith and divine worship, so that he neither asks nor thinks about God or His Word and heavenly treasures but clings only to the temporal and seeks only a god who may give him enough here on earth." In the same sermon Luther pointed out why covetousness is not readily recognized as idolatry and even may be considered a fine virtue when it is confused with God-pleasing diligence and hard-working ambition:

> . . . Idolatry always acts in this way. Before God it is the greatest abomination, and yet it has a striking appearance and reputation before the world. It does not want to be called sin or vice but the highest degree of sanctity and divine service. Thus also the idolatrous worship of mammon wears an imposing cover. It must not be called covetousness or a striving after unjust possession but an upright and honest seeking of support and a possessing of well-earned property. Covetousness can ingeniously clothe itself with the Word of God and plead that God has commanded man to seek his bread by his exertion and labor and that everyone is bound to provide for the support of his household. Hence no temporal government, nay, not even a preacher, may censure such covetousness unless it grossly betrays itself by robbing and stealing.[8]

In 1526 Luther preached a sermon on Matthew 6:24-34, that section of Scripture in which the Savior warns his disciples about the sin of worry and tells us that "you cannot serve both God and Money." The following excerpt from that sermon, in which Luther so effectively exposes the absurdity of making gods out of impotent coins and clothing, reminds one of the passages of Scripture which were quoted in Chapter Two, the denunciation and outright ridicule of idolatry expressed by Isaiah, Ezekiel, Jeremiah and the Psalmist in Psalms 115 and 135. Similarly Luther shows how love of money and created things mires people down in miserable and tragically ludicrous idolatry:

> Even if a man had the riches of all the world, he would nonetheless not for a moment be assured against death.
>
> What help do his great treasures and riches offer to the emperor when the hour comes in which he is to die? Money is a shameful, odious, impotent god who cannot even help one against an ulcer, nay, who cannot protect himself. There he lies in the chest and lets himself be served. Indeed, one must take care of him as of an impotent, powerless, weak thing. The master who has him must see to it day and night that thieves do not steal him. This impotent god can help neither himself nor anyone else. You should be ashamed of this dead god, who cannot help in the least and yet is so noble and precious, lets himself be taken care of in the most splendid manner and lets himself be protected with great chests and castles. And his master must watch and worry every hour lest he perish in a fire or some other misfortune befall him. If this treasure or god consists in clothing, one must watch him and protect him against the most insignificant worms, against moths, so that they do not ruin or devour him.
>
> Should not the very walls spit at us for trusting more in that god whom moths devour and rust ruins than in the God who creates and gives all, nay, who has heaven and earth and everything that is therein in the palm of His hand? . . . Shame on you, you accursed unbelief!
>
> The true God lets Himself be used and serves people. But mammon does not do this. He wants to lie still and let himself be served. This is the reason why the New Testament calls avarice idolatry, because it will be served. But to love and not to

246

enjoy — why, this is enough to disgust the very devil. Yet this happens to all who love this god mammon and serve him. He who is not ashamed now and does not turn red has an iron brow.[9]

We live today in a world where it is considered unmannerly and even un-American to say anything critical or negative about other peoples and religions. Luther would have stuck out like a sore thumb in modern society, as he did in his own time, because he was not afraid to deliver denunciations of false faiths when they were called for. His love for the truth of God's Word, for Christ, and for his misguided fellowmen led Luther to "tell it like it is." Again and again Luther railed against the error-ridden and idolatrous religious beliefs of the heathen, the Turks (Islam), the Jews and the papists. Some today would say that Luther was motivated by hatred, pure and simple; or perhaps by self-righteousness or deep-seated feelings of insecurity as he launched one broadside after another against ancient and contemporary forms of idolatry. As a Lutheran, I maintain that Luther's love for the true God and respect for his very first commandment moved the reformer to express himself as he did. Let the reader judge for himself as we consider the following statements of Luther.

Luther's compassion for pagan people shines through in the following statement which contends that man's reason is by nature idolatrous and therefore misleading:

All the heathen expected good things from God; so one invented this god, another that one, for no other purpose than that of finding aid and help from him when misfortune came. Thus the heathen made many idols, for it is a truth planted into our nature that God is a Being who helps all who call upon Him. The heathen were not wrong in believing that God is Someone who helps. This truth still inheres in human nature. Otherwise people would not say: Help me! They must have some knowledge of God. But reason is wrong, blind, and idolatrous because it ascribes divinity to other things, things that are not God, and does not recognize the true God.

> Human nature knows that it is God who helps; but who this God is it does not know.[10]

While Luther surely felt sympathy for the sad plight of pagan peoples whose reason led them astray, he did not mistake their deep sincerity or great devotion for truth. They were dead wrong, just as heathen and pagans are today, and Luther did not hesitate to agree with St. Paul who in Ephesians 2:12 declared that the heathen are "without God in the world." In the same vein Luther stated:

> By worshiping the sun and the moon — which they considered the true worship of God — the heathen have committed what is by far the greatest of their sins. This is why man-made godliness is sheer blasphemy of God and the greatest of all the sins a man commits.[11]

Luther unquestionably heaped ridicule on the false belief of the heathen, but at the same time he saw them as victims, duped by the devil. Luther observed that:

> No heresy is so absurd that it does not find its hearers. What could possibly have been more absurd than to teach the worship of Priapus and the male organ and the belief that Minerva was born from the head of Jove? Things so absurd were believed among the heathen, and all the world adhered to them. In short, the devil is the god of the world. Therefore the world accepts whatever this god inspires.[12]

The demonic origin of idolatry was also emphasized by Luther in the following comments in which he lumps together the idolatry of the Moabites and other heathen, papists and idolatrous Jews:

> The Moabites and other heathen did not knowingly worship demons but believed that they were serving the true God no less than did the idolatrous Jews and, indeed, no less than all our papists, even the holiest and most religious of them, are now doing. But their godlessness consisted in their assuming the right name of the true God and worshiping Him with rites

which he had not prescribed but they had invented. . . . Therefore their thought about God is of necessity a mere figment and a lie; and the god whom they fashion and form in this way is not the true God but an idol of their heart under the guise of which they are adoring the devil, the teacher and father of this lie. And so under the name of the true God they are, in reality, worshiping idols and demons under a false impression.[13]

What was Luther's attitude toward the Jews? William L. Shirer, the author of the best-selling *Rise and Fall of the Third Reich*, claimed that Luther was a "savage anti-Semite" and attributed much of 20th century anti-Semitism, including the atrocities of the holocaust perpetrated by Hitler and the Nazis, to Luther's evil influence. While it's true that Luther wrote a very bitter tract, *Von den Juden und ihren Lügen*, in 1542, four years before his death, that treatise can hardly be blamed for or associated with the hate-filled "master race" philosophy of Adolf Hitler. The learned Luther scholar, Roland Bainton, emphasizes that Luther's position toward the Jews, though he often expressed himself in harsh language and proposed their return to Palestine as well as the confiscation of their wealth which was unjustly obtained through the practice of usury, "was entirely religious and in no respect racial." The true motive of Luther toward the Jews of his day can be learned from the preface of his aforementioned tract: "We must indeed with prayer and the fear of God before our eyes exercise a keen compassion towards them and seek to save some of them from the flames. Avenge ourselves we dare not. Vengeance a thousand times more than we can wish them is theirs already."[14]

Although Luther was a child of his time who used language toward the Jews, Turks and papists, which we today might be inclined to classify as intemperate and harsh to the point of appearing loveless, yet on balance, the sincere love of Dr. Martin Luther for the true God and for all of his fellowmen shines forth brilliantly in virtually all of his writings and utterances. While it is most unlikely that Luther will ever be honored or canonized by organizations like the National Conference of Christians and Jews, we Lutherans should never be ashamed of Luther or feel constrained to apologize for what he said and wrote concerning the Jews.

Consider the following quotations from Luther, which undeniably contain denunciations of the beliefs of the Jews, Turks and papists, but they also reveal Luther's singleminded love for the true God and his determination that Jesus Christ receive the honor he deserves:

> . . . Now there is no other Mediator than the Lord Christ, who is the Son of God. Therefore that is not a true faith which is held by the Turks and Jews: I believe that God has created heaven and earth. The devil believes precisely this. But it does not help him. So men venture to appear before God without Christ, the Mediator. But St. Paul says Rom. 5: We have access to God by faith; not through ourselves, but through Christ. Therefore we must bring Christ with us, must come with Him, must satisfy God by Him, and all we have to transact with God we must do through Him and in His name.[15]

In Luther's day, as well as in our own, there were many people who contended that faith in some kind of god is all that matters and that if people are outwardly decent, sincere and well-intentioned, one shouldn't make too much of the Christlessness of their faith. But Luther did not accept that permissive pretense. He was disturbed about any belief in a deity that deviated from God's Word. Thus Luther issued the warning:

> . . . Therefore it does our clergy no good whatever to pretend that they are not serving an idol in their churches and chapters but only God, the true Lord. For here you learn that it is not enough to say and think: I am doing this for the glory of God; I intend it for the true God; I want to serve the only God. All idolaters say and intend just that. Intentions or thoughts do not

count. If they did, those who martyred the apostles and the Christians would also have been God's servants; for they, too, thought that they were rendering God a service, as Christ says (John 16:2); and St. Paul (Rom. 10:2) testifies concerning the Jews that they are zealous for God and says (Acts 26:7) that by serving God night and day they hope to come to the promised salvation.

Rather let each see to it that he is sure that his worship of God is instituted by God's Word and not devised by his own devout inclination or good intention. For whoever is given to a worship of God that lacks the approval of God should know that he is not serving the true God but an idol of his own invention, that is, his own notion and false idea and thereby the devil himself, and that the words of all the prophets are against him.[16]

Surely, the key issue which prompted Luther to express criticism of the Turks (modern-day Moslems or Islam) and the Jews was their rejection of the crucial role of Jesus as God's only-begotten Son and this sinful world's one and only Savior. It's good for us to remember that Luther, the devout Christian, simply had no choice but to oppose and condemn the beliefs of non-Christians like the Jews and Turks because of their stubborn condemnation and rejection of the God-man, the Lord Jesus. Luther's concern for Christ's honor permeates the following statements:

> Turks and Jews boast much of God and profess to have a better faith than we Christians. They say they cannot be wrong; for they believe in the one God, who created heaven and earth and everything. A faith such as this can certainly not be wrong, they think. Christ, however, concludes: He who hates Me hates My Father. Now since Turks and Jews hate Christ and persecute His Word, they certainly also hate the God who has created heaven and earth, do not believe in Him, and do not honor Him. For Christ is this same one God. . . . One should think of no other God than Christ. The god who does not speak through Christ is not God. In Old Testament times God would hear prayers because of the mercy seat; just so He will hear no one except through Christ. But the greater part of the Jews ran

hither and thither, burned incense and offered sacrifices here and there in order to serve God. They looked for God in many places, to the neglect of the mercy seat. So it is now. Men search for God everywhere; but because they do not search for Him in Christ, they do not find Him.[17]

For more than half his life Luther was a dutiful and dedicated member of the medieval Roman Catholic Church. It seems that when he first became a monk and then a theological professor, his loyalty and devotion to the pope as the visible head of Catholicism was unqualified. However, with the nailing of the 95 theses to the church door at Wittenberg in 1517 and the subsequent efforts of the papacy to squelch Luther's suggestions and proposals for reformation of the church, Luther gradually came to recognize the idolatrous elements in the pope-dominated church of his childhood, which he sincerely had wanted to serve as a priest and professor. Luther came to realize that Rome's preaching and teaching of salvation by works robbed Christ of his glory and made the pope a promoter and purveyor of out-and-out idolatry. Note how Luther mentions the papists in the same breath with non-Christian Jews and Turks in the following excerpt from a 1526 sermon on Exodus 3:1-6:

> Without this God, who died and rose again, let every man fear and hesitate, nor presume to draw near to God or to come to Him, no matter how pious and holy or full of good works he may be. For God the Father cannot tolerate anyone who wants to go to Him or approach Him unless he brings His beloved Son Christ with him. And so indeed the Son Himself says John 14:6: "I am the way, the truth, and the life: no man cometh unto the Father, but by Me." Here, then, all saints and all their merits are utterly excluded so that nothing is to rate in the presence of God except Christ. That is why Jews, Turks, and the pope, who despise this Son of God with His suffering, death, and resurrection and propose to come to God in a different way, stand condemned.[18]

Rome's propensity for saint worship led Luther to compare his former church with the polytheistic heathen of old. Note how Luther readily acknowledges that he also had been guilty of such idolatry. The word "we" in the following statement reveals this:

> The papacy was full of all manner of idols of silver, gold, wood, and stone. For although we knew that all of them were sculptured and fashioned by the hands of men, yet we fell down before these statues and adored them under the impression that God would graciously regard this or that image. And we fancied that St. Barbara, Anna, Christopher would regard their particular statues and hear our prayers. This cult was Egyptian darkness and quite the same madness and fury which in times of old was found among the heathen, who made up an infinite number of divinities; for thus they worshiped Juno, Bacchus, Ceres, Priapus, and others.[19]

In Chapter Three the subject of Mariolatry, the excessive, idolatrous devotion to the Virgin Mary within Roman Catholicism, was laid out in some detail. In this matter Luther also confessed that he had been in error. He had to admit:

> . . . I myself knew nothing but this confusion (about the distinction between Law and Gospel) for over thirty years and could not look upon Christ as being gracious to me: I wanted to gain righteousness before God through the merit of the saints. Thence arose the interceding and the invoking of saints. So St. Bernard was pictured worshiping the Virgin Mary, who was showing her Son Christ the breasts at which He nursed. Ah, how many kisses we gave Mary! . . . about the intercession, adoration, and prayer to departed saints there is nothing in Scripture. No one can deny that by such saint worship we have now come to the point where we have actually made utter idols of the Mother of God and the saints, and that because of the service we have rendered and the works we have performed in their honor we have sought comfort more with them than with Christ Himself. Thereby faith in Christ has been destroyed.[20]

Is the sin of idolatry really as common as this book would have readers believe it is? Are dead idols really as alive in the minds and hearts of misguided people as this writer insists they are? Is the writer of this book obsessed with idolatry to the point that he sees idols under every rock and behind every bush when they aren't really there? I must confess that the subject of idolatry has been much on my mind for a long time and I would even admit to it becoming a kind of obsession with me. But I have no regrets because I believe I'm in good company with faithful Christians like Luther who surely had a very similar obsession. He observed that "Without His (God's) Word all is idolatry and lies, however devout it may seem and however beautiful it may appear. . . ."[21] Indeed, Luther had a magnificent obsession: he was obsessed with the conviction that Jesus Christ is true God and true man and that ". . . outside Christ there is nothing but idolatry and merely a false, imagined notion about God."[22]

Time and time again Luther stressed the truth that knowing Jesus Christ as Lord God and Savior is the indispensable key to understanding the identity of the true God and avoiding the damning sin of idolatry. Certainly every Christian should share that obsession with Luther and should wholeheartedly agree with the following statements of the great reformer:

> No one is able really to recognize God or to speak of His divine Being and will except us Christians. . . . We firmly maintain . . . that no one is able to pray except a Christian. . . . He who does not know the Lord Christ from the Gospel may speak or know about God whatever he pleases (as the heathen, Turks, and Jews profess to know much about Him), his knowledge is nevertheless worth nothing. He does not know God aright and, therefore, must be without comfort in every temptation and sorrow and must fall into despair. . . . He who wants to know God, love God, worship God, and serve God should learn to know Christ aright, should love Christ, should worship Christ and serve Him. To know, love, worship, or serve God without Christ is impossible. . . . Outside Christ there is nothing but idolatry, an idolatrous and

false figment of God, whether it be called the Law of Moses or the law of the pope or the Alcoran of the Turk . . .[23]

The Apostle Paul once described himself and his fellow Christians as follows: "We are fools for Christ. . . ." (I Corinthians 4:10). Martin Luther was also a wonderful "fool for Christ," as every Christian should be. We live today in a world where words like compromise, moderation, liberal and broad-minded are highly-favored, while beliefs about Christ and idolatry, such as were expressed by Luther and have been set forth in this book are likely to be condemned as fanatic, too narrow and extreme. So be it! This writer is eager to be a fool for Christ. After all, it means being in the same camp with St. Paul and wholeheartedly agreeing with the following Christ-centered statements of Luther as they relate to idolatry:

> Christ herewith wishes to say: You have heard that you should rely on God, but I also want to indicate to you how you are really to find Him so that you do not fashion an idol under His name according to your own ideas. What I mean is this: If you want to believe in God, believe in Me. If you want to place your faith and confidence rightly so that they neither fail nor are false, then place your faith and confidence in Me; for in Me the entire Godhead is present and dwells, and (as He will say later on) I am the Way, the Truth, and the Life; and whoever sees Me sees the Father, whoever hears Me hears the Father, etc. If, then, you want to be sure of finding Him, then apprehend Him in Me and through Me; if you have Me, you also really have Him. The Father Himself testifies as much of Me. Thus Christ points out at various places in the Gospels that the Father has sent Him and that He speaks or does nothing of Himself, but that the Father commands and bids all the world to believe Christ as Himself. Accordingly, God enjoins that no one accept any other person or means whereby to apprehend Him than this one Christ and that we should be certain that if we rely on Him, we do not find any idol, as do the others, who deal with God apart from Christ. For God has depicted Himself through the Word with distinctness and sufficient clearness. Therefore it is decreed that whoever passes the Person of Christ

by will certainly never find the true God, for He is entirely in Christ. . . . He who would know God aright must know Him in Christ, that is, in that Word and promise which Scripture and the prophets have spoken and testified concerning Him. This is precisely the teaching and preaching of the Gospel: that this Christ is the Son of God, sent by the Father to become the sacrifice and payment for the world's sin through His own blood and in this way to remove God's wrath and reconcile us, so that, redeemed from sin and death, we might obtain eternal righteousness and life through Him. From this it must follow that no man can render satisfaction for his sin or remove God's wrath through his own work or holiness and that there is no other way or means to attain God's grace and eternal life than through the faith which in this way apprehends Christ. This is the right Christ, known aright. And he who knows Christ in this way knows the Father too. . . . Serving God and truly worshiping God consists in believing on Him whom the Father has sent, Jesus Christ. . . . Knowing Christ and knowing the Father are tied together and are one and the same knowledge. This is why I have often said that the Father is known only in Christ and neither will nor can be reached and found, worshiped and invoked, apart from this Mediator.[24]

Every Christian pastor and teacher has been asked a question like this: what will happen to the ancient heathen who never heard the Gospel or to pagan people of the present age in some remote part of the world who have not been told that Christ is their Savior? The proponents of universalism, mentioned in Chapter Six, would give the reassuring answer that somehow God will bring about the salvation of all sincere, well-intentioned non-Christians. In Luther's time that same question about the fate of the heathen was being asked. But Luther was no universalist. Following the guidance of the Scriptures, Luther rejected salvation by works and insisted that even the most upright and diligent heathen could not earn salvation apart from faith in Christ. Luther opposed the permissive position of his fellow Protestant reformer, Ulrich Zwingli, as follows:

> Zwingli recently wrote that Numa Pompilius, Hector, Scipio, and Hercules are enjoying eternal blessedness in Paradise together with Peter and Paul and the other saints. This statement is nothing but a frank confession of their idea that Christian faith and Christendom are of no importance. For if Scipio and Numa Pompilius, who were idolaters, have been saved, why was it necessary for Christians to be baptized or to be instructed about Christ? To a degree so horrible do men fall into deadly error once the Word is neglected and lost; they know nothing whatever about faith but hold and teach this doctrine: If a man does his best, he will be saved.[25]

Another question that has been asked and discussed by elementary school children and by learned philosophers for many centuries: why are there so many religions? If there is really just one true God and if that true God's revelation of himself, the Holy Bible, is completely reliable and pure truth, why is there such a bewildering diversity of beliefs about religion and the identity of God? Luther was also very familiar with that question and he knew the right answer! His answer comes from God's Word and it can serve as a fitting conclusion to this book, since it includes a simple, straightforward, scripturally sound definition of idolatry, that devilish worship of dead idols, which has led so many precious souls away from the Savior in the past and is very much alive in our own time. Luther explained why there are so many gods (idols) and false forms of worship in the world and what idolatry is as follows:

> There is an amazing confusion of religions and forms of religious worship in the world. This came about because all wanted to have and worship a god but proceeded without the Word of God, according to the opinion of their own heart. But this is, properly speaking, idolatry, when we ourselves give God a form and invest God with some sort of religious worship which He Himself has not instituted and has not commanded in His Word. For God does not want to be worshiped in any other

way than that which He Himself prescribed. Therefore those who try to worship him in a different way depart from the true God and worship an idol of their heart.[26]

Soli Deo Gloria

NOTES FOR CHAPTER SEVEN

[1]Ewald M. Plass, compiler, *What Luther Says*, 3 vols., anthology (St. Louis: Concordia Publishing House, 1959), Vol II, #2676, pp. 856, 857.

[2]Plass, *What Luther Says*, Vol II, #2677 and #2679 pp. 857, 858.

[3]Ibid., Vol. II, #2105 and #2106, p. 678.

[4]Ibid., Vol. II, #2111, pp. 679, 680.

[5]Ibid., Vol. III, #3631 and #3632, p. 1136.

[6]Ibid., Vol, III, #4082, pp. 1278, 1279.

[7]Ibid., Vol. II, #2110, p. 679.

[8]Ibid., Vol. II, #3061, pp. 972, 973.

[9]Ibid., Vol. II, #3071, pp. 975.

[10]Ibid., Vol. II, #1883, p. 616.

[11]Ibid., Vol. II, #1881, p. 616.

[12]Ibid., Vol. II, #2117, pp. 681, 682.

[13]Ibid., Vol. II, #2116, p. 681.

[14]quoted from John Warwick Montgomery, "Luther, Anti-Semitism, and Zionism," *Christianity Today,* 8 Sept. 1978, pp. 79, 80.

[15]Plass, *What Luther Says*, Vol II, #1680, p. 553.

[16]Ibid., Vol. II, #2113, p. 680.

[17]Ibid., Vol. I, #472 and #467, pp. 158, 159.

[18]Ibid., Vol. I, #546, pp. 187, 188.

[19]Ibid., Vol. II, #2114, p. 681.

[20]Ibid., Vol. III, #3996 and #3998, pp. 1253, 1254.

[21]Ibid., Vol. II, #2113, p. 680.

[22]Ibid., Vol. III, #5025, p. 1547.

[23]Ibid., Vol. I, #631, #632, #587, #476 and #471, pp. 159, 160, 202, 214.

[24]Ibid., Vol. I, II and III, #480, #1679, #5023 and #5024, pp. 163, 164, 553, 1546 and 1547.

[25]Ibid., Vol. III, #4017, p. 1260.

[26]Ibid., Vol. III, #5030, p. 1548.